MODERN THEATRE

Modern Theatre

Seven Plays and an Essay

PÄR LAGERKVIST

Translated, with an Introduction, by

THOMAS R. BUCKMAN

UNIVERSITY OF NEBRASKA PRESS · LINCOLN

Publishers on the Plains

UNP

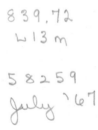

Contents

List of Illustrations

Introduction

Pär Lagerkvist is the major figure in Swedish literature of the last fifty years and by far the most widely translated. Some one or more of his works has been published in thirty-four languages. Beginning in 1913, Lagerkvist introduced a new spirit of modernism into Swedish poetry and prose, and especially into the drama. He was the first in Sweden to recognize the importance of Strindberg's later plays in the development of modern drama, and he became the chief Swedish inheritor of Strindberg's dramatic expressionism. Throughout his long writing career, Lagerkvist has remained faithful to the idea that the naturalistic portrayal of reality in literature is completely inadequate for the representation of modern experience. His writing is characterized by concentration on a few universal themes and a deceptively simple style expressive of a profound personal view. He shuns psychological interpretation, preferring what he describes as "simple thoughts, and uncomplicated feelings in confronting the eternal powers of life: sorrow and happiness, reverence, love and hate, expressions of broad human validity which rise above the individual."[1] In 1951 the Swedish Academy awarded him the Nobel Prize in literature, citing the "artistic power and deep originality with which he seeks answers to the eternal questions of mankind."[2]

Lagerkvist was born in 1891 in the small cathedral town of Växjö, in Småland, in south Sweden. His father, a railroad foreman, and his mother were from old peasant families. Both parents were faithful readers of the Bible; their religious view was one of quiet, reassuring pietism. Lagerkvist's maternal grandfather, with whom he spent his childhood summers, was, on the other hand, a stern believer in the religion of the Old Testament. The two religious attitudes were fundamental influences in his early years,

[1] *Ordkonst och bildkonst* (Stockholm: Bröderna Lagerströms Förlag, 1913), pp. 46–47.
[2] Artur Almhult, *Svenska Akademien* (Stockholm: P. A. Norstedt & Söners Förlag, 1954), p. 71.

ix

and evidences of them may be found in much of his writing. Later, attending the *gymnasium*, he learned a new doctrine. He rejected an orthodox belief in God, accepting evolution as the new truth, and at the same time embraced political radicalism. From 1910 through 1916 he published a number of revolutionary songs of struggle and a few poems and reviews in the Social Democratic journals *Fram* and *Stormklockan*.[3] Lagerkvist has described the environment of his childhood and youth and his spiritual and emotional conflicts of that time in the autobiographical novel *Gäst hos verkligheten* (tr. *Guest of Reality*, 1925), a work which is essential to an understanding of his life and writing.[4]

After a term at Uppsala, in the fall of 1911, Lagerkvist left the University, apparently dissatisfied with the academic milieu, and began studying and writing independently. In the spring of 1913 he spent several weeks in Paris pursuing his interest in the theories of modern painting and their possible application to writing. During the First World War, Lagerkvist lived in Denmark. In Copenhagen he began to study the history of theatre and drama, and in 1919 he was the theatre and art critic for the Stockholm daily newspaper *Svenska Dagbladet*. He resided often in France and Italy during the 1920's. Since 1930 he has lived in Lidingö, a suburb of Stockholm, but has traveled frequently in Europe and the

[3] *Fram* (1903–1912), monthly; and *Stormklockan* (1908–   ), monthly.

[4] First references to titles of Lagerkvist's works are in Swedish, followed in parentheses by the title in English and the date of first publication of the Swedish edition. Subsequent references are to the English title only. The abbreviation "tr." preceding a title in English indicates that the work has been published in English translation. For a complete listing of translations, the work by Anders Ryberg mentioned in the Bibliographical Note should be consulted.

For the benefit of students who do not read Swedish I have referred in this introduction almost exclusively to works by Lagerkvist available in English. Albert Camus' idea that "a man's sole creation is strengthened in its successive and multiple aspects: his works" is especially applicable to Lagerkvist. They should be studied, as Camus suggested in "Absurd Creation," not as "isolated testimonies," but "as a series of approximations of the same thought." (Albert Camus, *The Myth of Sisyphus and Other Essays* [New York: Vintage Books, 1959], p. 84.)

Near East. He was elected to the Swedish Academy in 1941, succeeding Verner von Heidenstam, the Swedish poet of the 1890's with whom he shares the classical ideal in poetry. Little more than the outline of Lagerkvist's life is known even in Sweden. He has always been very reluctant to communicate any personal information or opinions to literary historians or the press, and has repeatedly stated that what he has to say may be found in his writing.

Several dominant moods are discernible in Lagerkvist's work, beginning with extreme pessimism and passionate rebelliousness of spirit during the First World War. In the postwar decade he regained a sense of security and became reconciled with life, for example in the fable *Det eviga leendet* (tr. *The Eternal Smile*, 1920). But even though he achieved an attitude of acceptance, he still continued to doubt and question life. An invincible idealism emerges in his writing, based on faith in man, despite human evil, and hostility toward life which defeats human aspiration, as in the play *Konungen* (tr. *The King*, 1932) or in his widely known novels *Barabbas* (tr. *Barabbas*, 1950) and *Sibyllan* (tr. *The Sibyl*, 1956), both stories of believers, like Lagerkvist himself, "without faith." The tensions of Lagerkvist's position are also apparent in his modern satires *Bödeln* (tr. *The Hangman*, 1933) and *Dvärgen* (tr. *The Dwarf*, 1945), which warn against a new barbarism. His later poetry inclines toward calm, lyrical interpretations of nature and rural life, but this tranquillity is often interrupted by moods of troubled, restless seeking.

Shortly after his early trip to Paris, Lagerkvist's first programmatic work appeared, an essay "On the Decadence of Modern Fiction—On the Vitality of Modern Art" entitled *Ordkonst och bildkonst* (*Verbal Art and Pictorial Art*, 1913). In it he proposed abstract, mathematical concepts similar to those influencing cubist painting as a basis for literary composition, pointing to the example of the bold monumental patterns evolved by the chiefly anonymous authors of the classics of ancient cultures such as the Bible, the Avesta, the Koran, the Egyptian *Book of the Dead*, and closer to home, the Icelandic sagas, the Scandinavian folk songs and the Kalevala. He was critical of the planless improvisation which he saw in Swedish fiction of the first decade of this century, and urged instead the firm structure and uncompromising unity of artistic idea, imagination, and form which he saw in modern art and the primitive literatures.

Lagerkvist departed somewhat from this aesthetic ideal implying classical order and simplicity in his war-influenced poetry, *Ångest* (tr. *Anguish*, 1916), and in the stories *Järn och människor* (*Iron and Men*, 1915). Here he tried to achieve a strictly controlled style, but the tone is one of explosive bitterness and pessimism, leading him finally toward his second programmatic statement *Modern teater* (tr. *Modern Theatre*, 1918). Again he repudiated realism, and specifically naturalism, in the theatre, this time recommending the expressionism of Strindberg as an alternative.

The ideas in *Modern Theatre*, insofar as they establish guidelines for Lagerkvist's dramatic writing, reflect a creative temperament in opposition to the tendency of his earlier theories. In *Verbal Art and Pictorial Art* he is preoccupied with the severity of modern painting and with universal human feelings expressed in the relatively constrained and traditionally prescribed forms of the old literatures. But his deep spiritual involvement with events of the present demanded a much freer and more personal form, one which would accommodate his intense, subjective response to the life around him. He was attracted to the dramatic mode when he wished to comment more directly on the contemporary scene, and the form suggested by Strindberg's chamber plays seemed best suited to his needs, although later he moved toward a modified realism. Thus *Modern Theatre* is concerned with the artist's relation to the outside world and how its significant aspects may be used for the purposes of art, and, more specifically, in the writing of plays for a vital theatre.

Modern Theatre represents a further development of Lagerkvist's theory of writing and a greater maturity. He has emerged from the somewhat isolated aesthetic experimentation implied in *Verbal Art and Pictorial Art*; however, he does not discard its ideas entirely. They continue to be evident, especially in the style of his poetry and prose, but also in his plays, where in the midst of the particulars of time, place, and character there are symbolic figures and elements of ritualism. The metaphysical background is always present. His people have a dimension of timelessness and generality, even though they may also have a convincing reality of their own. Lagerkvist attempts in his dramas to unify a cosmic perspective with some primary aspects of individual experience.

In 1918, the psychological realism of Ibsen's plays, the literal transcription on the stage of drab, middle-class interiors, and the restrained, intimate style of acting were for Lagerkvist "no longer adequate as a means of expression . . . for the violent and abrupt contrasts in modern life." His brilliant characterization in *Modern Theatre* not only of the immediate day but of the entire modern period from the beginning of the First World War to the present, in which we recognize our own postwar years of international tensions, "limited wars," atom bombs, earth satellites, and feverish scientific activity, vividly makes the point:

> Our time, in its lack of balance, its heterogeneity, and through the violent expansion of its conflicting forces, is baroque and fantastic . . . . What a sea of brutality has broken over us, sweeping away and recreating! Is not every inner problem of mankind, which before lent itself willingly to give brilliance to the literary conversation, now suddenly transformed into objective, threatening realities? . . . If one looked more closely it might be possible to find profound resemblances between our time and the mediaeval period; between the age of faith, inwardness, and religious exaltation and the age of doubt, irreligion, and restless intellectual excitement, both chaotic, both a conglomeration of powers too resolutely storming heaven.

Naturalism, Lagerkvist wrote, ignores the fact that the world has changed; it can do no more than deliver a stereotyped view of a once settled existence that has now vanished. He also rejected the "escape" of the neoromanticists and symbolists from reality to a pleasantly wondrous land of dreams. He called not for a new classicism or a new romanticism but for an original, well-wrought expression which partakes of both. The modern writer must see "the fantastic in things themselves, and in very reality." The world is indeed a strange place, but it must be seen clearly and should be portrayed with a strong feeling for the external phenomena which surround the writer and inexorably demand his attention.

The essentially new features of Strindberg's drama in his post-1897 phase were attuned to the disquiet and uncertainties of modern life, Lagerkvist believed, and offered a broad range of expression and a multiplicity of new possibilities. He urged the would-be playwright to learn from them, but to use the method of Strindberg only if there is a profound inner motivation to do so, and only if his own dramatic expression could emerge naturally from genuine personal feeling and need; those who merely wish to borrow the externals of Strindberg's dramatic form in order to create a startling effect should leave him alone. In a few brief paragraphs he describes the characteristics of Strindberg's dramatic form:

> . . . everything is directed to one purpose—the liberation of a single mood, a single feeling whose intensity unceasingly grows and grows. Everything irrelevant is excluded even if rather important to the continuity or to the faithfulness of representation. Everything which occurs is meaningful and of equal weight. No minor roles, but all having an equal right to a place in the drama, and all equally necessary in order that the play will become what it is intended to be. And actually no "persons" in the usual, accepted meaning, no analysis, no psychological apparatus, no drawing of "characters." And yet, no abstractions, but images of man when he is evil, when he is good, when in sorrow, and when joyful. Simplification. But, nevertheless, richness. Richness too in the form itself, because of the fact that everything plays its part, nothing is lifeless, all is inspired and put into the drama as a living part of it; and because the theme is always shifting, and is clipped off, to be pursued on another plane. Confusion, but a confusion with meaning and order.

In *Modern Theatre* Lagerkvist declared the bankruptcy of naturalism, defined the importance of Strindberg to the new theatre, and stated his own program. His essay on the theatre is personal and provocative, but based on careful reflection and study. As the subtitle, "Points of View and Attack," indicates, Lagerkvist intends to take a stand, and therefore at times he is frankly polemical; thus it is not surprising that there is some lack of balance. For example, he may oversimplify to make a point and thereby do less than justice to Ibsen. His judgment of Reinhardt may have been based on insufficient acquaintance.[5] The work of Gordon Craig, the early Lagerkvist notwithstanding, retains its validity and power. But the essential arguments of Lagerkvist's essay stand on firm ground. Today naturalism has largely been banished from the theatre, its decline in Sweden hastened by Pär Lagerkvist's essay and plays. Likewise, the reforms in direction which he called for have all been realized. Still *Modern Theatre* is relevant, nearly fifty years after its first publication, as a classic statement of the case against naturalism and of the necessity to seek new forms of expression in theatre and drama, better suited to the modern taste.

The plays presented here are representative of Lagerkvist's expressionism: *Den svåra stunden, I–III* and *Himlens hemlighet* (tr. *The Difficult Hour I–III*, 1918, and *The Secret of Heaven*, 1919); of his reaction to the political events in Europe in the early 1930's (*The King* and *The Hangman*); and of his reflection, in the 1940's, on the nature of evil and the social responsibility of the artist and the scientist: *De vises sten* (tr. *The Philosopher's Stone*, 1947).

The four early plays project an inner state of the soul. Apparently confused and unrelated details produce a dominant effect created in the theatre by emphasis on externals: costume, lighting, color, and the arrangement of figures and very simple décor within the seemingly unlimited space of the stage picture. We are not aware of the normal plane of the stage but rather of an atmosphere of sound and light. The people in these plays and the words they speak are subservient to this aim, and thus there are no characters or dialogue in the usual sense, and no list of roles preceding the plays.

[5] Suggested by August Brunius in his review of the essay, "Ny svensk dramatik," *Svenska Dagbladet*, July 5, 1918, pp. 6–7.

The three later plays, on the other hand, make use of realistic settings and recognizable characters, not as ends in themselves, but in the service of allegory and symbolic meaning. A more conventional dialogue is employed, not so much to carry the action of the play forward, but rather to define the characters and to heighten the contentions between them. Generally, in these plays Lagerkvist does not seek a dramatic effect dependent on a single expressionistic mood or on the clash of wills, but rather on his own intense emotional and intellectual identification with the characters representing various aspects of a complex, paradoxical existence. Thus his use of reality is always informed by his vision of the ultimate forces of life and man's elemental attitudes toward them.

In a postscript to the original edition of *Modern Theatre*[6] Lagerkvist noted that the three one-act plays appearing in the same volume under the common title *The Difficult Hour* were not written to exemplify the principles that he had put forth in the essay. They were written, he said, before the essay was planned, and were quite independent of the author's later reflections on the philosophy of imaginative writing.

Nevertheless, the plays do illustrate his precepts to a remarkable degree, and it is in them that his ability as a dramatist first becomes evident. They are short, momentary views of crucial situations, sharpened by concentration and by abrupt and ironic contrasts. Here one finds Lagerkvist's expressionism arising out of the techniques of Strindberg's dream plays. Every unnecessary detail is sacrificed to create a sense of feverishness and torment. There is the fusion of the fantastic and the real, and the derangement of a dream, but nevertheless an underlying unity of meaning and order in which past and present are mingled. Lagerkvist has chosen the extremely dramatic moment immediately before or after death in which there is gradual realization of the brutality and emptiness of human existence as he saw it in 1918, but in which there is also the recollection of the beauty of life and the persevering desire for the communion of love. The action is the final struggle of conscious-

[6] Quoted in full in my article "Stylistic and Textual Changes in *Modern teater*," *Scandinavian Studies*, XXXIII (August 1961), 137–149.

ness against the mystery of death, the anguished last look into darkness dramatically conceived and executed.

The first two plays may be thought of as monodramas in which the inner experience of a man is expressed in external fragments of events. [7] The tentative, groping monologue of the first play shows us The Man in Tails as he gradually becomes aware of crucial events in his life, and of the fact of his death. Tension is created between his excitement and the indifference of The Hunchback, who is a vision from his earlier life. As in Poe, the memory of a painful detail from the past suddenly re-encountered takes hold of consciousness and bores more deeply into it until the breaking point is reached. The second play also takes place in the mind of a single person. A dying man experiences the anguish of death in a series of hallucinations in which all of life comes rushing past on the stage. This nightmarish parade is intermittently clipped off by the quiet, condescending conversation of the two old gentlemen, which serves both to explain and to increase the bizarre effect. The frenzy of the dream rises to an intolerable pitch, to be finally halted by the last shrill blast of the station master's whistle. The third play of this brief cycle is concerned with the reality of death. There are no dreams or visions, only darkness, voices, and undefined space inhabited by the dead. An innocent child's meeting with a world of hardened human misery is developed through contrasts between the lyrical quality of the boy's questions and reminiscences and the harsh crudities of The Old Man and The Old Woman who try to influence him. The wily adult perversion of youthful hope with its simple clarity and steadfastness is accomplished symbolically at the end of the play, and the boy disappears into darkness.

There are many points of similarity between Lagerkvist and the later Strindberg in these plays. For example, both the basic situation and the expressionistic mode and setting of *The Difficult Hour I* are suggested in many of the dream scenes in *To Damascus*, in a short passage in the fourth act of *Advent*, and in the fragment

[7] Here I have relied in part on Gösta M. Bergman, *Pär Lagerkvists dramatik* (Stockholm: P. A. Norstedt & Söners Förlag, 1928), pp. 76–109.

Toten-Insel. The technique of the dialogue is clearly reminiscent of Strindberg's brief but pointed dramatic scene *The Stronger*. An even more striking parallel is found in the scene in the middle play in which the young man is waiting for Elise; one thinks immediately of The Officer calling for Victoria outside the theatre in *A Dream Play*, in which Strindberg had also used the device of the revue, as he had earlier in *Advent*. The dead in *The Difficult Hour III* who sit in the dark and "sicken each other" are like the grotesque figures in *The Spook Sonata*. Other resemblances might be noted, but however strong the influences from Strindberg, there were important differences indicative of Lagerkvist's independence. His dream scenes are the work of a disciplined artist working within a form consciously limited in scope. They have a greater sharpness of focus and awareness of method, whereas Strindberg's longer dream sequences were created somewhat fitfully from the elements of his temperament and visionary world. There is an ironic sting in Lagerkvist's style which is foreign to the note of religious consolation in the later dramas of Strindberg. Lagerkvist does not share Strindberg's optimism, but sees the transition from life to death as from darkness to darkness.

The Secret of Heaven is Lagerkvist's most original and clearly conceived expressionistic play. Here, there is no projection of the sparks of a single consciousness onto a screen of darkness as in *The Difficult Hour*, but a distant view of a few individuals, hopelessly isolated from each other, inhabiting a Lilliputian planet which is a synthesis of the larger world, reduced in size to its most essential elements, as if seen through the wrong end of a telescope. Lagerkvist's subject is the brooding and disaffection of the Young Man in his search for meaning and for the love of Miss Judith, who in turn seeks, pathetically, a symbolic golden string of happiness. The rasping effect of this play depends upon the confrontation of selfishness, small-mindedness, and absurd vanity with youthful earnestness and desire, finally overcome by Miss Judith's preference for the strutting dwarf. In a sense the play is similar to a mediaeval mystery portraying suffering and death in an alien world, but its form is abstract in the manner of expressionism and its tone is one of Swiftian scorn.[8] This embittered attitude is quite different from Lagerkvist's later, more conciliatory view of life. Indeed, some of the figures in *The Secret of Heaven* appear in a more benevolent light in Lagerkvist's subsequent works and have a broader significance than they do here. The Woodsman, for example, becomes a well-meaning god-figure in the short prose fantasy *The Eternal Smile*, and the Dwarf returns as a sympathetic but evil genius and one of Lagerkvist's major symbolic figures in the short novel by that name published in 1944. The Young Man is related to Nadur in *The King* and Jacob in *The Philosopher's Stone*. These last three are all, to some degree, the young Lagerkvist seeking a place where life and love, in his understanding of these words, are possible.

The King is a philosophical dialogue in a dramatic context, concerned with class differences, the merits of contemplation versus social action, and the aims of revolution. The play was inspired by the restless political situation in Europe of the 1930's, but as in *The Philosopher's Stone*, Lagerkvist has chosen a historical setting to give perspective to the conflicts he deals with. In this instance he has developed an old Babylonian legend, mentioned by Frazer in *The Golden Bough*,[9] of a religious festival during which the people are allowed every kind of license while their rightful ruler is replaced for a few days, in his position of absolute power, by a condemned criminal. In the play, the usually harmless ritual does not end, as it should, in the execution of the temporary king. Instead the celebration turns into a wild revolt against established order, and the murderer, Iream-Azu, becomes the new leader. At first he is inclined to be fiercely vindictive, but by the end of the play he has become chastened by his new responsibility and the loyalties to others that he has discovered in the Captain and Nadur. Lagerkvist's theme is that a common bond of humanity must be the foundation for building a new world, in poverty and faith. The old king, Amar-Azu, and his young disciple Nadur may be

[8] Bergman, *Pär Lagerkvists dramatik*, p. 113, notes that Lagerkvist himself has stated that Swift influenced him in the writing of this play.

[9] J. G. Frazer, *The Golden Bough*, Part VI, "The Scapegoat" (3d ed.; London: Macmillan and Co., Ltd., 1913), p. 355.

regarded as different aspects of Lagerkvist's belief, reconciled here, but never finally resolved in the author's mind.

Of all of Lagerkvist's plays, *The Hangman* is still the most powerful and germane, despite its clear topical association with the violence of Hitler's Germany. It has the profound despair of Lagerkvist's expressionistic period and the concentration of the earlier plays, but here Lagerkvist, out of his wrath and indignation, has created a symbol—the Human Butcher as man's constant companion—which has a strength and validity unrivaled in any of his other dramas. The Hangman's presence is just as vivid, and the need that men have for him is, if anything, greater today than when the play was written. The hate, superstition, and violence evoked early in the play, in the mediaeval tavern, have their direct counterparts in the modern nightclub which appears in the second half. Lagerkvist employs naturalistic detail obviously growing out of considerable study and research, and gives his characters words and patterns of speech that seem to fit the mediaeval setting exactly; later he uses the familiar jargon of the Nazis and even some of Mussolini's phrases. The nightclub figures are all easily recognizable stereotypes, frightening because they so often appear in reality as people we know or know exist. The structure of the play is deliberately unreal. The abrupt change in time and the ever present figure of the Hangman, at once flesh and principle and therefore seemingly larger than life, underline the savagery common to the mediaeval and modern scenes and unify them in a terrible destiny.

Albertus in *The Philosopher's Stone* is related to the artist and inventor Bernardo in *The Dwarf*. Bernardo observes beauty and deformity with equal dispassion; he constructs war machines without concern for the misery and destruction they will cause. Likewise, Albertus, the alchemist, examines nature and establishes facts, but in order to do so he must exploit others, particularly his daughter, Catherine, whom he sells as a whore in order to obtain money for his work, and Jacob, whose death he indirectly causes. He and the Prince, who subsidizes his experiments, have a common bond of disregard for humanity. Albertus also symbolizes the artist seeking truth who may become a mere manipulator of human beings for his own ends. Lagerkvist seems to be asking: Does the artist or the scientist stand outside the normal laws of human responsibility? Does the search for truth free him from the burden of guilt? In this play, Lagerkvist places three kinds of faith in opposition to the Prince's cynical opportunism and to Albertus's science: the conventional belief of Maria, based on the prevailing religious system; Simonides' faith, which is that of a minority group cruelly tested and driven to flight; and the faith of Jacob, which is most characteristic of Lagerkvist, and which may be compared to Amar-Azu's longing for his land in the desert or to the world of lovers described in Lagerkvist's short story "Själarnas maskerad" (tr. "The Masquerade of Souls," 1930). In *The Philosopher's Stone*, the faithful are diminished or defeated by the arrogance of political power and scientific inquiry. Albertus's brief interlude of contrition is inspired by dubious motives, and he is evidently unchanged when the curtain falls. It appears certain that the philosophical oven will be relighted, that the search will continue, and that perhaps the cost will again be as great. In form the play is the most conventional of Lagerkvist's dramas. Although it is unnecessarily long and has a deliberate, contemplative quality which slows the action, it has a cumulative effect of great power.

Pär Lagerkvist's plays have a long record of successful production in Scandinavia. All of them have been performed except his first drama, *Sista mänskan* (*The Last Man*, 1917). The Schauspielhaus in Düsseldorf played *The Difficult Hour* in 1918, when Lagerkvist was still relatively unrecognized in Sweden, but subsequently Swedish audiences saw parts of the trilogy at the Royal Dramatic Theatre (*III*, 1921; *I*, 1927) and in performances by the Student Theatre of the University of Stockholm (*II*, 1930; *I–III*, 1947).

Lagerkvist's debut on the Swedish stage occurred in the spring of 1921 with the production of *The Secret of Heaven* at Gustaf Collijn's Intima Theatre. Einar Fröberg directed what must have been a fascinating performance with Harriet Bosse in the principal role, music by Ture Rangström, and a startlingly effective stage setting designed by Yngve Berg, consisting of a spherical acting area representing a small planet isolated in space, illuminated by an eerie light. The public and the critics, schooled in a dull and unimaginative theatrical tradition, were mostly unprepared for this bold experiment. A part of the audience was openly hostile, but its scornful whistling was drowned out by stronger applause. Although the notices were by no means entirely favorable, they were unexpectedly appreciative.[10]

The King, in part because it requires extraordinary technical resources, costuming, and an unusually large cast, has been staged only once. Soon after it was published there was talk of a production in Gothenberg and Stockholm, but in fact the first performance did not take place until 1950, when Lars-Levi Laestadius presented the play at the Malmö City Theatre. No expense was spared to create the "heavy, barbaric splendor" that Lagerkvist called for in his stage directions. The monumental décor, the rituals and entertainments, and the battle itself were impressive. At one point there were ninety-seven people on stage, and at another a war chariot drawn by two live stallions sped across the boards. It was to the director's credit that these externals were less obtrusive than expected, but still there seemed to be little proportion between this tremendous marshaling of effects and the rather subdued, philosophical discussion of the principals which, after all, is the essence of the play. Some of the leading roles were weak, and the mood of the play was diffuse. It was a magnificent evening but not quite the dramatic triumph that had been hoped for.

Per Lindberg, the Swedish director most closely associated with Lagerkvist, staged *The Hangman* in 1934, first at Den Nationale Scene in Bergen and later at the Vasa Theatre in Stockholm. Gösta Ekman's masterful portrayal of the title role in the Swedish production is still remembered as one of the great performances of the Swedish stage. In Sweden, surprisingly, the audiences were indifferent, despite the play's artistic success—the Stockholm production closed after twelve performances. In Norway, however, the

[10] For a discussion of the state of the theatre in Sweden at the time of Lagerkvist's Swedish debut see my "Pär Lagerkvist and the Swedish Theatre," *Tulane Drama Review,* VI (Winter 1961), pp. 60–89.

play was received with enormous enthusiasm, "which almost grew to the proportions of a folk movement," according to Lindberg.[11] *The Hangman* has also been produced in London and Amsterdam, and in the United States by university theatre groups.

The Philosopher's Stone was performed in 1948 at the Royal Dramatic Theatre and was revived on the same stage in 1952. Alf Sjöberg's direction fully summoned the playwright's dramatic intensity, so dependent on intimation rather than sharpness and progression of dialogue, and on symbolic figures which nonetheless become living characters, drawn with richness of detail, colorful and vigorous, like portraits in many of the later mediaeval miniatures. The play was warmly received by the public. In fact, judging from the number of performances in Stockholm—more than for any of his other plays—this was Lagerkvist's greatest success in the theatre. The critical response was qualified, but still many of the reviewers felt there was reason for superlatives. *Stockholms Tidningen*, for example, acclaimed *The Philosopher's Stone* as "one of Lagerkvist's great philosophical dramas" and the performance as "one of the Dramatic Theatre's most notable achievements of recent years in producing original Swedish drama."[12]

In translating Pär Lagerkvist's plays I have striven to be as faithful to the original as possible, but equally to convey the feeling of his language in effective English that can be spoken easily on the stage.

The translations are based on the collected edition of the dramas published in 1946 (item 252 in the Willers bibliography mentioned in the Bibliographical Note), except *The Philosopher's Stone*,

---

[11] See Per Lindberg, *Bakom masker* (Stockholm: Bonnier, 1949), pp. 25–34; and also his *Gösta Ekman* (Stockholm: Natur och kultur, 1942), pp. 221–223. For a Norwegian view, see Einar Skavlan, *Norsk teater 1930–1953* (Oslo: H. Aschehoug & Co. [W. Nygard], 1960), pp. 52–55. Information concerning the number of performances of Lagerkvist's plays is from an unpublished card file in Drottningholms Teatermuseums Bibliotek, Stockholm.

[12] Martin Strömberg, "Albertus kan göra guld. En lysande Dramatenrepris," *Stockholms Tidningen*, February 16, 1952, p. 11.

which was translated from the text in *Dramatik*, Vol. 3 (Stockholm: Albert Bonniers Förlag, 1956).

I should like to express my thanks to Fil. lic. Ulf Abel of the National Museum in Stockholm for many helpful suggestions on points of translation; to the University of Kansas for encouragement and support of this work; and to the John Simon Guggenheim Memorial Foundation for making possible a fellowship year in Sweden, 1964–1965, during which this book was completed.

THOMAS R. BUCKMAN

Modern Theatre:

Points of View and Attack
(1918)

The evolution of the theatrical art is so dependent on external realities which are not amenable to change that it may seem meaningless to come forward with any wish or assumptions concerning the direction its development might take. Without reflection the theatre has invariably regarded all well-meant theorizing as only that; and although one really cannot reproach it on this account, it does have on its conscience not a little ungratefulness for genuinely vital and sympathetic interest shown it.

Still, at a time when the art of the theatre itself seems not to have any guiding principle, but rather many conflicting ones, and when tradition is mingled with occasional experiments whose lasting value appears doubtful, when the whole outlook appears confusing to such a great degree, it is, of course, understandable if an author who works with drama, or wishes to do so, tries to orient himself a bit, tries to decide what would seem to be essential for the theatre both now and generally, and thereafter attempts to take a stand in regard to the different trends. Anything less would hardly do. He must of his own accord form an idea of the means of expression and of the aims proper to the theatre so that he will, in every case, have a fixed point from which to proceed.

A personal view. But preferably not one which is merely personal. Not a view leading him to the conviction that he in fact requires a theatre for himself, which he ought to question to the last. But one which is suitable both to him and to his time. And which, instead of superciliously disregarding the external requirements of the theatre that at the present moment actually exist, on the contrary, uses these very requirements as a foundation.

A highly limited freedom of movement and a difficulty in finding new form and of making practical use of it, if it is discovered—this may well be said to characterize the art of the theatre. And if the theatre in all ages has shown an intractable conservatism and an anxious respect for traditional forms, this is in part understandable. Yet it cannot, therefore, be completely excused. For it has a great partiality for stereotype which is not deserving of the name of piety or reverence for tradition or any other such pretty phrase, but is surely mere convenience and indifference. The theatre has a tendency to enclose itself and exclude the outer world, disregarding the fact that the life which moves beyond its walls changes its forms little by little, which has caused it to believe, with a good conscience, that it could do without many sound impulses from the outside. Not only from life itself but also from other adjoining spheres of art which have reacted far more strongly to contemporary events. In this not even the drama can be excepted, although it is the theatre's indispensable support. For if a tendency toward renewal has become evident in the drama, the theatre has not hesitated even then to struggle against it. This resistance places too great an emphasis on its independence. It is to regard the theatre as something apart, without any appreciable connection with the rest of the world.

An isolation of this kind in a time so full of change such as our own has been felt too unnatural. And a breach has been made, here and there, in the wall. There have been attempts, some already successful and others as yet not quite as felicitous, more or less to recreate the theatre and give it a form intended to better satisfy contemporary taste.

Still, when faced with these attempts, one must again acknowledge, willingly or unwillingly, to what degree the theatre actually seems to be bound by certain forms, how difficult these are to unite with others, and how much in the old forms, which at first glance appeared to be empty conventionality, upon reflection— especially when it is no longer there—evidently originated in a genuine feeling for tradition, that is to say, quite simply, in a feeling for what is right and natural in the theatre, even if this is unnatural and artificial outside it.

The march of naturalism into the theatre must be regarded as the foremost of these attempts. It is not of very recent occurrence, but at this moment its effects may everywhere be observed and possibly

evaluated. Other attempts at renewal may be found in some probably rather ephemeral manifestations, tendencies, and experiments
in the modern theatre. These are too near us to really make
possible any evaluation, but they do not therefore appear any less
bewildering. There will be occasion later to consider them briefly.

The realistic portrayal of people and milieu, which almost fifty
years ago was meaningfully and fertilely new, gives contemporary
drama its basic character. The art of dramatic production has also
stood for the most part on the same foundation since the break-
through occurred with the inclusion in the repertoire of Ibsen and
the naturalists who followed him.

Naturalism appears to dominate the stage almost completely.
The actor's art turns to it both when it wishes to give its best and
when in need. Stage direction with all its technical perfection
serves naturalism. And yet on closer inspection one cannot help
noticing that from the very beginning its position has seemed
rather insecure, just as in recent years it has been threatened by new
tendencies within the theatre.

First, with reference to the physical setting, it seems that this
entire studied art of illusion, of which the naturalists are so proud,
is misdirected because so little—and never perfection—can be
achieved in this way and also because the direct illusion does not
belong on the stage at all. If a completely natural illusion is
achieved, it becomes evident that it does not correspond with what
is right for the theatre. It breaks out of its framework, offends the
eye, if it does not actually seem extravagant or absurd.

For it is undoubtedly a fact that reality cannot simply be moved
onto the stage, but must first be given a new form consistent with
its new purpose and new surroundings. Naturalism, it seems, has
very little observed this precept, and that is why, even from the
most superficial point of view, because of the visible stage picture,
it appears foreign to its environment as if accidentally placed there.

And, of course, when naturalism appeared it encountered a
theatre built according to a view of the means of expression and
aims of the theatrical art which was much unlike its own. Here was

no structure designed for the exposition of a harsh and inhibited realistic story, but rather for the free play of the fantasy, for magnificent passion, sweet pleasure, for reckless romance or classically heightened ideality—for a little of everything, not merely the even grayness of everyday life. Greater proportions and more splendid forms.

But without troubling itself with scruples on that score, and without considering if the view expressed here was really not more correct and less transient than its own, naturalism moved resolutely into this alien environment and tried to feel at home. Like a bolshevik in a *palais* from *l'ancien régime*.

A printing press can deliver edifying books one day and shilling shockers the next. It pays no attention to such small matters. And the reader of either product will not therefore sense anything unsavory.

However, the relationship between the theatre and the drama is something else. The theatre as architecture, and therefore also as artistic idea, encloses the drama. It is always present, making its influence felt, intervening and participating more than is generally understood even though one never ceases to be aware of it. It approves or disapproves, gives emphasis or effaces, breaks asunder or concentrates everything more compactly.

Naturally the drama should not be adapted to the theatre building, nor should the dramatist speculate on how suitable his work will be on the stage. But he has reason to observe and to consider if the view of theatrical art which has been expressed here is not, perhaps, really correct and acceptable also to him. He has even greater cause to do so because it is not a chance innovation, as his own notion *could* be, but rather a view which has been tested through the centuries and found to be good, after it had become established. A view valid despite the many changes of fashion. In fact, so generally valid that a variety of different forms—although not all of them—could and still can be in harmony with it.

If he turns his back on it, quite possibly he will forfeit the opportunity of being initiated into much which has always been of great importance for the theatre.

Actually, there probably has never existed anything so inimical to the essence of the theatre as the modern interior drama, the one-wall-away drama in which naturalism has excelled, and the art of acting and stage production which has been derived from it. One sits in one of these magnificent, gilded, pleasantly ingenuous playhouses where one really feels the genuine mood and festive anticipation of the theatre, and then suddenly the curtain rises, revealing a narrow, brownish, dirty interior on which the director has worked and slaved in the sweat of his face to make as exact and natural as possible with rugs on the floor, tables, chairs, *fauteuil*, chaise longue, and with people who move slowly and thoughtfully across the stage, carefully and minutely unmasking each other. There is something foolish in this, something which does not cohere as it should. One is compelled to admit that it is the theatre that has the right on its side in the matter and that the drama has broken out of its framework because it has not made use of the means of expression which are most natural for the art of the stage.

This playhouse, with its peculiar form directly adapted to its purpose, its rows of seats and boxes, its pleasantly spacious interior, is the most fantastic of all rooms which wholly belong to our own time. Filled with people and light, it gives an enticing impression of something extraordinary; and for my own part I must confess that often before the curtain has gone up I have been able to form, as I think, a better idea of what the theatrical art actually wishes to be and should be than I have succeeded in doing on the basis of what I observed afterwards on the stage—if the play were a naturalistic drama of the orthodox type.

Away from the theatre!—that seems to have become the watch-word of the drama, and the stage picture has been forced to conform to its intentions. Even the actor's art has followed in this direction.

The actor has become more and more fearful of the theatrical (by which I mean not empty sawing, but the movements on the stage which are most directly expressive), and his style has become increasingly intimate. He prefers little gestures and movements and the imitative rather than the creative art of acting, in general, means of expression which are as unobtrusive as possible. The portrayal of character has moved toward familiarity, inhibition, and dislike of all externals.

Gradually the playhouse and the audience have become something rather irrelevant to the real actor—almost a necessary evil. If one wants to look at him—well, please do. But otherwise he goes about at ease in his room and has nothing to do with these unknown persons. A wall has been removed because it seemed desirable, but he is, in any case, at home and behaves accordingly. If, when the play is over, he does not unwillingly see—for after all he is still an actor!—the audience, politely indicating its presence and trying to show that it seemed to understand, this is, nevertheless, as long as it lasts, only his own little secret understanding.

No one will deny that this kind of acting has directed attention to values which before have been less recognized and that as reaction it was understandable and natural. But to try to hide the fact that it is for the audience that the drama is played is rather frivolous. And to demand that the little, intimate means of expression should form the basis of an idea of what is really distinguished on the stage must surely be an unsuccessful venture. For just as the theatre is and will remain a very public institution, the art that is presented there must necessarily be an art directed outwards—but not, therefore, empty.

Goethe, in his otherwise not very instructive *Regeln für Schauspieler*, has expressed that view of the theatre and acting which in our day, it has been urgently felt, should be left as far behind as possible:

> The stage and the auditorium, the actors and the beholders, consist above all of a whole.—The actor must constantly consider that he is there for the sake of the audience.—They (the actors) should not therefore, because of misunderstood naturalness, play to each other as when no third person is present.

That is the simple view that has been held hitherto in this matter. And in accordance with it the attempt was made to bring the public as close to the actor as possible, to remove the borderline between stage and audience in different ways: by means of direction, décor, through the acting itself, and often through the use of a prologue and epilogue in which the actors addressed the audience directly—all this which has now been discredited. For now it seems the purpose is first and foremost to mark the borderline as sharply as can be, to make the distance as great as possible. The art of acting has adjusted itself to this idea to such a degree that one sometimes really sees a drama played with an indifference toward the audience which is almost impressive.

But still, all of this takes place in the name of truth, honesty, and naturalness. Well, nature—the word can mean so many things. Perhaps it is unnatural that a person on a stage, before an audience which never takes its eyes from him, behaves as if he were alone with his God. And natural that his performance becomes something quite different.

If the role is an experienced inner reality for the actor, the form will *always* be inspired by it. He does not need to be afraid to use the means of expression which are most suitable for the theatre, and he only does the audience a disservice by not using them.

Naturalism has so long let us understand that it alone represents the "genuine," the "true," and the "real" that we have developed a mistrust of every other mode of expression except that protected by naturalism's own patent, despite the fact that we could see that its form as often as any other was merely the cleverly constructed covering of nothing. One can indeed with reason reproach naturalism itself for having elevated form—its own!—to the position of being an end in itself, preaching the necessity of its use also in areas where it does not belong and onward in a time in which it only seems constraining, as if naturalism in itself possessed an undeniable general validity. Naturalism has been rather far from understanding that every form in itself is dead and is simply a product of the search of the individual and his time for their own expression. Or—when it is a question of theatre, that form merely means an adjustment to the *relatively* constant external conditions of a particular art.

Actually, we can hardly doubt that, for example, a Kean or a Ludwig Devrient was capable of giving a greater and more powerful portrayal of human character than any naturalistic actor of our own day. And yet their performances, from the point of view of what is "natural," certainly would have seemed both "affected" and "theatrical" and much else deserving of contempt. But did they not have, in addition to all their other resources, an advantage which our contemporary actors lack, for the very reason that the forms they used were eminently suitable to the theatre?

Fear of the "theatrical" is understandable, as often as it has, no longer supported by authentic personal qualities, degenerated to empty pose. But we usually base our impressions of that style on how it appeared in its decay, not as it was when it sprang from sound and genuine feeling. And we are used to thinking that it is entirely out of the question that our time which is so "natural" in every way could be guilty of a similar crude caricature—in the opposite direction.

Like every other style, the so-called theatrical, quite naturally, conceals nothing but lurking dangers whenever one thinks that it can replace inspiration, instead of making easier, insofar as it can, the creation of an outer form in which the inner vision is truly expressed. And if one wishes to see an example of this style in hopeless deterioration—and this can be salutary—it is only necessary to read the previously mentioned rules for actors in which Goethe raises his stern pointer before the, we may assume, raptly listening troop of actors in Weimar. They also deserve to be quoted because they are rather amusing. Here are some of them:

> He who stands on the right side gestures with the left hand, and likewise, he who stands on the left side with the right, so that the breast will be covered as little as possible by the arm.
>
> The two middle fingers should always be held together; the thumb, index finger, and little finger should be somewhat bent.
>
> The movement of the arm always takes place in succession. First the hand is raised or moved, then the elbow, and then the whole arm . . . for otherwise the movement would be stiff and ugly.
>
> The actor does not take out his handkerchief in the theatre,

much less blow his nose, and even less does he spit. In a work of art it is horrible to be reminded of these natural things.

Among the gravest of errors which must be avoided is that an actor, in order to move his chair farther forward, grasps between his legs, takes hold of the chair, and then raises it slightly and draws it forward. It is not only incompatible with Beauty but even more so with Decency.

Likewise, there is little doubt that if naturalism on the stage were driven to similarly minute perfection—practically impossible to achieve in the one case as well as the other, thank God—the result would be just as forbidding.

Naturalism on the stage means, in short, a denial that theatre ought to be theatre, a new and revolutionary idea which, if it were correct and viable, would surely mean that we now, after hundreds, if not to say thousands, of years of mistakes, had finally discovered the essence of the matter.

But if, on the other hand, it is *not* correct, and we have good reason to believe that it is not, then the situation will be different. Then it can only imply a distortion and a corruption.

Actually, naturalism has only been able to constrict, to make narrower, and to cramp the drama and the art of the theatre.

In its dislike of all externals, of everything which seemed of the theatre, and in its resolve to force upon the theatre its *own* means of expression, naturalism had only one way to go: to concentrate the drama in the spoken word and to cut away from it, and therefore from the art of stage production as well, all other means of expression.

The spoken word was ready and tractable. It could be used for debating problems; and later, when the discussion was over or the matter removed from the agenda, it could give us a picture of man as he stood and moved in our midst. This was fine; the stage was an excellent platform for pronouncement and psychopathological analysis.

The consummation of both good and bad are achieved in the

typical Ibsen drama with its silent tramping on carpets throughout five long acts of words, words, words. Here intimacy and restraint were driven to the point of becoming virtues; and because an author of extraordinary talents used them, they seemed inviting to a whole generation and more. Even now when the worst of the Ibsen affliction has passed, there is certainly no one who will deny that it was a great blessing that we were stricken with it, but likewise also a happy occasion that we have recovered. One can perhaps hazard the assertion that Ibsen is a great author because of his merits, not his mistakes, and not because, through his authority, he came to work more than any other for the limitation of the modern drama to a rather confined area.

Naturalism has also implied a more severe and one-sided definition of the dramatic, a more forbidding demand on dramatic structure, the elimination of all lyric elements and all immediate poetic effects as basically irrelevant. What is alone of importance is the gradual development and clarification of the inner conflict. And here there is no use for anything but the quick reply, the dissecting dialogue, because the conflict is not one between undivided passions, instincts, and feelings, but rather a case of the author's slow picking to pieces of the characters and grim feeding of them to the public. Lyric portrayal of moods, poetic ecstasy, all of the like unnecessary and frowned upon.

This involves still another contraction of the boundaries which, admittedly, is only a necessary consequence of naturalism's basic idea, but still not a happy one.

But the objection can be made: is not the word the one element which is really essential? And is it not an advantage for drama to be free from the burden of lyric ornament which only makes the action less clear?

One can point to the greatest examples of the past such as the theatre of antiquity which, with almost no technical stage devices and with abstract scenery often irrelevant to the action, had to depend only on the spoken word and yet truly succeeded. But that is a matter which concerns us very little. The same limitation does not exist for us. The modern stage is a sorcerer's magical box full of a thousand possibilities, and we make a mistake if we do not use them. It is not only imprudent, but also artificial and unnatural. If the various possibilities of the modern stage are not properly used, then we cannot avoid the more or less unpleasant feeling that they have been neglected and that we have voluntarily limited ourselves more than was necessary.

Moreover, our theatre did not develop from the theatre of antiquity, but from that of the Middle Ages. Despite indirect lines of development, it traces its ancestry to the latter.

When Tieck and the Neo-Romantic movement in general reeled with vast plans to give the theatre and drama new power through associations with the Middle Ages, this occurred with a genuine feeling for where our theatre had its origin. The mistake was that in his enthusiasm for looking backward Tieck quite forgot what was more important—to look forward. When in our day we have occasionally moved in the same direction, we have also found ourselves to be on solid ground. However, this has meant little in those instances where it was deemed sufficient simply to seek a more or less archaic form.

The theatre of the Middle Ages is so rich and diversified that it can always be worth the effort to take a little interest in it. Was the spoken word the only essential element here? Far from it. Here everything, and nothing by itself, was essential. From the point of view of the diversity of means of expression, it is the richest conceivable form of theatre; in any case, the freest which has ever existed.

The spoken word, dialogue and lyric, played a great part, but the ability to tell a story on the stage and the art of scenic arrangement played as great, or even greater, a part. In this there is something sound and correct. The theatre does not deny itself the means of expression at hand; it uses them all, one having as much value and excellence as the other, the end really being a *show*, something to see, not just to hear.

The medieval theatre used to a great extent purely external means of expression. Its technical apparatus was developed, and, what is more important, its ability to tell a story on the stage was

vital as never before or after. On the stage itself there were so
many possibilities and such a rich imagination to make use of them
that the effect of the play depended to a great degree on what was
done there. It is true that later, during the period of decline, this
imagination degenerated to nothing more than clever ingenuity,
dispelled and subdued the drama instead of strengthening it, and
made itself the master instead of the servant. But it cannot be denied that as long as the drama itself was vital, it made for greater
richness and opportunity, and besides was sound and valid.

But, it will be said, this relates to the theatre of the Middle Ages,
and even if it were ever so excellent for its own time it cannot have
very great importance for us; we have nothing to learn from it.

No, perhaps nothing to learn, but certainly an observation to
make, namely, that our own modern theatre possesses the very same
richness of possibilities. The only difference is that we use them so
poorly. We have the opportunity of releasing on the stage an imagination which creates form genuinely and dramatically, not
lowering ourselves to the taste of a barbaric time, but using externals entirely as an expression of an inner vision. But we do not do it,
and it is naturalism in the drama and on the stage which holds us
back.

Of course, we make use of our resources, but only for an anxious
art of illusion, complicated and meticulous, in itself flat and
empty. Or, in a certain quarter, for the creation of a noisy, heavy,
and bulky apparatus, a puffing machinery which disperses the
mood it aims to hold fast and leaves both actors and audience
gasping.

We lack the simple, self-evident, living dramatic power *to tell a
story*, and the scenic imagination which, with a light touch, as our
indoor theatre requires, really *creates* and *forms*, and does not merely
illustrate. And yet this is just what the modern theatre seems to
call for.

Of course, the responsibility must be placed on the playwright,
not on the director. It is the playwright who must bring it about,
who must step down on the stage, writing directly for it, not for
the street, for the public or the "glade in a grove." Only from the

world of reality can he draw his material, just as only from it, his inspiration, but he has a right to use them for his own purposes, and in so doing he can achieve an effect which is more expressive and genuine.

It is surely this in particular which makes the position of the modern art of directing so weak: that, despite its great resources, it exists only to deliver an illustration of the action; it is merely a little, all too unessential addition to the inner life of the drama. There is no reasonable proportion between what it *can do* and what it now *conveys*.

If there is to be a thunderstorm in a naturalistic drama and the available resources are used to recreate the storm just as it appears in reality, neither more nor less, with lightning and crashes, rain and driving clouds, then about ten times too much has been done. All this means essentially so little for the drama itself, no matter how much talk there is of thunder and lightning. And we have an irritating feeling that too much is made of it. We object not only because we know we are in the theatre and feel that this does not belong on the stage, but also because the drama and the director's art are too much isolated from each other.

Here, one might say, is an example of the medieval theatre at the time of its decline when the master machinist looked after his duties and the playwright attended to his. We should have had more reason to observe how drama and direction in the medieval theatre in the time of its flower flowed together into a unity in which both were naturally dependent on each other, and how the drama came to life on the stage itself, making use of all of its possibilities to truly unloose its fury.

The modern stage invites this kind of cooperation just as much as did the medieval, even if our theatre, our tastes, and all of our assumptions and aims are so widely separated from those of the Middle Ages that in nothing else can resemblances be found.

The stage devices ought not to be materials for illustration brought in afterward to heighten the mood. They should be created directly out of the writer's imagination and should be a link in his

line of thought just as important as any other, and therefore presented in a form just as pronounced and to just as great a degree
animated by his inspiration. Would not this mean a richer scale of
expressive elements for the dramatist, a freer hand, and room for
more active imagination? And does not the theatre have here a
sound and natural line of development, the theatre for which externals play such a large part that they must be used, yet not as
such, but as expression for something within?

The stage devices should then, even if they were complicated,
always seem motivated, not clamorous, disturbing, meaninglessly
intrusive. And, of course, it would not be a question of trying at all
costs to develop as much activity on the stage as possible or of setting into motion a great complex apparatus. On the contrary.
The heavy devices, the purely external elements of great dimen-
sions, and the most violent effects of the stage are not suitable for
our indoor theatre. Enclosed within its four walls, the theatre re-
acts against too much noise. It demands a light touch, vigor of expression, distinction, not raw strength. Not machine culture. But a
living imagination.

This, then, is an attempt to affirm that the spoken word does not
alone have the right to dominate the stage, and that such a circum-
stance, especially in our modern theatre, is opposed to that which is
natural.

And now this question: is the drama's limitation to dialogue, to
the exclusion of the lyrical elements, wholly an advantage?

It implies something new in any case. Until the advent of
naturalism the lyric had its accepted though limited place in the
drama, and its justification was not questioned. Yeats, the Irish
dramatist and man of the theatre, in a foreword to *Plays for an Irish
Theatre* has considered this relationship:

In poetical drama there is, it is held, an antithesis between
drama and lyric poetry, for lyric poetry however much it move
you when you read out of a book can, as these critics think, but
encumber the action. Yet when we go back a few centuries and
enter the great periods of drama, character grows less and some-

times disappears, and there is much lyric feeling . . . . Suddenly it strikes us that character is continuously present in comedy alone, and that there is much tragedy, that of Corneille, that of Racine, that of Greece and Rome, where its place is taken by passions and motives, one person being jealous, another full of love or remorse or pride or anger.

It is clear that there must be a great difference between our own understanding and formation of motifs and that of these earlier periods. For us, people, moods, and passions are much more complex. But it is doubtful that we must therefore eliminate all lyric from our drama, as doubtful as it is that we should for that reason be compelled to shrink from a sound and graceful naïveté in our view of people and motifs and a fair simplicity in their formation.

Certainly lyric elements as rallying points and intervals of rest in drama are as fully justified now as in the past. It is simply evidence of the author's shortcoming if he does not understand how to use the lyric in this way or if he does not wish to do so. And without it there will be a deficiency, a great impoverishment in the drama.

Is it not just this deficiency which comes to mind when, as we view the modern drama, it seems to us monotonous, an endless dialogue which is taken up again at the beginning of every act where it ended in the previous one, like a chewed thread which is never bitten off or taken out of the mouth, an accumulation of words, feelings, and ideas which tire us and cause our interest to flag? In this kind of drama there are no real contrasts in the form; the same means of expression are used all the time, and the viewer's receptivity must necessarily be dulled.

Here again is another contraction of form, a striving in a single direction, with a denial of other possibilities, which cannot be counted as advantageous for the drama even if the greatest writers have veered off on this tack.

The explanation seems to be that most often there has been less interest in drama as such than in either the idea one wished to put forward or the persons one wished to bring to life. And yet the drama itself, the impression which it as a concentrated whole makes on the audience, is surely the essential thing. Here the writer opens his world for those who wish to see into it, reveals his view of people and things generally, not by allowing a character to talk about what he has on his mind but by introducing something personal into the form of the drama itself and into its atmosphere and light, something which gives just that perception of life which is his own. The effect of the whole must certainly be vital to him; the effect of a single character, which is merely a detail, far less important. In the former instance he includes all he essentially intended, in the latter only a part.

The characters may be splendidly conceived and drawn, but the drama poor just the same, merely leaving behind a vague and unsatisfactory impression. And in modern drama we find time after time the characters very carefully shaped, nuanced, and worked out in too great detail and the plot likewise exploited to the extreme, while, on the other hand, the drama itself as poetry and vision has been neglected. It is lost for us and becomes vaporous; only a few types remain and what they do, think, and believe.

The older drama is superior in that it aims primarily at a strong unity of effect, and in that detail is kept in its place and the structure raised with different materials, complementing and strengthening each other. And here the lyric element, especially, plays an important role.

In the recollection of a Shakespearian performance many details may be erased, but all that which *is Shakespeare*, all that world of wonder and poetry, remains vividly alive for us, opens like a beautiful flower which still has all of its fragrance remaining. While of Ibsen we remember a few isolated types—a Borkman, a Stockmann, a Mrs. Alving—and otherwise merely that it was something about illness, or the compact majority, or perhaps only that it was something very complicated and very long.

Naturalism means for the theatre constraint and curtailment of its possibilities in many respects, a one-sidedness which once had its importance as reaction, but which now seems only bare and oppressive because, basically, it is incompatible with so much that is essential for the art of the theatre. That is why one must oppose it.

But there is also another reason which concerns not only the theatre and drama, but imaginative writing generally.

Naturalism seems no longer adequate as a means of expression and does not answer to the time in which we live. Much of what we observe around us and even much more which we only darkly surmise cannot be made clear or suggested in this form. It cannot find expression for the violent and abrupt contrasts in modern life, for all of the complexities and the confused and fantastic elements which we see.

Naturalism has its definite, rather severely limited form. It is confined to a continuous developing of theme which allows everything to lie on the same plane. People and things appear in the same plane so that, despite all changes and shifting of scenes, we always have the feeling of wandering along through a flat and treeless landscape where, as we approach, the writer little by little exhibits his people and settings.

It is this form we must now find inadequate if we would try to present that perception of life which the modern stream of events even in its outward appearance imparts to us. It allows us to *describe* a feeling or a view as thoroughly as we wish, but it does not allow us to shape directly, in the very form of poetry, the most profound, indeterminate, and beautiful strains of our feeling into a whole and living expression, as is the intention of all art.

Our time, in its lack of balance, its heterogeneity, and through the violent expansion of its conflicting forces, is baroque and fantastic, much more fantastic than naturalism is able to portray it. In our daily lives we scarcely possess the feeling of security which naturalism's form gives, but rather an acute need of finding expression for all of the anguish we feel as life wells up against us. It is here that we are left in the lurch—when we try to understand ourselves and our own time.

Our age is directed outward perhaps more than any other; and when the attempt has been made to impugn it, this, especially, has been a point of criticism. But hardly in justice. In the first place, it is inconceivable that it could be otherwise. Besides, this extroversion should not be thought of simply as the equivalent of shallowness. Basically it means nothing more than a stronger feeling for reality and a need to see the inner condition expressed in something external and tangible; in art this is a preference for a more firm and concise form, colder perhaps, but just the same more intense. As reaction against the intimacy of a previous period and against all the introversion of the nineteenth century which gave to its cultural life the atmosphere of quiet and peaceful interior, even when battle was the watchword, this new requirement is both understandable and sound, though we may also see much beauty in the past. It represents a cooler spirit, which may also imply fresher air.

And if this development does no more than fill us with anxiety and bitter irony, must we not look upon it unflinchingly just the same? Does not the writer's own period force upon him irresistibly its way of seeing, if not its manner of valuing and judging, its form, even though his writing is a single thunderous protest against the time? Can he reject this influence if he really, in all seriousness, wishes to understand the essence of his own day? He can close himself in, cut off all contacts, become absorbed in other periods and other moods, and entirely, without reflection, live other people's lives. And he need have no fear on that account of not being appreciated. But one should take pleasure in him, as in the fragrance from an old scent bottle, of old lavender found in a bureau drawer, and shed a tear and become a bit sentimental at the thought of all that has been lost. No, one should let bygones be bygones.

The truth, the bitter, scornful, alarming truth about oneself— that can only be heard from one's contemporaries.

What a sea of brutality has broken over us, sweeping away and re-creating! Is not every inner problem of mankind, which before lent itself willingly to give brilliance to the literary conversation, now suddenly transformed into objective, threatening reality? Is not every emotional persuasion by force of necessity now entirely transformed into embattled resolution?

And how powerless the writer stands in the midst of all this! How little his word weighs in the struggle. It counts for nothing.

The importance of imaginative literature has diminished quite considerably. From the place of first importance it occupied, stared at, recognized, the leader of the debate, it has been pushed down toward the door. But what is there to say about this? Only that it is right and natural. Poetry and art forced back into their proper places as the comparatively subordinate factors they are in life and also in culture. Finally there is liberation from that suffocating atmosphere, that stifling overvaluation of the aesthetic which allowed the values and judgments of art to be decisive and final and made the author regard himself almost as the creator of time, while he was at the most a spectrum in which the different rays could be examined and identified close at hand, or more often only the little window mirror which showed the man who dared not go out himself what was happening down on the street.

It is inconceivable that imaginative writing which, even when it attempts to describe reality directly, must isolate phenomena and to a certain extent tell a story and distort, or when it wants to give a total view can only express it as a vision, in ecstasy—that this art could continue to be decisive during a period which has so many clearer and more authoritative sources of knowledge from which it can derive its certainty and doubt. From these and from hard and threatening realities we derive the driving forces of our lives. And in just this, surely, lies the strength and greatness of our time.

Poetry and art, however, can find expression for all our anguish and rapture, our pleasure and pain, in the presence of what comes to pass, in face of that which is built up and that which crushes us, for our clinging to what we own and our longing for what we most bitterly lack. Is this not enough? Does this not satisfy our aspiration? If not, then one may enclose and cultivate himself within a hothouse atmosphere in silent adoration.

But blessed be life, the strong and inexorable.

If the outward appearance of our time did not correspond completely to its inner state, then art and literature could be unmoved by it all. But in its very foundations our time is just as shattered and disharmonious and as divided against itself as its outer shell suggests. A chaos, but not in dissolution—a chaos which is on the verge of integration into something which as yet we know little about. And in that uncertainty and on that unsteady foundation there is a feverish work of building, a recklessness and boldness which is found only in a world still at the point of just coming into existence. There is a fortuitous application of all the impelling forces, a baroque towering up of all things on top of each other until the whole structure trembles, cracks at the joints, and threatens to fall to pieces.

Even though we may have been able to hide the fact before, recent events have suddenly illuminated our world as if by a flash of lightning. We have been forced to see everything, all of the madness in the picture, its incoherence and incongruity, the deep clefts and the grinning chimeras. And the unloosed passion of the time which, nevertheless, will only cause it to build on and on and on, as if in feverish intoxication and frenzy, untroubled by the gaping abyss.

In this fury, in this mania and ecstasy, there is something of the Gothic spirit; just as in the lack of moderation, balance, and harmony there is something of the complex character of the Middle Ages.

If one looked more closely it might be possible to find profound resemblances between our time and the medieval period, between the age of faith, inwardness, and religious exaltation and the age of doubt, irreligion, and restless intellectual excitement, both chaotic, both a conglomeration of powers too resolutely storming heaven.

Someday, surely, out of the confusion a new age will arise having narrower limits, but also restored balance, an age with tempered boldness, with style and grace, when beauty will have time to blossom and become fragrant, and not suddenly spring forth full grown, a rich and brilliant renaissance.

But as yet nothing of this can be discerned. As yet all is shattered, torn asunder, hard, incongruous; light and dark stand in sharp opposition to each other. And we must live in that which surrounds us, in that time which is ours, sensitive to it and attempting to understand.

Perhaps the genuinely vital interest of our time in the Middle Ages and in both the Gothic spirit and its works, and the direct influence from that period which one can find in the fine arts and even elsewhere are not just matters of coincidence or of taste, but have more profound causes in a secret kinship which gradually brings forth similar expressions and a related feeling for form.

And perhaps the often disdained and misinterpreted striving for a particular form is actually a little link—if possibly not a very important one—in the struggle to understand what is peculiarly our own.

A new romanticism? A more variable, more violent and ecstatic form? A more unexpected and simpler view?

But it will become clear that naturalism, even though it primarily must be opposed by a future form of imaginative writing, has left behind many profound influences. Or perhaps one could more correctly put it this way: that the rapid development of the natural sciences and the interest in, and increased knowledge about, reality which first called forth naturalism are still decisive in shaping our ideas, even if in another way than before. We cannot withdraw from reality; it has thrust us too close to life. Everything in our surroundings is inescapably real to us, and there is no release from this feeling.

Neo-Romanticism, tired of the gray, trivial, everyday existence, could tear itself away entirely from all of that and project itself into a fantasia which denies reality, an alien world of dreams; however, we could not, if we felt a similar need, free ourselves from the external world in this way, but, surely, are compelled to see the fantastic elements in things themselves and in reality itself.

The violent and conscious reaction of symbolism against naturalism was actually without great result. Must this not be explained by the fact that the symbolists tried to deny the foundation on which they themselves stood? They wished to cast a beautiful mist over a period which was cool and clear, causing all the firm con-

tours to be erased and making everything appear vague and in-
definite. But the fog withdrew, and the world remained, harsh
and unexplained as before.

Hence, naturalism's great genius—Strindberg!—who after all
was not a naturalist, never became ensnared by this form even
though the new need for which symbolism was an expression was
also evident in him, and despite the fact that the appearance of
symbolism coincided with a crisis in his life similar to the religious
emergence which influenced other writers to follow the new movement. He had too many associations with strong contemporary
currents, even if he often went against them, to be content with this
casually arranged form. And so he becomes instead, as a dramatist,
the creator of a new, deeply personal form, entirely the outgrowth
of inner compulsion, wholly a ruthless, personal expression, but
none the less conditioned by the time itself.

Thus finally to Strindberg.

There could have been reason to mention him before, and with
reference to some of the statements in the foregoing one could not
help making the comment: but still this cannot be said about
Strindberg. Or: yet all of this is found in Strindberg.

And it is a fact that he has meant the renewal of the modern
drama, and thereby also the gradual renewal of the theatre. It is from
him and through him that naturalism received the critical blow,
even though it is also Strindberg who gave naturalism its most intense dramatic works. If one wishes to understand the direction in
which the modern theatre is actually striving and the line of development it will probably follow, it is certainly wise to turn to
him first of all.

We can discuss only his form here since this little essay is, on the
whole, concerned with it alone. Not because this point of view is
the most fruitful, but because in this particular connection it has its
importance.

Strindberg's distinctly new creative work in the drama, where he
is, more than in any other area, an *imaginative writer*, begins first
after he has gone through the religious crisis out of which he

emerges, on the whole, free of alien influences, entirely absorbed in himself, enclosed in his own suffering and his own shattered, agonizing world. It is as if, confronted by the need of finding expression for these new, complex conditions of the soul where nothing is at rest, where all is unquiet, anguish, a never ceasing vacillation, where feeling is replaced by feeling, faith by doubt, when existence itself and the external world seemed to him to crumble, to dissolve, as if he then no longer found the old form sufficient, but had to press forward, seeking a new one in which all this could be reflected, one which was as restlessly changing and complex as the conditions of the soul which it should make intelligible.

From his letters one sees that he himself is conscious of this and, at the age of fifty, with an immense production behind him, is anxious and doubtful about the result. Thus he writes to Geijerstam[1] from Lund when he sends him *Advent*:

> Here is the Mystery in the spirit of Swedenborg! Never have I been so uncertain as now if I have succeeded or missed the mark. Have no idea whether it is good or worthless. Tell me frankly!— Approbatur, Cum laude, Non sine, or the like. One word only! But no judgments of friendship. A criticism, Sire!

Hereafter, the drama—and the direct, intimate confession—is his true expression. And it is conceivable that it was to be the drama because it is in all respects his most personal form, his finest tool.

Strindberg himself characterizes *Advent* as "a mysterium." And not only here but also in *To Damascus* there is a mood of the Middle Ages, of Catholicism, and of severe and naïve religiosity which afterward always remains. I do not know if Strindberg specifically had the medieval drama in mind when he created this motif of the passion play to which he returns time and time again. But in the freedom with which the dramatic theme is handled, in the seeming looseness and the apparently fortuitous juxtaposition of the scenes which one feels in reading but which on the stage is not noticed,

[1] Gustaf af Geijerstam (1858–1909).

and in the immediacy and richness of the narration there is much of the medieval drama. But still, quite naturally, everything is entirely new.

As there are in Strindberg's historical dramas evidences of Shakespeare (for whom, toward the end of the century, Strindberg shows renewed interest and says that he has then really discovered for the first time), likewise in the dramas which are his most remarkable and most ruthlessly personal there are vestiges of the Middle Ages. And his interest in Shakespeare can, of course, explain his movement toward the medieval view, since Shakespearian drama in its complexity, luxuriance, and liveliness still retains so much from that period. Now, certainly, he had in all respects a keen interest in drama and a need to seek new dramatic forms, new and richer means of expression.

In regard to form, he succeeded completely for the first time in making a reality of all that he was profoundly seeking, in the chamber plays, in these extraordinary dramas which open a whole new world to our eyes, as rich in human experience as they are in poetry.

Here everything is directed to one purpose—the liberation of a single mood, a single feeling whose intensity unceasingly grows and grows. Everything irrelevant is excluded even if it is rather important to the continuity or to the faithfulness of representation. Everything which occurs is meaningful and of equal weight. No minor roles, but all having an equal right to a place in the drama and all equally necessary in order that the play will become what it is intended to be. And actually, no "persons" in the usual, accepted meaning, no analysis, no psychological apparatus, no drawing of "characters." And yet, no abstractions, but images of man when he is evil, when he is good, when in sorrow, and when joyful.

Simplification. But, nevertheless, richness. Richness, too, in the form itself because of the fact that everything plays its part, nothing is lifeless, all is inspired and put into the drama as a living part of it, and because the theme is always shifting and is clipped off, to be pursued on another plane. Confusion, but a confusion with meaning and order.

Here naturalism is entirely cast aside, its straight line abandoned, and instead a much richer form is created implying an incomparably broader range of expression, a multiplicity of new possibilities.

In the presence of these dramas no one can fail to see how insufficient the naturalistic form is and how narrow its limits. For no one can doubt that Strindberg, if he had been forced to develop the themes in *The Spook Sonata*, *The Pelican*, and *The Black Glove* in one fixed realistic plane, never could have wrung from them that fullness of moving humanity which has made them stand as the most profound and remarkable imaginative writing that he produced. Nor can anyone doubt that it was just through the new mode of expression which he created that Strindberg was able to speak so directly and openly to us, to touch hidden strings in our consciousness which we perhaps had sensed but whose sound we had never before heard.

One may add that Strindberg is not a great dramatic writer because he found this new form.

But that this form allowed him to show the full magnitude of his greatness.

Strindberg's drama such as it gradually became signifies in all respects revolt and renewal. And one cannot imagine that it will have anything else but a revolutionary effect on modern drama because it so completely destroys the old foundations, creates new ones instead, and so clearly shows a way which leads forward.

Ibsen, who was long the modern writer *par préférence* because he exhaustively plodded through all of the social, sexual, and mental-hygienic ideas and ideals which happened to come up for discussion, merely weighs us down with his perfectly consummated and fixed form, impossible of further development, and besides, only fills, in an admirable way, an unoccupied place which otherwise would have been empty. Strindberg, on the other hand, opens a perspective forward which is stimulating and exciting and allows us a premonition of what lies deepest within us, not because he informs us about what we think or ought to think—for how often do we really share Strindberg's opinions?—but just because in him we find the very disquiet, uncertainty, and faltering pulse of our own day.

A new form has never been created more beautifully or more completely as a result of inner personal compulsion.

And yet, as the form finally appears to us, it is never purely and simply the fruit of personality; innumerable other factors have also had their influence: everything which lives and moves about the writer, all he has seen and experienced, all of the life and time which was granted to him. The *form* never becomes entirely his personal property, but that of his time and perhaps posterity's as well.

Had Strindberg lived some hundred years ago, the result would never have been this form, but another. It developed as it did because it was natural, obvious, and necessary that it do so.

If we take a similar turn we shall do so not only because it is right, but also because it is unavoidable, provided we wish to go forward and not backward. And the rightness of it is all the greater for there being nothing to gain without a new quest, nothing finished, clarified, and benignly arranged which only requires that we adopt and use it. Whoever would simply appropriate Strindberg's scenic devices would not profit much by the attempt. Everything must naturally be derived from his own feeling and need. For Strindberg himself this form was fully realized; for his contemporaries and for posterity it is still something which is coming into being.

But the quest is open to anyone if the motivation is instinct and not secret agreement with oneself.

In that sense, however, it seems there is no seeking to be found. What has been taken by force is something that, in a much higher degree, remains Strindberg's inviolable personal property. It is that genuine Strindbergian atmosphere in a drama, the storm and eruption—the violent outburst of a morbid and raging genius. This is what they have hurried to take possession of. In Germany—with a shriek as from jubilant dervishes—and even, if much more modestly and decorously, in Sweden.

What else can the result of this be but a Strindberg in an inferior edition? And where do they intend to go with this thunderbolt in their baggage? So fateful when it flashes and flames against a world, so tame when it merely seems to threaten the author.

Whenever this has happened it has been partly because more attention was given to Strindberg's earlier naturalistic production than to his later work, which raises a front against naturalism. Thus he became easier to place, could be put into a familiar pattern and utilized without so much trouble.

But however strong and passionate Strindberg's earlier dramas are, the emphasis still does not lie there. His later plays, from the point of view of humanity, are richer, finer, more profound and fervent. And as imaginative writing, far more powerful, and liberating in a quite different way. For here, in spite of everything, the light has finally broken through. Here one can breathe and live and believe also in the good.

But it has been Strindberg's fate—and probably will continue to be for a long time yet—that he is valued first and foremost for his bad qualities, both as a writer and as a man. All of his repellent and morbid features were seized upon; these have been regarded as the most interesting. For this suited modern literature best.

Perhaps, however, Strindberg can be viewed more reasonably without thereby losing any of his magnificence or interest. Perhaps one may love the beauty and the value in his work and understand, but not love, its inferior qualities.

It would then be easier to see entirely without prejudice where he is greatest as an imaginative writer and where he falls short.

The sweeping renewal of the modern drama which Strindberg represents in his later development cannot be explained away. It is a revolt against the old, not a development from it. And it is this, his last achievement, that makes it impossible to circumvent him even if one has entirely different purposes and goals.

Ibsen can be circumvented, like a milepost with a Roman numeral on it. But Strindberg is in the middle of the road and one is allowed to pass only after one first understands him and what he actually signifies.

Naturally I do not mean that Strindberg should quite simply be taken as a tutor in the art of dramatic writing. Indeed one cannot be taught in that way, not even if it merely is a question of form. And one "ought" in this case to do nothing other than that which is compelling; otherwise the whole endeavor will be floating in mid-air.

The inner compulsion must be there no matter how it may have originated. That inner compulsion which alone gives imaginative writing meaning and vitality. That compulsion which in youth seems less threatening, and perhaps even is lacking, which explains why most of what a young literature creates is of rather little value. This greatest wonder of life—that everything becomes more circumscribed, shrinks about us until there is finally only one way. No longer a choice or an external chance. But the compulsion from within.

If the struggle for a new form does not also mean the struggle for a deeper personal view, then for heaven's sake it should be avoided. And if one does not need to understand Strindberg's importance, one ought to leave him alone.

All I want to affirm is that Strindberg's newly created dramatic form, despite all its subjectivity, nonetheless corresponds to an artistic instinct in our age.

So much for the drama.

But the modern theatre? Has something similar happened here? Has the art of acting, and the art of play production generally, abandoned its old platform, looked for new forms of expression, proposed other goals than before?

Many attempts which have been and are being made to find newer and freer forms indicate that there has been dissatisfaction with naturalism. From different points of departure and with different concepts in mind concerning what is essential on the stage, attempts have been made to create anew from the older forms or in spite of them.

Foremost may be mentioned the intimate theatre which arose from the drama of Strindberg and whose founding Strindberg himself brought about through his remarkable preface to *Miss Julie*.

"First and last a small stage and a small auditorium" is the de-

mand he makes. And afterward he always holds fast to it, throughout his entire development. His own theatre comes into existence
chiefly to put this idea into practical effect. And here it acquires its
most interesting form through the introduction of the so-called
"drapery stage." This is the most extreme consequence, and it is
better and more sensible than stopping halfway.

But whether this way is, on the whole, the right one is another
question. Many of his plays—like much of naturalistic drama in
general—could be played to advantage on such a stage. But many,
and among them the most important ones, could only lose by it.

The fact cannot be avoided that a small stage implies, first and
foremost, reduced possibilities. Such a stage is confined within a
small space from beginning to end. When an effect built upon contrasts is necessary it is helpless and can do nothing. It has no possi-
bility of expression through proportions, distance, and antitheses.

Therefore, as long as the drama makes only small demands on
décor or is only loosely and temporarily attached to its outer framework, all may be set in order. It is merely necessary to retrench all
along the line, to make a virtue of bareness. But where the external,
as in Strindberg's later dramas, is intimately associated with the in-
ternal, where it participates and intervenes, and where the fantastic
in the concept and figuration also demands a fantastic scenic form,
it will not do at all.

The tendency is negative throughout, goes back to the most
primitive forms of theatre, such as, for example, the theatre of
India of which the intimate theatre with its drapery stage is a conscious or unconscious copy. (Strindberg also gives sometimes quite
the same stage directions as those found in the Indian drama—that
a person shall pretend to open a door, etc.) But while the Indian
theatre was satisfied with this because it had to be, in our day it can
only seem artificial; and one cannot believe that the theatre would
ever seriously choose this path of self-sacrifice and meagerness, even
if it were so bidden by Strindberg.

The merit surely lies in the fact that in a time of confusion in
such matters this theatre really implies a definite style. But in this
there lurks a danger for the actor which weighs even heavier and

which has already been felt—the danger that instead of enriching his acting skill and liberating his imagination, he is led to *stylize* his presentation, killing his individuality. Stylization is the antithesis of all art, and in our day it is the spectre which threatens everywhere. One need only think of a "stylized" landscape painting hung as a background to give "atmosphere"—as happened in Strindberg's theatre and which he insisted upon in, to choose an example, the last scene of *The Spook Sonata*[2]—in order to understand what the end would be.

On this point, and for that matter, in his whole attitude toward the theatre, in his suspicion of it and his wish to see it changed quite simply into an awe-inspiring pulpit for the playwright, Strindberg is no more than the exponent of his own generation's taste and ought not to be regarded as anything else. It would be unfortunate if his instructions were taken *ad notam*. Unfortunate both for the effect of his own dramas and for later development.

Undeniably, the building of a tradition has to some small degree already begun, so that we have a certain *manner* of playing Strindberg, just as we have long had a definite Ibsen tradition. And what is almost even worse, we have acquired—from Germany—a taste for playing his fantastic dramas within a frame of turbid *Jugendstil*, pretentious, empty, meaningless.

All of which shows how little *the theatre* has understood how it should utilize the new elements in *drama* which appeared with Strindberg and that it will probably be Strindberg's fate, not only as a man and as an imaginative writer, but also in his capacity as the greatest dramatist of our age, to be swallowed whole without an attempt to distinguish the better from the worse, the meaningful from the less meaningful.

Max Reinhardt, in his so widely noted work in the theatre, seems to have arrived at the view that the intimate style on the stage is not able to satisfy entirely our demands and taste, that we are beginning to stand in need of something else. After first having been

[2] Böcklin's "The Island of the Dead," pseudo-art's much praised triumph.

interested in the theatre of the chamber play, he has turned more and more to the creation of novelties in the grand style.

He has indisputably achieved many important results. And yet, regarded as a whole, his contribution seems to be ineffective, if he intended—which he undoubtedly did—a renaissance of the art of the theatre. As a whole, unsuccessful because, generally speaking, his work lacks all unity and consistency and does not build on any solid ground.

It is not possible to find any guiding principle in his work. A reaction against naturalism is evidently intended on several points. But on others naturalism is driven to the furthest extreme, to the most minute imitation of reality. And this mingling is so unconstrained that the effect can often be completely grotesque. Such as when—to take a crude example!—real trees are placed in a fantastically stylized forest. Should the former give us the idea that this is reality? And the latter let us understand that it is, nevertheless, a very strange story? Or is nothing at all meant by this?

A multitude of whims and ideas—that is the general impression one has of Reinhardt's theatre. Sometimes very brilliant and picturesque, but more often too heavy, with an apparatus greater than the effect produced.

A theatre, and much less a renaissance of the theatre, is not built on random caprice. It demands consistency and firm ground and a relationship with what has gone before and shall come after. Thalia is, strange as it may sound, the least whimsical lady one can think of. She would rather be re-engaged on the worst terms than venture out on an uncertain enterprise which could be pleasant as a change but later might leave her high and dry. Therefore, one must feel very doubtful about this new trend—of course, a school has already been formed—in the German theatre, even though amidst the confusion there may perhaps be found some of the first impulses toward genuine theatrical refinement in the future.

For it should be noted that much of Reinhardt is good and that this release of the imagination in order to create "theatre" is sound and entirely justified and designed to save us from the drought in which the art of the theatre finds itself because of the naturalistic drama; it gives the dramatist, the director, and the actor a freer hand. But one important point is demanded unconditionally: that everything should develop naturally, should not be forced, but should be simple and self-evident. Otherwise, it all hangs in the air like a more or less resplendent fireworks display until it is extinguished and falls to the earth.

Self-evidence—it is that which is lacking in Reinhardt's theatre. His display of power is not suited to the milieu which is the modern theatre, and he often seems to work without a thought that such an agreement is necessary. Thus, between the stage and the audience a great gulf is fixed. When we, sitting there between four walls, see this enormous and heavy apparatus with its revolving stage and sculptural décor, and when the whole splendid business is put into motion, we feel, it must be admitted, that it is too much for us, that it is too cumbersome and formless for its purpose, that by finer and simpler means something not only as good but better and truer must be possible of achievement, that here it is necessary to use a gentler touch, not the crowbar and hydraulic jack which cause the stage and auditorium to creak at the joints and the audience, which never doubted the power, although it would rather have seen it take other forms, to be too much and unnecessarily impressed. Upon seeing one of these typical Reinhardt bravura performances, one has a feeling of staring down into a stone quarry where visible and invisible persons are working so that the sweat drips, so heavy everything seems.

Ehrensvärd[3] has a line which might be brought to mind here, although it seems to lead us rather far from the subject: "In what does the beauty of the tree consist? In that one sees such a great thing appear so light. . . ."

Reinhardt actually achieves his best results when he proceeds more carefully, in the chamber plays, for example, when without too much clatter he seeks a certain style and refinement.

His directly original creative work, however, does not convince.

[3] Carl August Ehrensvärd (1745–1800), Swedish artist, author, and aesthetician.

The Englishman Gordon Craig has attempted with more consistency to solve the problems of the modern theatre, however, through a predominantly theoretical contribution[4] of which, it might be added, Max Reinhardt seems to have made considerable use.

Craig has kept in mind an undoubtedly much neglected matter: the stage picture as a unity of pictorial and sculptural effects and, in association with it, the costuming. The stage, according to Craig, ought to show us a fantastic painting having depth and space, and the actors ought to be expressive foreground figures within it. By these means he wishes to achieve an intense effect of mood.

And as certainly as painting in the real meaning is a very foreign concept to the modern theatre, this calls attention to a deficiency. If Craig himself had only quite clearly known in what painting, on the stage and elsewhere, really consists, for one cannot say that this is the case. His point of view is entirely that of the quasi-modern idea of art; for him it is merely a question of stylizing—that is the whole of the matter. When the designer wishes to get away from nature he destroys it, instead of trying to understand it and afterward making use of it for his definite purposes. It is strange that such a view can be used as a foundation in a time when the feeling for the genuinely pictorial is more vital than it has long been. Here especially, modern painting has made its most important contribution. To this art, which at once leads away from nature and also tries to avoid empty stylization, one must obviously turn if he wishes to introduce pictorial quality to the stage.

Actually, the *sculptural* seems to be of chief importance to Gordon Craig. By placing on the stage a few imposing forms he aims to give the onlooker an impression of something voluminous and expansive, and consequently, to create just that dizzying feeling which seems to him the most essential of all. (Thus, for example, his setting for *Macbeth*, which consists almost entirely of a gigantic column which, it seems, is supposed to disappear high in the darkness, perhaps even in heaven—the real one, that is, not the theatrical heaven.)

4 The periodical *The Mask*, Florence.

Why the sculptural décor should be regarded as better at all, as now seems to be the case here and there, than the older method using backgrounds and side scenes or than any other conceivable method, is difficult to understand. It is ill-suited to the modern theatre. And why bind oneself to one definite kind of décor when, on the contrary, the stage ought, surely, to be an arena for the imagination, where one has a right to do everything one has a notion to, if only it can be motivated and made to appear natural and in its place.

In conformity with his general view, Gordon Craig has played Shakespeare in fantastic costumes suited to the décor, without troubling himself about historical matters. If one has not seen the results of these sporadic practical experiments, it is, of course, impossible to have any idea about what their advantages may be. But the purpose seems to have been to produce a beautiful picture, something captivatingly picturesque in which, after the audience's enthusiasm concerning Craig has subsided, even Shakespeare might also have been allowed to speak.

The distortion in this way of viewing things is easy to see. One side of the theatrical art has been assigned an importance so disproportionately great that everything else has been swept aside. The décor has become an end in itself, although it is justified only to the extent that it is motivated by the action. It stands there pretentious and motionless, without any proper inner relationship to the drama.

Craig's entire reform program falls on the fact that theatre is not a specially sculptural-pictorial problem, but one infinitely complex, in which the pictorial—the stage as picture, as well-balanced composition—is a comparatively unimportant part.

But the merit lies, as has already been emphasized, in the indication that a pictorial problem also really exists in the theatre. Modern painting will probably make a contribution here sooner or later. In its extroversion and clarity it is as if made for the theatre, and it ought, if properly used, to fit well into the frame. It should be able to liberate the modern stage from meager naturalism as well as from strained stylization in décor.

And it is conceivable that it also would have its influence in other respects, that it would lead the actors to create more freely, with less fear of the fantastic, the violent, and the unique, that through an effect on the formation of character and the manner of expression generally it would contribute to the birth of a new and more vigorous art of stage presentation.

In spite of everything that can be said against it—or its practitioners—modern art, through its sharp observation of what is typical of the present and of the unheeded but essential aspects of the life which moves around us, possesses the conditions necessary for creating style in even other areas than its own. It is possible that it could by degrees favorably influence the taste of both the public and the people of the theatre. And since—*mirabile dictu*—it generally seems to be more inclined toward the heightening of taste than toward tasks which could seem more urgent for itself, perhaps here one may, with reason, entertain real hopes.

Looking at these attempts toward a renewal of the modern theatre, one must admit that as a whole they are not very successful, that they are too inconsistent to imply a firm foundation for something new. And that the means of expression most natural for the existing theatre have not really been used.

The principal concern—and this in a quite unfortunate way—has been those problems posed by the arrangement and use of space on the stage itself, leaving the art of acting to keep even step with these reforms as best it could. A renaissance of the *actor's art* has not emerged, even though there have recently appeared scattered representatives of a new type which perhaps foreshadow what will come. But they are still isolated, without milieu. The Reinhardt school has not created any new style—and how could that be possible when, generally speaking, it does not strive toward a definite goal. Gordon Craig's ideas have been all too little tested in practice for there to be any question of such a thing. And the intimate stage has been satisfied with a naturalistic art of presentation, possibly with some tendency toward stylization.

If a genuine renaissance of the theatre is to come about, of course everything must be infused with new life and new principles, everything must be revised and take on a new form in a natural way.

But do we, then, really stand on the threshold of such a revolution, as one might assume, judging from the rather numerous experiments?

Probably not a revolution which would overthrow and destroy the external theatre and which would lead us instead to an intimate meeting hall or circus. We are fully satisfied with the external form of our theatre. It seems right for us and our conditions, and we will not conceive of it as being otherwise. We long for nothing new on that point.

But a revolution—or more correctly, evolution, for here there can hardly be a question of any bold leaps in development—which re-creates the forms of the art of the stage so that they are more suited to modern taste and demand and which, above all, liberates us from the narrowness, one-sidedness, and barrenness which came into the drama and onto the stage with naturalism. An evolution of this kind is not only conceivable but extremely desirable.

A theatre which gives the imagination of both dramatist and actor greater freedom of movement and greater audacity, a simpler, more immediate, and more expressive form. And above all, a theatre which stimulates the dramatist and the actor to *seek* instead of being satisfied and which opens perspectives forward instead of enclosing us in the present and the past.

The Difficult Hour:

Three One-Act Plays
(1918)

I

In the darkness on the stage, transparent forms are discernible: farthest to the right the blue gable of a house leans sharply in toward the audience; up to the left a barrier which cuts obliquely across the entire stage opening; in the background the fragment of an arch, illuminated from below by light, billowing smoke which whirls in under the arch and disappears; above this, in the darkness a red dog rushing wildly forward; to the right of the dog two great hands stretched out as if in terror; to the left a large pale head without hair, and still higher up the number S 8007, in large print.

All of the forms are in different depths and in planes that cross each other, all in confusion. The colors fantastic, but dull. The stage in a blue-violet half-darkness.

A MAN, *in from the right with cape and tails, wavers like a sleepwalker, seems to be talking with someone*: Yes, I tell you, it was just as we drove into the tunnel. Top speed, you know! . . . A smash, you can imagine, as if heaven and earth came crashing down! . . . Oh, God . . . Dead white with fear!—you can understand that!

A HUNCHBACK, *a thin man withered by illness, supported by his cane, comes forward from the background and follows the man in tails like a shadow, listening with his head craned forward, tapping with his cane as he walks*: Yes, yes, of course . . .

THE MAN IN TAILS *does not look at him but continues as before*: I sat by the window and looked up toward the barrier and the street up there . . . The dog, you see, that ugly dog, he tore out of there! . . . —oh, well, makes no difference . . . Beautiful weather, nice and sunny . . . And . . . —Yes, superb as a matter of fact, really superb! . . . 8007 . . . S 8007— — — Oh, I'm mixing it all up . . . that automobile . . . smart, it was! . . . —But then it seemed as if the car we were in went off in the middle, you know, and then into a thousand bits! . . . And I was thrown way forward as if I'd been fired out of a

cannon, way into the tunnel. Dark, I can tell you! Pitch-black.
And then it seemed as if I had scalding steam on my face . . .
and somebody screamed horribly! . . . oh, oh . . .
Sighs. Wavers. But recovers himself again.
Well, it wasn't so bad for me anyway, I got off easily . . . Only
hit myself in the back of the head here a bit . . . no, it's not
important . . . —Amazing, how easily I got off . . . almost as if
you'd like to believe in a gentle providence . . . "God's good
angels stood on guard. . ."
Laughs.
Only hurts a little here in the back of my head . . . —God only
knows what happened to the rest of them! . . . But I got up
after a minute . . . just a little unsteady at first . . . And then
I went into the tunnel . . . Because, at that end, you understand, at that end I couldn't get out . . . no, you see, there
wasn't a chance, it was completely plugged up down there!

THE HUNCHBACK: Hm. Yes, quite right.

THE MAN IN TAILS: Not the smallest crack, you understand! Just as
if it were walled up. —So I had to go in the other direction . . .

THE HUNCHBACK: He, he.

THE MAN IN TAILS: But listen, George, I didn't think this tunnel
was so terribly long. How long is it really?

THE HUNCHBACK: Well, that's hard to say exactly.

THE MAN IN TAILS: Good that I met you anyway! —I feel so strange
somehow . . . It's as if my head were swimming . . . And I see
so many jumbled things here in the dark . . .

THE HUNCHBACK: So-o-o.

THE MAN IN TAILS: Don't you?

THE HUNCHBACK: No, I don't see anything.

THE MAN IN TAILS: What! Don't you see anything?

THE HUNCHBACK: No.

THE MAN IN TAILS: That's strange. —Well, you know, I hit my
head a little here in back and I'm still a little dizzy . . .

THE HUNCHBACK: Hm. Quite.

THE MAN IN TAILS: And there seems to be so much of that horrible
accident floating around in my brain yet . . . It's good that I

met you, George . . . —But how can it really be that you're here?

THE HUNCHBACK: Huh, God knows.

THE MAN IN TAILS: Kind of you anyway . . . Won't you give me your hand, I feel so . . . Whew, how dreadfully cold you are!

THE HUNCHBACK: He, he, he.

THE MAN IN TAILS: Kind of you anyway . . . I wanted especially to meet you. Just happened to think of you, don't know why, and wanted so much to see you again . . . Say, you're not angry with me are you?

THE HUNCHBACK: Talk!

THE MAN IN TAILS: Well, you see, I couldn't help it. I really couldn't help it . . . She just went and fell in love with me, what could I really do! I didn't make a move. But I was young and all the rest of it. I guess that's what it was. And you . . . you . . . well there was that matter of the hump, you understand . . .

THE HUNCHBACK: Yes, of course, I understand perfectly well.

THE MAN IN TAILS: Yes . . . you see, she was probably very fond of you too . . . in one way . . . But then I turned up and so naturally she had to run off and fall in love with me . . . My God, you know how they are. They're all like that.

THE HUNCHBACK: So? She did?

THE MAN IN TAILS: Certainly! She was madly in love!

THE HUNCHBACK, *who follows him all the time while he wavers to and fro*: So-o-o. I thought it was you who . . .

THE MAN IN TAILS: Yes . . . yes, of course . . . naturally I . . .

THE HUNCHBACK: Yes, that's what I mean. I heard someone say that she . . . well, that she really didn't care as much.

THE MAN IN TAILS: Who said that!

THE HUNCHBACK: Come, come, don't get so worked up. That was only something she said in passing . . .

THE MAN IN TAILS: She!

THE HUNCHBACK: Yes.

THE MAN IN TAILS: It's a lie!

THE HUNCHBACK: Maybe, but that's what she said anyway.

THE MAN IN TAILS: It's a lie that she said that!

THE HUNCHBACK: No, my friend, I heard it, myself. She told me. But good heavens that was so long ago . . .

THE MAN IN TAILS: Yes . . . yes, that's how it was then!—But later, my boy, later it was something entirely different . . .

THE HUNCHBACK: So-o. —Was it now?

THE MAN IN TAILS: Yes, yes! —But you mustn't keep after me this way. I can't sort it out . . . I have all this in my head too . . . *Suddenly grips his arm.*

Watch out there! It's going to crash! Help! Help! It's crushing my chest! I can't breathe! Pull me loose! Pull me loose! God! I'm choking!— —

Quiets down. Smiles at his own terror.

Come now . . . it's not so bad . . . Actually I managed quite nicely . . . Only hit my head a little here in back . . . no, it's not important . . . —Listen! Do you hear how they're screaming over there . . . See it's all blocked off . . . as if someone slammed a cellar door . . . can't slip out there . . . Better try the other end . . . Is it far do you think? . . . Oh, no it's not so far . . . —But I have to rest here a bit first, I'm so dead tired. . . . I'll soon feel better though . . . — —Yes sir, I pulled away from that nicely . . . and lucky too because I'm going out tonight. You see, I'm all decked out . . . Haven't torn anything have I? Oh, no . . . A little late dinner at Phoenix, you know the place . . . *chambre séparée* . . . with *her!*

THE HUNCHBACK: With her? So-o-o . . .

THE MAN IN TAILS: Yes, sir. What do you say about that, eh? *Dances a couple of steps unsteadily, whistles.*

— —Can you keep a secret? If you can I'll tell you . . .

THE HUNCHBACK: Well?

THE MAN IN TAILS *leans over and whispers:* Tonight . . . tonight, my boy, I'm sure of it!

THE HUNCHBACK: Hm. Sure of what?

THE MAN IN TAILS: Oh, you understand . . . sure that . . . that I'll have . . .

THE HUNCHBACK: But you've been sure all the time.

THE MAN IN TAILS: Yes . . . yes, certainly. Of course, I have!
—But, well, you know . . . have and have . . .

THE HUNCHBACK: He, he!

THE MAN IN TAILS: What are you laughing for? — —A lady won't
let herself be carried away like that . . . ah, you should have
seen that almost unnoticeable little smile when we parted and
she gave me her hand . . . just the least bit scornful and
coquettish . . . A man doesn't mistake little things like that,
I'll tell you.

THE HUNCHBACK: He, he, he!

THE MAN IN TAILS: What kind of a hollow laugh is that? Sounds as
if you had a hole in your chest! And of course, you have, you
poor wretch! That's why you can't bear the sight of someone
who is happy. Your kind never can!

THE HUNCHBACK: I see, so we're going to quarrel now? Maybe you'd
rather I'd go?

THE MAN IN TAILS *takes hold of his arm*: No, no, don't go, don't leave
me George . . . I feel so strange . . . so done in . . . hit my
head, you know . . . here . . . here, in back . . . no don't go,
George! I'm so afraid!

THE HUNCHBACK: Afraid?

THE MAN IN TAILS: Yes, afraid . . . I can't tell you how afraid I
am . . . oh, God in heaven!

THE HUNCHBACK: But what's the matter with you?

THE MAN IN TAILS: I don't know . . . I feel so washed out . . . I can
hardly . . . I can hardly lift my arm even . . . Look how it
trembles. Oh, God! — —George, there isn't a hole there in
back . . . in the back of my head? George?

THE HUNCHBACK: What nonsense! There isn't even a lump.

THE MAN IN TAILS: No . . . no . . . it's just my imagination . . .
I'm so upset by all this . . . Why, good heavens, I got off scot-
free . . . But the others, George, the others . . . the devil
knows what became of them!—
Breaks out in laughter.
Ha, ha, ha! That fat one . . . oh, that was comical! . . . he got

it right in the stomach so that his eyes stuck way out of his head! . . . ha, ha, ha, I thought I'd split! He sat there with his hands in his pockets so damned sure of himself . . . but he got it all right! — —I managed very well though, George . . . Just a little tired . . . but it doesn't matter . . . Bad luck it should happen just tonight though, when I was going to meet her . . . —I really didn't have to take the subway you know, could have taken a taxi instead as I thought of doing at first . . . but it was a little cheaper . . .

THE HUNCHBACK: He, he! Certainly, certainly.

THE MAN IN TAILS: What in hell are you laughing for? Envious because it isn't you! Little hump that didn't get any of the steak and can't have a decent feeling for anyone that does. Beggar! Damned if ever I've seen such a miserable lot!

THE HUNCHBACK: There, there, not so hasty.

THE MAN IN TAILS: That's just like you! I remember how anxiously you slunk about that time I showed up. Crouched down like a mouse afraid of the cat, scowling as if you wanted to bite if you only dared! Green with envy! Why anything as pitiful as the figure you cut then, I've seldom seen!

THE HUNCHBACK: Come now, quiet down a little, otherwise I'll have to go . . .

THE MAN IN TAILS *changes his tone*: No! — —No, don't go! You mustn't leave me, George—I can't stand being alone . . .

THE HUNCHBACK: Are you frightened?

THE MAN IN TAILS: Yes . . . I'm afraid . . .

Takes hold of his arm.

Don't you hear how they're screaming over there? Oh, it's horrible!—Don't you hear it?

THE HUNCHBACK: No, I don't hear anything.

THE MAN IN TAILS: What are you saying? You don't hear anything?

THE HUNCHBACK: No, not the least little noise. It's as silent as the grave here.

THE MAN IN TAILS: Whew.

THE HUNCHBACK: He, he.

THE MAN IN TAILS: Don't laugh like that, George. It sounds so
ghastly, makes me shudder . . . —and don't keep after me in
that dreadful way, I can't stand much more . . .

THE HUNCHBACK: Why, my boy, I've said hardly a word. You have
been the only one talking all this time.

THE MAN IN TAILS: Have I? —But anyway it seems that you have
been driving me to it . . . And I'm so tired . . . I can hardly
hold myself up any longer . . . —George, you mustn't be angry
with me . . . It wasn't my fault . . . that's the truth, it wasn't
my fault . . . —She was all that I longed for. Oh, all that anyone longs for . . . and there I was young and strong . . . and I
wanted to live . . . My God, everyone wants to live . . . and
you . . . well, you were so frail . . .

THE HUNCHBACK: Yes, my friend, I know very well.

THE MAN IN TAILS: But it's horrible anyway. Horrible . . . If you
knew how I have suffered, how my conscience has tortured
me! . . . Oh . . . a stinging in my chest every time I think of
you . . . And yet I can't stop thinking of you . . . it's so
strange . . . you press in on me, it's just as if you were the one
who . . . —Yes you! Now I see how you force yourself on me!
Against my will! You won't leave me in peace, you keep after
me again and again . . . until I fall . . . that's what you want,
of course!

THE HUNCHBACK: Come, come . . .

THE MAN IN TAILS: Yes, I'll try to calm down, George . . . You're a
good fellow . . . I don't mean what I'm saying, you know. You
understand that . . . Oh, it's frightful to see you again . . . and
live through all that once more . . . frightful . . . You loved
her very much, didn't you?

THE HUNCHBACK: Yes . . . yes, surely I did. Although perhaps in
another way than you. I had so little hope. Hardly any hope.

THE MAN IN TAILS: No . . .

THE HUNCHBACK: That's why I loved her more humbly and submissively . . . —But, that's not worth talking about.

THE MAN IN TAILS: Yes, yes, tell me, George! It's as if . . .

THE HUNCHBACK: Hm . . .

THE MAN IN TAILS: Tell me about it, George . . . oh, it's dreadful . . . how long had you loved her then?

THE HUNCHBACK: Well . . . about six years, I think.

THE MAN IN TAILS: Six years!

THE HUNCHBACK: About that—I waited, you see, waited for her to understand . . . Followed her . . . No, not so that I bothered her. I didn't even mention anything to her. Only loved her in secret . . . in humility . . . Because of the hump . . .

THE MAN IN TAILS: Yes . . . yes, I know . . .

THE HUNCHBACK: But she didn't seem to notice anything . . . just as if she hadn't even seen it . . . She sang or smiled—you know that strange smile that would make you tremble and really feel how far away she was . . . You remember it, don't you?

THE MAN IN TAILS: Yes . . .

THE HUNCHBACK: That's what I mean—She joked with me because she thought I looked so comical . . . And I would smile too and humble myself even more . . . And would wait for her to understand how much I loved her. Followed her submissively like a dog . . .

THE MAN IN TAILS: Yes, but you see . . . you could never win her that way. Good heavens! No, that was all wrong, George! You should have taken her masterfully, George, masterfully! Like a man, damn it!

THE HUNCHBACK: Yes, yes, but there was the hump . . .

THE MAN IN TAILS: Yes, that's right . . . — —But George, she would never fall for you that way. Never! Why immediately the first time I met her . . . master of the situation, you know, and, well, rather indifferent. And she was head over heels from the first minute. From the first minute! Couldn't see anything but me, you understand—in short she was in my power.

THE HUNCHBACK: So-o? Really?

THE MAN IN TAILS: Yes, you see that's the only way, the only way.

THE HUNCHBACK: Maybe. But it wouldn't do for me. I couldn't ask anything but could only imagine that she might want to give me something anyway, out of pure goodness . . . And so I waited humbly and submissively— Finally I thought I noticed that after all she was a little fond of me. No, no, she didn't love me . . . But she didn't poke fun at me any more because of my defect. I thought she treated me so gently— And then one time . . . one time when we parted she kissed me on the forehead . . . Oh, it was so strange . . . — —but you came and then I understood . . .

THE MAN IN TAILS: Oh, that's terrible! Terrible! What suffering I must have caused you, what suffering I must have caused you!

THE HUNCHBACK: Yes, my friend, but as you said yourself, it wasn't your fault . . .

THE MAN IN TAILS: No, no, you don't believe that! And it's not true. I took from you the only thing you had to live for, the only thing! What you had dreamed about all your life! . . . Oh, it's dreadful . . . How could I do it, how could I! You fell, crushed . . . nothing more to live for . . . nothing . . . and you got that pain in your chest, too . . . Oh, I remember how you went around . . . like a shadow . . . little and hollowed . . . with feverish eyes . . .

THE HUNCHBACK: Hm.

THE MAN IN TAILS: I remember how you watched me with your sickly, frightened look that was nothing but anguish, immeasurable anguish! . . . Oh, those eyes, those eyes, I'll never forget them! . . .

THE HUNCHBACK: Won't you?

THE MAN IN TAILS: I've never been able to forget them, never!

THE HUNCHBACK: Hm.

THE MAN IN TAILS: Oh, it's dreadful, dreadful! . . . It was I . . . *I* who was responsible for it. It was I who drove you to desperation! . . . Oh, George, George! . . . I drove you to your death! *He suddenly gives a start, draws back in terror, staring at him.* God in heaven! You are dead! You are dead, George! — — Help! Help!

THE HUNCHBACK *follows after him*: Come, come, calm down, calm down . . .

THE MAN IN TAILS: Help! Help! You're dead!

THE HUNCHBACK *follows him. Pokes him with his cane*: He, he, he!
—And you are too.

THE MAN IN TAILS: What do you say! I! . . . Am I dead?
Falters.

> THE HUNCHBACK *nods affirmatively.* THE MAN IN TAILS *wavers,
> collapses to the ground with a scream.*

THE HUNCHBACK, *standing over him*: There . . . there . . . quietly
now . . . you feel so exalted . . . just in the beginning . . .
There's so much to think about . . . you stir everything up . . .
The forms slowly fade away.

There . . . now it will be better, don't you think . . . quieter
. . . oh, yes, you feel so exalted . . . Now you don't see so
many strange things, do you? . . .
It is completely dark.

Now you don't see me either, do you? No, just as I said . . .
—There . . . there, now it's better, isn't it . . . quieter isn't
it . . . — —Well, I'll be on my way again . . .
*He is heard, walking slowly, tapping his cane on the ground until his
steps die away in the distance.*

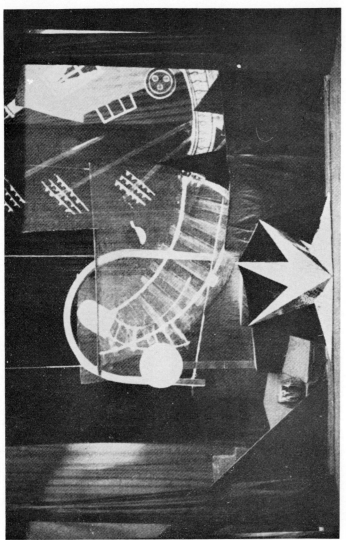

The Difficult Hour I
Klubbteatern, 1927
Director: Per Lindberg
Design: Jon-And

II

Along the footlights, a strip of the stage a couple of yards wide is sharply illuminated from above. The rest of the stage in darkness, except that in the middle, also lighted from above, there is a white hospital bed where an elderly man lies motionless as if dead.

People pass rapidly by in the strip of light along the footlights, always from right to left.

Some workers, hunched forward. Fashionable young men. A ragamuffin. A boy pushing a cart loaded with enormous cardboard boxes. A butcher's helper with a skinned and split steer on his back. Then a man of almost double human proportions with cane and broad-brimmed hat. Again fashionable young men in lively conversation. A man with a clubfoot which strikes loudly on the ground. A carpenter carrying a door. A deformed dwarf with a barrel organ tied to his waist, which he grinds. A Negro grinning so that his teeth shine. A little girl pulling a wagon with a doll in it. Again the man with the steer. The fashionable men. The giant-like man. A laughing, parched old woman. A man carrying on his shoulder a large illuminated Christmas tree with a shining star on top. Two men with a trunk. Immediately after them a stationmaster far down by the footlights blows a whistle and extends his arm.

Two old gentlemen dressed in gray and with gray top hats. —While they converse the stream of people continues as before but more slowly and sparsely.

THE FIRST MAN: He is weak, I hear.

THE SECOND MAN *nods affirmatively*: Very weak.

THE FIRST MAN: Likely be over by tonight.

THE SECOND MAN: Likely that.

THE FIRST MAN: Fine man.

    THE SECOND MAN *nods in agreement.*

And so kind-hearted.

THE SECOND MAN: Ah, so kind-hearted.

THE FIRST MAN: But tell me, where did he get that idea of always going around with a blue cane?

THE SECOND MAN: Hm. Whimsy. —One day I met him with violets in his mouth.

THE FIRST MAN: Ha, ha, ha.

THE SECOND MAN: Just whimsy. —Fine man all the same.

THE FIRST MAN: Quite. —Maybe a little too soft. And a little too concerned about himself.

THE SECOND MAN: Suppose so.

THE FIRST MAN: But so kind-hearted.

THE SECOND MAN: Ah, yes, so kind-hearted.

They go. DWARF *in, playing. Stands and grinds out a music-hall song to its end. Then holds out his hat, turned in toward the stage.*

DWARF: Thank you, thank you. A thousand thanks.

Bows, bows again. —*But then flings the barrel organ into the darkness where it lands with a crash just by the bed.*

Damn your old stinking carcass!

Laughs scornfully and goes.

The man with the steer. The man with the clubfoot. The cart with cardboard boxes. The man with the Christmas tree. The fashionable men. The men with the trunk. The stationmaster in as before, blows his whistle and extends his arm. An old man comes straight out of the darkness around the bed and strews spruce greens where the people are passing by.

AN OLD MAN: Tsst . . . tsst. Schsch, schsch . . .

No more people pass by. Goes back into the darkness.

Stage is empty. A laborer with leather apron and glasses comes in carrying a large chandelier. Sits down, takes out a file and files the prisms one after another so that they screech. The old man in the bed restlessly turns his head a bit. Then the laborer goes out. The two old gentlemen.

THE FIRST MAN: There's only one thing I don't understand, and that's his idea of going about with a blue cane. —Where did he get it from? You can't buy them.

THE SECOND MAN: Well, good heavens . . .

Shrugs his shoulders.

—Would you like a cigar?

THE FIRST MAN: Thanks.

They smoke.

—Soon over, I should think.

THE SECOND MAN: Should think so.

THE FIRST MAN: They say he'll die at nine o'clock.

THE SECOND MAN: Oh? —Wouldn't it be better a little later, say eleven o'clock, for example?

THE FIRST MAN: Maybe so, but it's been decided once and for all. *Severely, seriously, in another voice.*

AND IT CANNOT BE CHANGED!

Strikes his cane on the ground. The giant-like figure slowly across the stage. After a moment.

For that matter he never really had a chance to live.

THE SECOND MAN: Ohh?

THE FIRST MAN: No, I often heard him complain about it.

THE SECOND MAN: Ohh?

THE FIRST MAN: He used to say that the only bad thing he'd ever done in his life was that as a child he once threw a red-hot penny to one of those old fellows who grinds a barrel organ down in the courtyard. —No, he never had a chance to live . . .

THE SECOND MAN: Poor Henry.

THE FIRST MAN: No, he didn't . . .

THE SECOND MAN: But wasn't there a great deal, in a way?

THE FIRST MAN: Well, yes . . . but it never did amount to much, you see.

THE SECOND MAN: But wasn't there a woman once in his youth?

THE FIRST MAN: Ha! That's just it. —She was called Elise. You didn't know her?

THE SECOND MAN: No.

THE FIRST MAN: She was delightful. Really a sweet little child, I'll tell you.

Clacks his tongue.

Fine, delicate. A vision, quite simply; yes, she was. Perhaps a little too impertinent. —Naturally, he loved her. Loved her quite madly, in fact. And she was just right for him, just what he'd been yearning for.

THE SECOND MAN: Oh, well now!

THE FIRST MAN: Mm. That's not the idea, you understand.

THE SECOND MAN: It isn't?

THE FIRST MAN: Mm. Stupid. God meant something entirely different, you know.

THE SECOND MAN: Oh?

THE FIRST MAN: Quite— —

Turns in toward the bed, takes off his hat.

Thank you, well. I have my corns, but otherwise I'm fine, thanks. As usual. And yourself? —So. Oh my, that is too bad. Well bye-bye, old boy!

Turns back to THE SECOND MAN.

— —Well, you see . . . Because . . . as soon as she'd really caught him, it was a different tune! Just as if she'd gotten a little hint, you know . . . psst! . . . from on high one might say.

THE SECOND MAN *questioning.*

And she became another person entirely, you see. You could hardly recognize her even. She became big and fat, like a man, her walk was awkward and noisy and her face coarse, her voice loud and vulgar like a market-woman's. That's the way she changed, you see. —And the way she ate! Why you can't imagine it! She gorged everything she could find and when there was nothing left in the kitchen she started gnawing on the wood bin. But when she began to feel a little full she would sit down and embroider green sofa pillows or paste picture postcards all over the walls, or put paper flowers and gilded grass, you know, in every nook and corner of the house and china cats on the chiffonier. Oh, yes, what an imagination she had! There just weren't any limits.

THE SECOND MAN *shakes his head, troubled.*

Really it's not very difficult to understand God's purpose in all that, do you think?

THE SECOND MAN: God's purpose?

THE FIRST MAN: But Henry never did understand it. It just disgusted him. He became ill and tired. Utterly distressed with it all. —It irritated him especially, I remember, that even out among people she couldn't stop chewing her nails. And he would cry all day long because of her. He didn't understand God's purpose in all that. When God wanted to muddle it up a bit for him so the whole thing wouldn't be so damned simple —then he didn't understand any longer. Poor Henry.

THE SECOND MAN: Poor Henry. —And so?

THE FIRST MAN: So she left him, of course. That was clear. And he was left sitting there, little and elegant, with his blue cane between his legs.

THE SECOND MAN: Alone?

THE FIRST MAN *nods in affirmation.*

Poor Henry.

THE FIRST MAN: He didn't understand God's purpose, you see. And it's dreadful when one doesn't understand what God intends for him. Isn't that right?

THE SECOND MAN *shakes his head*: Dreadful . . .

THE FIRST MAN *puts his hands behind his back, starts to go*: Nice weather, by the way!

THE SECOND MAN *follows*: Nice weather, indeed! It will soon be time for the full moon.

THE FIRST MAN: Yes. But I can't believe what you said about tadpoles because I won't be getting my sacks of wheat until Wednesday.

Two blackened laborers in, one carrying a snorting blowtorch. They lift up a manhole cover in the ground and the one with the torch crawls down in the hole. To the one that remains above.

What are you going to do down there?

LABORER: Something wrong with the cable. The telegraph cable, you know. An important telegram is caught down there and can't get loose. But we'll repair it, you can be sure. It'll be cleared up all right.

THE FIRST MAN: What does the telegram say?

LABORER: Don't know.

THE FIRST MAN: Where is it going?

LABORER: Teneriffe.

THE FIRST MAN: Ohhh.

The other laborer is heard striking and hammering down in the hole, the torch hisses. The two old gentlemen go. A YOUNG MAN *comes in, dressed in a light, handsome summer suit. Looks happily and expectantly around. Goes over to the* LABORER *at the manhole. Lifts his hat.*

THE YOUNG MAN: Pardon. —I am the man lying in there who's going to die. Oh, of course, long ago when he was young, you know.

LABORER, *indifferent*: Oh, that so.

THE YOUNG MAN: But it wasn't that I wanted to say. I only wanted to ask if you had seen little Miss Elise?

LABORER: Don't know the lady.

THE YOUNG MAN: You don't know her! Oh, she's so delightful. So sweet. Simply *charmante*! I'm crazy about her, you know! Haven't you really seen her?

LABORER: No, 'pon my soul.

THE YOUNG MAN: Strange. I was going to meet her here. She promised to come.

LABORER: Hoo! They're always going to come. But damned if they ever do.

THE YOUNG MAN: Shame on you talking like that. I know very well that she'll come.

LABORER: Oh, well, then.

THE YOUNG MAN: What are you busy with down there?

LABORER: Something wrong with the cable. A telegram's caught.

THE YOUNG MAN: What does the telegram say?

LABORER: Don't know.

THE YOUNG MAN: Where is it going?

LABORER: To Teneriffe.

THE YOUNG MAN: Oh, that's a long way off, isn't it?

LABORER: You bet it is. Way off on the other side of the globe.

THE YOUNG MAN: Then it must be something important.

LABORER: Must be.

THE YOUNG MAN *walks to and fro, looking around. The butcher with the steer passes by. The youth steps toward him.*

THE YOUNG MAN: Pardon, but you haven't seen little Elise, have you?

THE BUTCHER, *puffing under the burden*: Puh! Can't even see you! Look after my job, I do.
Goes.

THE YOUNG MAN *restlessly to and fro. After a moment, the laughing old woman comes in.*

THE YOUNG MAN *speaks to her*: Old lady, you haven't seen my little Elise, have you?

THE LAUGHING WOMAN *puts her hand behind her ear*: What?

THE YOUNG MAN: Miss Elise!

THE LAUGHING WOMAN: What say?

THE YOUNG MAN: I'm asking if you've seen my little Elise, old lady.

THE LAUGHING WOMAN *puts her head forward*: I'm a little hard of hearing.

THE YOUNG MAN: Have you seen Miss Elise, silly old thing!

THE LAUGHING WOMAN: Hi, hi, hi! Hi, hi, hi! God have mercy on you, boy, saying that sort of thing to an old hag like me. Hi, hi, hi! Hi, hi, hi! God forgive you, boy!
Goes.

THE YOUNG MAN *looks desperately around. The figures from before hurry across the stage. Boy with the cart, ragamuffin. The Negro. Man with the clubfoot. The organ grinder. The man with the Christmas tree. The man with the steer. They rush past more and more rapidly.*

THE YOUNG MAN *runs among them and calls in confusion and desperation*: Elise! Elise!
The men with the trunk hurry past. The stationmaster in, more quickly than before. Puts the whistle to his lips. THE YOUNG MAN *rushes forward and seizes his arm.*
Don't blow it! Don't blow it!

Stationmaster, unmoved, blows a shrill signal. THE YOUNG MAN, *crushed, staggers away; disappears in the stream of passersby. It becomes quiet. The two old gentlemen slowly walk across the stage.*

THE FIRST MAN: God's purpose, you see, God's purpose . . .
Out.

The giant-like man slowly across the stage. Then empty and silent for a rather long time. Only THE LABORER *at the manhole. The blowtorch hisses down below. A white-haired old gentleman dressed in a distinguished manner, in black with black top hat, silently comes forward from the darkness around the bed. Goes slowly forward and back. Looks at his watch. —Stops by the manhole, stands for a long time and looks down.*

THE OLD GENTLEMAN: Won't that telegram ever get free?
LABORER, *below*: Oh, sure, it'll come loose.

THE OLD GENTLEMAN *again slowly forward and back. A fat middle-aged woman in, glaringly dressed. Chews on her nails.*

THE OLD GENTLEMAN *hurries forward to her. Takes her hands*: Elise! Elise! Is it you!
THE WOMAN: Well, what's it about?
THE OLD GENTLEMAN: Is it really you!
THE WOMAN: Who else?
THE OLD GENTLEMAN: Darling!
THE WOMAN *grunts. Pulls back her hands in order to chew her nails.*
Elise, I love you! I love you!
THE WOMAN, *chewing*: Well?
THE OLD GENTLEMAN: Oh, now I see it all differently. Now I understand the meaning of it all—finally! And now I love you as you are—you, you!
THE WOMAN *chews. Anxiously, whispering.*
Elise! I am lying in there and I'm going to die!
THE WOMAN: I heard talk about something of the sort.
THE OLD GENTLEMAN: Nine o'clock, Elise, at nine o'clock . . .
Looks at his watch.
THE WOMAN: Poor baby.
THE OLD GENTLEMAN *takes her hands again*: I love you, Elise! Love you!
THE WOMAN: Yes, I hear you.

THE OLD GENTLEMAN: But then can't you love me too, can't you
. . .?

THE WOMAN: Sure, you old dear, I don't mind.

THE OLD GENTLEMAN: Is it true! Is it really true!

THE WOMAN: My lord, sure—sure it's true.

Draws her hands away again in order to bite her nails.
—Well, then. We're going to begin all over again. Let me see
now, where did we break off?

THE OLD GENTLEMAN: No, no, all the old life is forgotten. This is
going to be new, the old life is forgotten, Elise!

THE WOMAN: Oh, no you don't. Don't try to skip. No skipping,
my friend! —Now. We're going to begin again and share
everything as before. Right?

THE OLD GENTLEMAN: Yes, darling, at last we'll be together, finally
before I die . . .

THE WOMAN: Well, then. You think we can live here in your
house? Do you have things—things for the kitchen I
mean?

THE OLD GENTLEMAN: Oh, yes, yes, I have them. But, Elise . . .

THE WOMAN: Don't interrupt. All right. We begin tomorrow.

THE OLD GENTLEMAN: Tomorrow, tomorrow . . . but I'm going to
die!

THE WOMAN: Do you have beets in the house? If not, then buy
some. And ten pounds of meat. The best. Must be there when
I come.

THE OLD GENTLEMAN *fingers his watch*: But I'm going to die, Elise,
I'm going to die! . . . At nine o'clock, nine o'clock! . . .

THE WOMAN: No, now you listen to me. Put away that watch! We
have to get things ready, don't we? It's all going to be neat
and tidy! Right?

THE OLD GENTLEMAN *confused*.

WELL! DO YOU WANT IT NEAT AND TIDY OR
DON'T YOU!

THE OLD GENTLEMAN: I'm going to die, I'm going to die . . .

THE WOMAN: TELL ME, DO YOU WANT IT NEAT AND
TIDY OR NOT!

THE OLD GENTLEMAN *tries to take her hand*: Elise, I am going to die, to die! . . .

THE WOMAN: That's none of my business!

Man with the steer rushes by, pushes her away from THE OLD GENTLE-MAN. *After him all of the others. The man with the clubfoot, carpenter with the door, the man with the Christmas tree, the laughing old woman, the Negro and the organ grinder. All of them rush wildly by, pushing her along with them.*

THE OLD GENTLEMAN: Elise! . . . Elise! . . .

All in confusion.

I am dying!

Totters back into the darkness.

The men with the trunk rush in. And the stationmaster hurries forward, blows a long shrill, screeching signal, extends his arm. Then suddenly, darkness all over the stage. Only the light glaring from the manhole. Silent. Only the hissing of the torch. No more passersby, the stage is empty. Finally the two old gentlemen come in. The darkness is impenetrable, but they are illuminated somewhat by the light shining up from the manhole.

THE FIRST MAN: Must be over now.

THE SECOND MAN: Yes, must be.

THE FIRST MAN: Is it nine o'clock?

THE SECOND MAN: Likely is.

THE FIRST MAN: Oh me, oh my. —And so there's nothing more to say about that: Kind-hearted boy, downright kind-hearted . . . Perhaps, a little too soft and a little too concerned about himself but such a kind heart, such a kind heart . . .

THE SECOND MAN: Quite right.

THE FIRST MAN, *after a moment*: Well . . . —He couldn't quite manage things here. Didn't seem to understand it. And so he was let off from it all. It slipped away from him, it did . . . and that's all there was to it.

THE SECOND MAN: But how much more dreadful, to die!

THE FIRST MAN: I wouldn't say that. But, at all odds it must be an experience.

LABORER *comes up out of the hole with the torch, which throws a light on their faces.*

Well, what did that telegram say?

LABORER: Uh, it was nothing at all.

THE FIRST MAN: It wasn't?

LABORER: It only said: The canary bird died, you swindler!

THE FIRST MAN: So . . . nothing more. —What can that mean . . .?

LABORER: Huh, I can't make heads or tails of it.

They all go out.

III

The stage entirely in darkness. A BOY, *carrying in front of him a half-burned candle, advances straight across and high above the open stage. No steps are heard. Only his face is lighted.* —*When he is almost across, an old, hoarse voice is heard down in the darkness.*

VOICE: Hallo, who are you?

THE BOY, *stops, turns around*: I'm only a poor child . . .

THE OLD MAN, *below, mumbling something to himself*: Where are you going?

THE BOY, *in desperation*: I don't know, I don't know . . . Where shall I go! . . .

THE OLD MAN: Hm. You don't know. —Huh, might have known. Ha!

THE BOY: Oh, tell me how I shall find my way!

THE OLD MAN: Ha, ha. —Come down, let me get a look at you.

> THE BOY *goes obliquely down through the darkness until he stands in the middle of the stage.* THE OLD MAN, *who is still hidden by the darkness, mutters to himself.*

THE BOY: Oh, it's so terrible! . . .

THE OLD MAN: So-o.

THE BOY: I've looked and looked in the darkness but I can't find anything and I don't know where I'll go . . .

> THE OLD MAN *mutters.*

Tell me, if you know, which way I should take!

THE OLD MAN: Ha. —My soul and blissful days, take any way you like. There's nothing to stop you here!

THE BOY: But that's the worst of all. I can go any way, up and down, in any direction! Wherever I set my foot I can go, and it feels right . . . But just the same it isn't right. There's nothing, it's empty, empty . . . Oh, God!

THE OLD MAN: Ha, ha.

THE BOY: First I went up a great big stairway, it seemed . . . a great

high stairway . . . up, up, higher and higher . . . It was so pleasant, as if I dreamed . . . up, to the highest place in heaven . . . and up there God and all the good angels waited for me. I knew it would be so light, if only I could get up there . . . Oh, it was just as mother used to tell me . . .
Begins to cry.

THE OLD MAN: Come now. Don't howl. —How long did you go up that stairway?

THE BOY: I climbed and climbed without resting . . . It's strange, though, I didn't get tired at all!

THE OLD MAN *mutters.*

But it was just as dark all the time, not the least bit of light. . . —and finally I began to think that maybe it wasn't a stairway at all and I only thought it was . . . and when I put my foot straight ahead I could walk that way too and go straight out . . . And now it was as if I were in a great desert . . . Oh, God! . . . But then I knew that it wasn't a desert either and then I went deep down as if I were in a narrow valley and looked all around me with my candle. . . . Then up a high mountain because I thought I might find something up there . . . But it wasn't a mountain at all because when I got to the top, I went straight, I could do that too . . . I could walk any way . . . Oh, won't you please, please tell me where I shall go and how I shall find my way!

THE OLD MAN *mutters.*

If you know please tell me!

THE OLD MAN: Say, what is it you are really going around looking for here?

THE BOY: I don't know exactly either! —First I thought it was God and the good angels but now I know it must be something else . . . I don't know what! . . .

THE OLD MAN: So, you don't even know.

THE BOY: But if I only found it I would know that very instant it was what I'd looked for all the time!

THE OLD MAN: Ha. —That really must be a sweet little something, that must.

Pär Lagerkvist

THE BOY: You're bad!

    THE OLD MAN *mumbles.*

Maybe you want to hurt me! Who are you?

THE OLD MAN: Just a poor old man . . . an old carcass . . .

> THE BOY *leans down and shines the light on him. We see a horrible, dried-up face with a long thin beard.* —*Rises again.* THE OLD MAN *is once more hidden in the darkness.*

THE BOY: Are you dead, too?

THE OLD MAN: Yes, but it's been so long ago I hardly remember.

THE BOY: How long have you been sitting here then?

THE OLD MAN: Oh, along about three thousand years.

THE BOY, *frightened, takes several steps back. Stands there oppressed and silent*: But what do you do here, how do you spend your time?

THE OLD MAN: Ho, I don't know. I sit here and pick my toes.

A CHUCKLING VOICE, *farther down in the darkness*: Hi, hi, hi!

THE BOY, *frightened*: What was that?

THE VOICE: Hi, hi. It's only me.

THE BOY: Who is it? Where does it come from?

THE OLD MAN: Oh, it's someone a little farther down. An old witch.

THE VOICE: Witch, did you say? I'll show you who's an old witch. Tsch!

THE BOY: Aren't you alone?

THE OLD MAN: No-o, there are a few others.

A ROUGH VOICE, *from below*: Brummeli—brummeli—brummeli—brum! Boom, boom, boom!

A SQUEAKY VOICE: Bimmeli—bimmeli—bimmeli—bim. Chim, chim, chim!

> *Scattered cries below* THE BOY *and* THE OLD MAN; THE OLD WOMAN'S *voice is shrillest.*

THE BOY, *in wonder and fear*: Who are those people?

THE OLD MAN *whispers to him*: Oh, don't pay any attention to those lackwits.

THE BOY: Are they dead?

THE OLD MAN: Certainly, they're dead. Long ago. That's why they're so stupid.

THE BOY: But what do all of you do here?

THE OLD MAN: What we do?—We just sit here and sicken each other.

THE BOY: But why don't you leave each other! Why don't you go your own ways!

THE OLD MAN: No-o. —You don't understand this, you know.

THE BOY: No. I don't understand a bit of it . . .

THE OLD MAN: We're happy together in a way, you see. That's why some of us are here . . . it goes so slowly, you know . . .

A howl from below.

THE BOY, *frightened, gives a start*: What's that!

THE OLD MAN *calls down*: Oh, you be quiet!

A prolonged howl again.

THE BOY: What is it?

THE OLD MAN: Oh . . . it's an old howling monkey, or baboon or whatever it's called. —That was never the idea at all, you know . . .

THE MONKEY *howls toward them.*

But they thought she was so intelligent.

THE MONKEY: Buuh! Buuh!

THE OLD MAN: Shut up when your betters speak, you idiot!

THE OLD WOMAN: Idiot! If you were only half as smart, you dolt. —Don't you dare say anything about Molla; she's so cute!

THE OLD MAN *mutters something to himself.*

THE BOY: Oh, it's dreadful . . . where shall I go? . . .

THE OLD MAN, *friendly*: Yes, where are you going to go, dear child . . . The candle will soon be burned out.

THE BOY: Won't I get any more candles then?

THE OLD MAN: No, by heaven, you certainly won't. —That little stump of a candle is what you take along from down there, you know. It's just enough for everything a person has within him, no more, no matter what kind he is. About four, maybe five inches, that's about all there is. That's what you leave with. —And when it's gone and you haven't found anything, well, you just sit down and stare. There's nothing else for it, you know.

THE BOY: Oh, that's terrible . . . What shall I do?

THE OLD MAN: Hm. Yes, what's one going to do.

Mutters.

THE BOY, *after a moment*: Did the monkey get a candle like this, too?

THE OLD MAN: Oh, sure! But she ate it up.

THE BOY, *after a moment*: How shall I be able to find anything out there . . . There's neither beginning nor end.

THE OLD MAN: Hm . . . All you'll find I guess will be a few people sitting and hiding in some cubbyhole.

THE BOY: Bad people!

THE OLD MAN: Hm, yes . . . likely be that.

THE BOY: Oh, it's dreadful, dreadful . . . and soon it will be quite dark . . . God, dear God! . . .

THE OLD MAN *mumbles to himself; then* —: Was it any better down there?

THE BOY: What do you mean?

THE OLD MAN: Was it better down there—living, I mean. Ah well, you didn't even have time enough for that, of course!

THE BOY: Living! Oh, it was wonderful . . .

THE OLD MAN *mutters in objection*: Hm, guess you didn't have time enough for that.

THE BOY: Oh, yes, I did lots of things. And everything was so beautiful . . . You have no idea all the things I saw and did!

THE OLD MAN: So-o?

THE BOY: I was out in the woods every day and I had a mill wheel out there. You should have seen how it went around in the springtime. Wheee how it went! In the spring I was going to make a sawmill. —Oh no living wasn't bad at all. It was all so wonderful.

THE OLD MAN *mutters to himself*: Hm . . . I'd forgotten . . .

After a moment.

But what about when you died?

THE BOY: It was in the middle of summer and the window stood wide open. And the whole garden was full of flowers . . . and all the bushes . . . And the birds sang all evening until far into the night. —And in the morning a little baby bird came and sat on the window sill and looked at me with his head cocked a little to one side . . . I think it was a finch.

THE OLD MAN *mutters*: Yes . . . Yes . . . I'd forgotten that . . .

THE BOY: Oh, I had time for a lot of things . . .

THE OLD MAN, *after a moment*: But . . . did you love someone too? . . . I mean really love someone?

THE BOY, *pausing*: Love?

THE OLD MAN: Yes . . .

THE BOY: Certainly! I loved mother, of course.

THE OLD MAN: Nobody else?

THE BOY: Yes . . . yes, the others too. But not like mother, of course.

THE OLD WOMAN, *from below*: Hi, hi, hi!

In a disguised voice.

Come let me see you, little darling!

THE OLD MAN, *urgently*: No, don't go down there, don't go!

THE OLD WOMAN: You be still! —Well, come now little boy. Otherwise I'll come and get you, I will.

THE BOY *afraid*.

THE OLD MAN *whispers to him*: She can't because she has gangrene in her legs, that's what she died of! —But that damned monkey found her some place and pulled her along up here!

THE OLD WOMAN: Well, come now little boy . . .

THE OLD MAN: Don't go, don't go for God's sake! She's the worst scum you can imagine. For God's sake, don't go down there!

THE OLD WOMAN, *shrieking*: Listen to who's talking! You old geezer. You who begged and pleaded for several hundred years to kiss me somewhere— —what was it you said? Tsch! —Did you get to? Nix to that, old boy. And so you started wailing like a little brat that can't have the nipple. Boo, hoo, hoo. You callous old swine! Devil take you!

Noisy laughter from everyone below. THE MONKEY *joins in the laughter with his howling.*

Hi, hi, listen to Molla, she's laughing at you, too, hi, hi!

THE MONKEY *gives an angry, resounding howl. The voices laughing again.*

THE BOY, *in desperation*: What kind of a horrible place is this?

THE OLD MAN *whispers*: It's hell, hell, my child.

THE BOY: But isn't it up in heaven?

THE OLD MAN: That doesn't help when people come together like this, you see.

THE BOY: But go away from each other then!

THE OLD MAN: No, no! . . . Heaven, you see, heaven is even worse, a thousand times worse even, because it's just nothingness!... One would go mad there of having nothing around. Crack-brained, you understand! That's even worse, watch out for it! Some people have tried it but they've become quite dotty and have gotten all kinds of queer ideas, everything turned upside down for them and hardening in the head, you know, hardening in the head, watch out for it, boy! . . . No, we have to put up with what we have, there's no other way. —But sit up here with me, I'll be good to you, I will, I'll take care of you, you'll see . . . We won't pay any attention to them down there . . . They're so stupid, the lot of them . . .

THE OLD WOMAN: What are you cackling about?

THE OLD MAN *mutters something to himself. In a disguised voice.*

Dear little child, don't stand there and listen to him. He's daft, you can hear that! He's got hardening in the head, you can hear that! Has had it all his days, that's what he died of, you know. —Watch out! Don't stand so close! First thing you know he'll spring up and bite you!

THE BOY *shyly takes a step backwards.* THE OLD MAN *mutters.*

Poor little thing. Oh, what a pity it is, poor little boy. How are you going to get along? You can't manage by yourself here, poor thing.

THE BOY, *desperate*: Oh, God, where am I going to go . . .

THE OLD WOMAN: Don't go away! Come here, I'll take care of you, I'll be good to you, you'll see . . .

THE OLD MAN: Don't go down there, for God's sake, don't go!

THE OLD WOMAN: Watch out for that foul old man, little boy!

THE BOY: Where shall I go!

THE OLD MAN: You must go out and seek, seek as long as your candle lasts, you know!

THE OLD WOMAN: For shame, luring that poor thing straight to his ruin! —Come, little one, you can sit on my knee . . .

THE OLD MAN: You have to keep seeking as long as you have the candle left! As long as you have the least bit left! That's what I did! As long as I had a bit left!

THE BOY: But you didn't find anything anyway?

THE OLD MAN *whispers cautiously*: Didn't I? . . . How do you know? . . . — —That's not true . . . Tst! . . . *I've found mine!*

THE BOY, *closer, excitedly*: What was it! What was it you found!

THE OLD MAN: Tsst! . . . You see . . . when the candle was almost burned out, when I only had a little tallow left in the palm of my hand and the wick was floating . . . and I broke out in a cold sweat . . . Then, you understand, I thought that I saw something shimmer up in front of me in the darkness . . . couldn't quite see what it was . . . —I poked up the wick, you know . . . It burned, I'll tell you . . . But anyway then I saw!

THE BOY: What was it?

THE OLD MAN: Tst . . . what was it? —Something like a little whit lying still . . . or maybe floating around . . . a little whit, you see . . . —I clutched it, you understand. Snatched it up! — — at the last minute! Just when the candle went out!
Grunts contentedly.

THE BOY, *shyly, away from him*: Where is it?

THE OLD MAN, *cautiously*: Hm . . . I'm sitting on it. —So that no one can steal it, you see. This is a fine nest of thieves, I'll tell you!

FROM BELOW: Ha! Ha! Ha! — Ha! Ha! Ha!

THE OLD WOMAN: Hi, hi, hi. Hi, hi!

THE OLD MAN: They're so envious of me because I have it, you see, all of 'em. That's why I am sitting up here so high, I'll tell you! —That's why I can stay up here above them, you see.

THE OLD WOMAN: Hi, hi, hi, he thinks he's sitting on top.

All break out laughing.

Listen to me, you old scarecrow, do you want to know something? We all turned upside down a while back so now you are sitting on the very bottom. Hi, hi! We're all sitting above you! Idiot!

THE BOY, *confused and alone. Finally begins to cry*: Oh, mother! . . . *Begins to walk slowly away, obliquely up to the right.*

THE OLD WOMAN, *before he disappears*: Where are you going, poor little thing?

THE BOY *stops, crying*: I don't know, I don't know . . .

THE OLD WOMAN: Poor little child, how do you think you can manage out there! How can you be so foolish! —Come now . . . that's a good boy, come over here . . .

THE BOY *stands silently*.

Come now, my child . . . And I'll let you sit on my lap . . . are they so bad to you . . . there, there, poor little thing . . .

THE BOY *silent*.

Where do you think you'll go, dear child . . . Come now and you can sit on my lap, poor boy! . . . And nobody will hurt you . . . You and I shall talk about so many things . . . Come now, my child . . .

THE BOY: Who are you?

THE OLD WOMAN: Oh, shame on you! Don't you recognize me?

THE BOY: How could I know you?

THE OLD WOMAN: For shame, boy! Your mother should hear you!

THE BOY: Who are you then?

THE OLD WOMAN: Your old grandmother, of course! —And you pretend you don't know me. Shame on you, boy!

THE BOY: Grandmother? Is it grandmother?

THE OLD WOMAN: Yes, your own grandmother. —Don't you remember her? She was so nice to you.

THE BOY: Yes . . . yes, she was.

THE OLD WOMAN: Don't you remember how you sat on her lap and she told you stories and gave you candy too, didn't she?

THE BOY: Yes, yes, I remember . . . Certainly, I remember! Oh, grandmother, is it you, is it really you?

THE OLD WOMAN: Surely, my child . . . And you didn't even recognize me!

THE BOY: Oh, yes, now I hear that it's you. Oh, grandmother . . .

THE OLD WOMAN: And you didn't even want to sit on my lap any more . . .

THE BOY: Yes, yes. I want to be with you, I want to be with you! *Steps downward.*

— —Oh, grandmother, when I was about to die I thought of you so often because mother said maybe I would go and meet you . . .

THE OLD WOMAN: Yes, there, you see!

THE BOY: And mother was so unhappy, you know, because I was going to die . . . But I wasn't so sad because I didn't really understand it, she said . . . But now I understand it. —Oh, I'm so happy that I can be with you!

THE OLD WOMAN: My dear little child . . .

THE OLD MAN *mutters.*

THE BOY *pauses*: But, grandmother . . . ?

THE OLD WOMAN: What is it?

THE BOY: Shouldn't I look for something in heaven?—Shouldn't I, grandmother?

THE OLD WOMAN: Dear child, of course, you should; of course, you should . . . You shall do exactly as you wish.

THE BOY *silent.*

You shall do exactly as you yourself wish. Don't bother yourself about me, dear child. No need to bother yourself about me . . .

THE BOY: No, no, I want to be with you! Only with you, grandmother. Always!

Goes downward.

THE OLD WOMAN: Well, well, I thought so . . .

THE BOY *stops again*: But what about the candle?

THE OLD WOMAN: Oh, you can give that to little Molla, she'll be so happy! —Up now, Molla, and you'll get some sugar!

THE MONKEY *comes up, contentedly yelping. Stretches out a long hairy hand for the candle which* THE BOY *gives her.* THE BOY *down into the darkness.* THE MONKEY *up the same way that* THE BOY *first came until she is in the middle of the stage. She sits and turns the candle this way and that, yelping delightedly. Opens her mouth and swallows the candle. Smacks and chews. —Runs back down into the darkness howling cheerfully.*

The Secret of Heaven
(1919)

A huge blue-black sphere rises into the space above the floor of the stage which divides it slightly above the middle; the sphere appears to extend downward into the darkness. Diagonally from above and to the left, a conical-shaped beam of light, verdigris-green in color, shines down through the darkness and sharply illuminates the visible portion of the sphere, leaving only a part of it to the right in the shadow.

High up on the arch of the sphere an OLD MAN *stands, sawing wood. He doesn't ever raise his head or look around, but simply tends to what he is doing. He takes pieces of wood from a pile to the right of the sawhorse and lays the finished pieces in a stack to the left.*

On the slope, a MAN ON CRUTCHES *walks about with difficulty, and near him a* DWARF *with short little legs trips along. The dwarf has broad breeches, a little cane that he swings, and a large, brilliant-red vest which is too big for him.*

Straight ahead and down near the sharp contour between light and darkness, a wizened little MAN WITH A SKULL-CAP *and large spectacles sits on his haunches, mumbling to himself, his head on his hands. Left of him, an* OLD WOMAN *with a broad, continuous, and toothless grin; her knees are pulled up; she has dirty feet and great pigeon toes which she picks. To his right a* GIRL *with bewilderment in her eyes, red untidy hair, and a guitar on her knees.*

Far out to the left a large heavy-limbed MAN DRESSED IN FLESH-COLORED TIGHTS *and a black belt around his loins sits in profile. From a pile on his right he takes up dolls of medium size, different kinds of people in miniature, men and women, old and young. Takes one at a time, looks at it, puts it on his knee, makes it bow or curtsy. Lops off its head with his finger so that it flies off into the darkness. Then he puts the bodies in a pile to the left. — Sometimes the head is fixed too securely, and then he twists it off, making a face as he does so, and throws it right out into the darkness. He never looks up, is completely absorbed in his task.*

OLD MAN IN THE SKULL-CAP *mumbles while he presses his fingers against his forehead*: I'm sure to get the hang of it all soon, I'll understand the whole thing before long . . .

THE MAN ON CRUTCHES *snorts*: Huh, what is that you understand?

OLD MAN *looks up at him in confusion, straightens his spectacles. Crouches down again, continues mumbling.*

THE YOUNG GIRL *plucks a string on the guitar—a discordant note—while she sings monotonously*: Pling pling plingeli-pling. Pling—pling——pling.
She touches her cheek, pulls at her hair helplessly and sighs, the guitar slides off her knees.

The WOODSMAN *saws.*

THE DWARF *trips about, swinging his cane. —Toward the cripple, in a conceited, squeaky voice*: Nice weather, isn't it? Just right for a morning walk, hee hee.

MAN ON CRUTCHES *sniffing, turns his back on him, stumbles along with difficulty.*

THE DWARF *pokes his thumbs in his armpits, stands puffing himself up in his red vest, looks up at the light, lets it shine on him.*

OLD MAN: The meaning, the actual significance of the whole thing, it is . . . it is this . . . that . . . That we must whirl around, yes that's it. Everything must whirl around, that's it. —That's the meaning, that's the real significance of it all . . .

OLD WOMAN: Haha.

OLD MAN: Up to that point there's no trick to it.

The WOODSMAN *saws.*

The MAN IN THE FLESH-COLORED TIGHTS *lops off a head.*

THE GIRL *picks up her guitar. Discordant sounds again*: Pling pling plingeli-pling. Pling—pling——pling.
Places her hand on the side of her head, stares out in front of her, sighs heavily.

THE DWARF *skips down to her, swaggers about*: Nice weather, Miss Judith, nice weather, isn't it?

THE GIRL *frightened, gives a start, looks at him, bewildered. But then her face brightens, she smiles and stretches out her slender arm toward him:*

Oh, is it you, my pet! Is it you!
She sinks down again. Tired, preoccupied.
What do you want with me?

THE DWARF: Alas, you played so beautifully, Miss Judith. So enchantingly!

THE GIRL: No, no, I cannot . . .

THE DWARF *with hand on heart*: So enchantingly!

THE GIRL: On no, oh dear no. I am only trying to find a string, just one . . .

THE DWARF: So-o?

THE GIRL: Just one . . . — —It doesn't seem to be . . .
Looks at the strings.

THE DWARF *indifferently*: Which one is it?

THE GIRL: Oh, it's not like the others. It's pitched so high, so high. Almost as if the string would break . . . And when one touches it, it seems as if it were of gold . . .
Touches the strings.
— — —There doesn't seem to be a string like that, no string like that . . .
Offers him the guitar.

THE DWARF *looks at the strings, gives it back to her*: No, there isn't.

THE GIRL *bursts into tears.*

THE DWARF *consoles her*: Oh, Miss Judith, you play the others so beautifully. Play all the others!

THE GIRLS *cries.*

THE DWARF: But Miss Judith, if it doesn't exist . . . ! Why try to find it!
Pokes her with the cane: It *doesn't exist*, little lady.

THE GIRL *looks at him in bewilderment*: What did you say?

THE DWARF: It doesn't exist, little lady.

THE GIRL *in a moment—confused and helpless*: But why . . . Why do I try to . . . ?

THE DWARF: Yes!

THE GIRL: Why do I try to find it then . . . ? If it doesn't exist!

THE DWARF: Yes, that's what I say! Why . . .

THE GIRL *bursts out in a long, hysterical laugh. Grabs the guitar, tears at all the strings at once; makes a grating, squeaking, clattering noise, while she shrieks*: There's no such thing, no such thing!

OLD WOMAN *chimes in with a clucking laugh that shatters the air around her.*

THE DWARF *begins to jump around in time with the clattering music, while he sings*: There's no such thing! There's no such thing! Cheem-cheem-cheem. Cheem-cheem-cheem. There's no such thing! There's no such thing! Cheem-a-leem-a-leem. Cheem-a-leem-a-leem.

MAN ON CRUTCHES *spits, turns his back.*
THE GIRL *suddenly becomes silent. The others too, just as suddenly. —She sits quietly. Draws her fingers over the strings, carefully, anxiously. Listens. She sags down.*
The WOODSMAN *saws.*
The MAN IN TIGHTS *lops off a head.*

MAN IN THE SKULL-CAP: I'll soon get the hang of it, I'll understand it all before long . . .

A YOUNG MAN *comes up from the other side of the sphere, he stops on top of it, timid and anxious. Looks around him in wonder. Only* THE DWARF *and* THE MAN ON CRUTCHES *notice him.*

MAN ON CRUTCHES *peers sideways at him, then after having a good look*: Who are you?
THE YOUNG MAN *afraid*: I don't know.
MAN ON CRUTCHES *turns his back and goes*: Maybe you ought to find out.
YOUNG MAN *embarrassed, but bold enough to take a step toward him*: Yes . . . I know. That's what I've come for, to try to find out.
MAN ON CRUTCHES: Well then . . . hmm, go ahead.
OLD WOMAN: Ha!

YOUNG MAN *continues to stand there, looking shyly about him.*

THE DWARF *skips up to him, struts about, puffing himself up*: Hum. — —Hum.

YOUNG MAN *looks down at him in wonder. —Carefully takes a few steps down the slope. Sees the big* MAN IN TIGHTS. *Curious, he goes behind his back to see what he is doing. The man is looking at a little doll, turning it over. Lets it do a few tricks. Then he twists its head off and flings it far out into the darkness; lays the headless body in the pile at the left.*

THE YOUNG MAN *shrinks back in terror, hides his face in his hands, screams*: Oh God, oh God . . .!
OLD WOMAN: Hahaha, hahaha!

THE DWARF *sniggers.*

YOUNG MAN: Oh my God, my God . . .!
He totters about, takes a wrong step, falls headlong.
THE DWARF *breaks out in a violent, hicking laugh*: Watch out . . . hehe . . . watch out, my boy, so you don't fall off! Hehehe.

YOUNG MAN *gets up. Puzzled, he looks from one to the other.*
THE DWARF *trips triumphantly forward and back, measuring him with an amused and condescending look.*

A SWARTHY MAN *has crept up out of the darkness, up the slope. He crawls on his knees, covered with leather pads; his trouser-legs drag along behind, empty. Instead of a hand he has an iron hook. He continually scratches in the earth with it, scratches and looks for something. —When he catches sight of the young man, he stretches his iron hook out toward him*: Give a poor man a penny. —But with a hole in it. It has to have a hole in it.
YOUNG MAN *steps back. Takes out his purse and looks in it*: I don't have one.

THE MAN: No. No one has. There's never anyone who has.

YOUNG MAN: But don't you want an ordinary one, without a hole? *Offers it to him.*

THE MAN *with a hostile look*: Keep it yourself, you bastard!
Mumbles. Begins to scratch again in the earth.
YOUNG MAN *gets out of this way.*
THE DWARF *insulted, steps back when* THE MAN *crawls close to his feet.*

MAN ON CRUTCHES *after watching him for a moment*: What are you rooting around for?

> MAN WITH THE IRON HOOK *looks up, hunches down again, mumbling*.

MAN ON CRUTCHES: Why don't you have any legs?

> MAN WITH THE IRON HOOK *looks up. Mumbles. Digs again*.

MAN ON CRUTCHES *to himself*: He doesn't have a hand either. Ho, ho!

THE DWARF: Oosh, there are no healthy people left in the world!

MAN ON CRUTCHES *whispers to him, pointing with his crutch at* THE YOUNG MAN: That one? Who's he?

THE DWARF: Him!

> *Snorts in contempt.*

MAN ON CRUTCHES *observes the* YOUNG MAN. *After a moment*: Who are you?

> YOUNG MAN *perplexed*.

MAN ON CRUTCHES: Are you someone special?

> *To* THE DWARF: Damned how he stares.

> YOUNG MAN *goes away*.

THE GIRL *plays*: Pling pling plingelipling . . .

MAN ON CRUTCHES *takes a stance and looks at her. To* THE DWARF: That one, she's crazy.

THE DWARF: Mmm yes, she's a little crazy. But it doesn't matter.

THE GIRL: Pling—pling— — — —pling.

MAN ON CRUTCHES: Was she that way when she came?

THE DWARF: Yes, she was that way when she came. It doesn't matter.

> THE GIRL *lays the guitar on the ground, holds on to it with one hand, pulls and tears furiously at the strings with the other, while she screams wildly, gratingly. —Exhausted, she falls down, the guitar under her, her face in the ground, hands in her hair.*
> *They stand there indifferently, watching her.*

A LARGE MAN *old, white-haired, with a long white beard, comes up from the other side. On his chest is a sign which says* BLIND. *He gropes about with his hands, calling*: Help me home, help me home! I can't find the way!

MAN ON CRUTCHES *stumbles away*: Devil take him.

THE DWARF *takes a stance with his cane on his shoulder, looks up at him.*

BLIND MAN *groping about*: Help me home, help me home . . .

MAN ON CRUTCHES *after a pause*: Where do you live?

BLIND MAN: Seventy-eight steps up, farthest up, all the way up to heaven . . .

MAN ON CRUTCHES: So-o. —But where?

BLIND MAN *confused*: I don't know . . .

THE DWARF: In a house, if I may ask?

BLIND MAN: I don't know . . . —Seventy-eight steps, seventy-eight . . . farthest up, all the way to heaven! . . . If I can only reach the hand rail, I'll know, I'll find it myself. I'll find it myself.

They laugh at him.

BLIND MAN *continues to grope about, in desperation*: I live in heaven, I live in heaven! Help me home, I can't find my way home . . .
He stumbles over THE MAN *on the ground scratching with his hook, falls over him.*

THE MAN: What in hell do you want!

Pushes the BLIND MAN *off him.*

BLIND MAN *completely mixed up. Fumbles about, moans*: Where am I? . . . Where am I? — — —
Touches the man.
Who are you?

THE MAN *looks up at him; scratches again.*

BLIND MAN *touches his arm*: What are you doing?

THE MAN *crossly*: Me? —Looking for worms.

BLIND MAN: Worms? Are you looking for worms? —Why are you doing that?

THE MAN: It suits me.

BLIND MAN *wondering. Tries to get up, but he can't*: Won't you help me
  up . . .
THE MAN *scratching*: I can't.
BLIND MAN: Won't you help a poor old man?
THE MAN *curtly*: I can't.
BLIND MAN: Can't?
THE MAN: No.
BLIND MAN: Why?
THE MAN: Because I can't get up myself.
BLIND MAN: So-o. You can't get up yourself? Why?
THE MAN: Because I haven't any legs.
BLIND MAN: No legs? . . . You haven't any legs? . . . Hehehe.
  *Giggles, his hand to his mouth. —Tries to rise again, but can't.
  Reaches out his hand, imploring*: My dear friend, give me your
  hand . . .

  THE MAN *offers his hook.*

BLIND MAN *lets go in surprise. Then*: Hehe— —hehehe— — —Hehe-
  hehehe!
  Manages to struggle to his feet. Wavers.
  I live in heaven, I live in heaven . . . !
  Gropes along again.
  Help me home, help me home . . . I can't find the way
  home . . .!
  Goes to the other side of the sphere.

  YOUNG MAN *stands there uncertainly.*

MAN IN THE SKULL-CAP: I'm sure to get the hang of it all soon, I'll
  understand the whole thing before long . . .
OLD WOMAN: Haha.
  The WOODSMAN *saws.*
  The MAN IN TIGHTS *lops off a head.*
MAN IN THE SKULL-CAP: The meaning, you see, the real significance
  of it all, it's this . . . it's this . . . that . . . that . . .
YOUNG MAN *goes down to him, on his knees beside him, takes his hands be-
  seechingly*: The meaning! Do you understand the meaning!

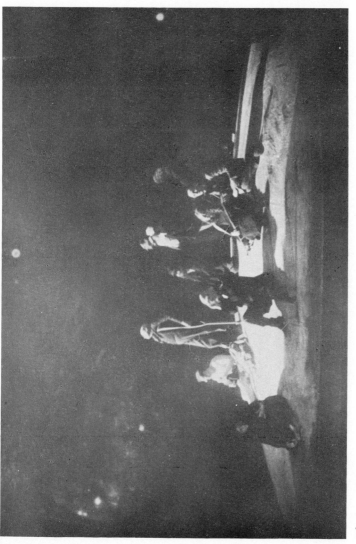

The Secret of Heaven
Intima teatern, 1921
Director: Einar Fröberg
Design: Yngve Berg

MAN IN THE SKULL-CAP *dumbfounded. Curtly*: Of course I understand the meaning.

Straightens his spectacles, looks at him: I understand everything.

YOUNG MAN: Everything?

MAN IN THE SKULL-CAP: Yes. Everything. — —Except him.

Points over his shoulder with his thumb.

YOUNG MAN: Who?

OLD MAN *sullenly*: Him. —The one sawing wood.

YOUNG MAN *surprised. Looks at the* OLD MAN AT THE SAW HORSE: Him . . . —Why don't you understand him?

OLD MAN *irritated, withdraws his hands, settles himself again.*

YOUNG MAN: But everything else! All of these dreadful things! Oh tell me, what is the meaning of all this! Is there really any meaning in it all?

OLD MAN: There's a meaning in all of it together, it's not hard to understand. But if you take each thing by itself, then there's no meaning in any of it.

YOUNG MAN: Then what is the meaning of it all together?

OLD MAN *straightens his spectacles. Thoughtfully*: The meaning, the most profound significance, my young friend, is this: that up there we have what we call the sun. —Do you understand?

YOUNG MAN: Yes . . .

OLD MAN: And here, here we are. —And the sun whirls around. And we, we whirl around. Do you understand?

YOUNG MAN: Yes . . .

OLD MAN: And so we whirl around the sun. That is to say, the sun whirls around us. —Do you follow me?

YOUNG MAN *perplexed.*

OLD MAN: Everything whirls around. Everything. —And therein lies the *meaning*, my young friend. Therein lies the real *meaning*. That's what I've found out.

YOUNG MAN *desperate*: And nothing more . . .

OLD MAN *offended*: *Nothing more?* —That's all there is. Huh!

YOUNG MAN *stands up, in anguish he presses his hands to his chest. —Be-*

side himself, he rushes confusedly up the slope to the MAN ON CRUTCHES *and grips his arm*: Oh help me, help me!

MAN ON CRUTCHES *snorting, turns his back.*

YOUNG MAN *despairing, goes to* THE DWARF.

THE DWARF *turns abruptly, precipitately. Stops a little way off, measures him patronizingly from head to toe. Draws himself up and begins to strut around, swinging his cane.*

MAN IN THE SKULL-CAP: Hehe, they don't know!

YOUNG MAN *to* THE MAN *with the iron hook, throws himself down beside him, lays hold of him.*

THE MAN *pushes him away*: Oh, go to hell!
Keeps on scratching.

YOUNG MAN *wanders about in distress and agitation. Finally sinks down on the ground. Lies with his face hidden in his hands.*

THE GIRL *begins to play again. Slowly. Listens to every note.*

YOUNG MAN *raises his head. Begins to listen. Listens to every note, as she does. Gets up, stands looking at her. —Finally goes slowly down to where she is sitting. Stands very close to her, but she doesn't see him*: What is it you're playing?

THE GIRL *in a fright, looks up. Then*: Oh, it's nothing. No, nothing at all.

YOUNG MAN: It's as if you were looking for something?

THE GIRL: Yes . . .

YOUNG MAN: What are you looking for?

THE GIRL: Oh, I'm trying to find a string. Just one . . .

YOUNG MAN: What kind of a string?

THE GIRL: Oh, it's such a strange one. It's not like the others . . .
It's pitched so high, so high. Almost as if it would break . . .
And when one touches it, it seems as if it were of gold . . .

YOUNG MAN: Mmm? —So strange . . .

THE GIRL: Yes, it is strange. —And when I play on it everything is so beautiful. The whole world is beautiful.

YOUNG MAN: What are you saying! The whole world!

THE GIRL: Yes, yes. Then the trees blossom. The whole earth is in bloom. And then the world is sweet, oh so sweet. And the little birds come and sing for me, the trees are full of them. —Yes, they'll sing for you too. If you're good.

YOUNG MAN *listens, enchanted.*

THE GIRL: They sing like that string, just as high and full of joy. They come when they hear its sound. —Oh, the whole world is filled with the sweetest music. And people stand and listen, everyone must listen.

Whispers to him: Because it comes from heaven. You see, it comes from heaven!

YOUNG MAN: Oh, play, play on it!

THE GIRL *sits silently, absently, as if she were dreaming:* And my head is clear. And I understand everything so well, everything . . . so well. For it comes from heaven, from heaven . . .

YOUNG MAN *kneels down beside her:* Do you have that string there! Do you!

THE GIRL *shakes her head, touches the strings:* There isn't one like that . . .

YOUNG MAN *bends down to see. She hands him the instrument.*

THE GIRL: It should feel as if it were of gold.

YOUNG MAN *looks at the strings, feels them. —Puts the guitar back in her lap, hides his face in his hands:* It's not there.

THE GIRL *stares in front of her.*

OLD WOMAN: Haha.

THE WOODSMAN *saws.*

THE MAN IN TIGHTS *lops off a head.*

THE GIRL *when she hears him sniffing, strokes his hair slowly, but absently, without seeing him.*

YOUNG MAN *looks up at her:* So good you are!

THE GIRL *doesn't hear, stares ahead of her.*

YOUNG MAN *after a moment:* You . . . you are good. —All the others are so evil, and ugly. But you, you are beautiful and good.

THE GIRL *doesn't hear.*

YOUNG MAN *after a moment*: You have strange eyes. — —What are you looking for?
She doesn't hear him.
Say, what is it you're staring at?
She doesn't answer.
Tell me! What are you looking so hard for?
Seizes her hand in a firm grasp.
THE GIRL *gives a start; clutches her brow.*

YOUNG MAN: Was it something you saw?

THE GIRL *her gaze wanders helplessly.*

YOUNG MAN: Did you see something?
THE GIRL: No . . .
YOUNG MAN *after a moment. Holds her hand in his*: Won't you talk with me?
THE GIRL: Yes . . . — —Who are you?
YOUNG MAN: No, don't say that. Don't talk like the others, you who are so good.
THE GIRL: Am I good?
YOUNG MAN: Yes, you are good. I can see it in your eyes.
THE GIRL *her hand at the side of her head*: No, no, you musn't talk so oddly.
YOUNG MAN: Yes, you are good. That's why I understand you. The others are a puzzle. But you, you are so pretty. Oh everything about you is lovely . . .
Caresses her hand.
— —When I sit here and look at you, suddenly I feel so happy and in good spirits. Inside I feel so peaceful, not anxious as I did before. I'll tell you . . .
Whispers: I'm so frightened of all this! I think it's dreadful . . . Don't you?
THE GIRL: Yes.
YOUNG MAN: And I don't understand a thing about it . . . Do you?

THE GIRL *shakes her head.*

YOUNG MAN: I don't understand it, that's why I think it's so

horrible . . . Oh, I was so desperate I wanted to cry. And I felt
something pressing against my chest, every minute it was harder to breathe, and finally I couldn't, it was so heavy and so
frightening . . . —But when you let me sit here and hold your
hand, I feel calm. Everything is different when I hold your
hand. May I?

THE GIRL: Yes.

YOUNG MAN: But you ought to talk with me too. Oh I don't know
what it is! I feel so many strange new things that I didn't feel
before. What is it? I don't know . . . — —It's so odd. I'm
very happy. You should talk with me!

THE GIRL: What shall I say?

YOUNG MAN: I don't know . . . —Whatever you like.

THE GIRL: I can't.

YOUNG MAN: Can't you? —But that's all right, it doesn't matter.
If I may just sit and hold your hand I'll be happy. —Oh your
hand is so soft and warm. It's just like a dove's heart, so warm
and tender.

THE GIRL: No, no . . .

YOUNG MAN: Yes . . . —I saw a dove once. It lay on the ground and
was about to die. Then I took out its heart so that it too
wouldn't die. And it was just like your little hand, so warm,
so . . .

THE GIRL *her hand touching her forehead*: No, no, don't talk so
strangely.

YOUNG MAN: Do I speak strangely? But I don't know any other
way. I don't know anything, I can't say anything right. — —
Would you rather I not say anything?

THE GIRL: Yes . . .

YOUNG MAN *sits silently, looking at her. Finally*: Oh you are so lovely.
The whole world is lovely. — —
Troubled, seizes both her hands: But there is so much of it, and I
don't understand it! I don't know what it is! What is it, what
is it! You must help me! You must help me!
Embraces her impulsively, clings to her, hides his face. —He breathes
heavily, moans. Then he becomes quiet. Rests happily against her breast.

*Caresses her arms and hair. Hides himself again, close to her, a long
time as if he had gone to sleep and was dreaming.*
Finally he lifts up his head, looks around, listens intensely: Judith!
—What is it? — — —Listen . . .!

THE GIRL *doesn't answer.*

YOUNG MAN: Is it you? —Are you playing . . .?

THE GIRL *shakes her head.*

YOUNG MAN: But don't you hear, don't you hear it . . . ! —Oh, it
sounds so sweet. — —And don't you see the flowers! The trees
are blossoming, and the earth is green, don't you see, don't you
see! . . . Oh, you're playing, you're playing for me!

THE GIRL *confused.*

YOUNG MAN *caresses her hair, her cheek:* Oh, beloved, you are playing
for me . . . that's why everything is so beautiful, the whole
world . . . And look, the people stand and listen. See how
gentle their faces are when they listen . . . They've forgotten
all that's evil, and see only the good . . . — — —Now I understand everything so well, everything! — —It comes from
heaven, it is coming from heaven! . . .

THE GIRL *bewildered:* No, no!

YOUNG MAN: You found it, and you are playing on it, the string
that only you could find! . . .

THE GIRL: What string?

YOUNG MAN *looks at her in wonder:* The string you were looking for,
which felt like gold . . . — —Oh, you have found it, that's
why the world's so lovely and new. Look, look! Listen to the
birds singing! See the flowers, how they are bursting out! Oh,
it's so beautiful and lovely . . . And you have given me all of
it. You! You!

Kisses her passionately.

I love you! Love you!

THE GIRL *wanting to free herself:* No, no, you are so strange! . . .

YOUNG MAN: I love you, I love you! —And you love me too, don't
you, tell me, don't you!

THE GIRL *with her hand to her forehead:* No . . . no . . .

YOUNG MAN: Don't you like me? Can't you be fond of me?

THE GIRL *shakes her head.*

YOUNG MAN: Aren't you fond of me?

THE GIRL: I don't understand it, I don't understand anything . . .

YOUNG MAN: Don't you want to like me, to love me?

THE GIRL: Yes, yes, but I can't.

YOUNG MAN: You *can't*?

THE GIRL: No, because I don't know what anything means, and I
   don't understand a word of what you're saying.

YOUNG MAN: You don't understand what I'm saying?

THE GIRL: No, no, not a word. I'm not quite right, you know, here,
   at the back of my head. Oh, it's so pitiful.

YOUNG MAN *consoles her, caresses her slowly.*

THE GIRL: I want so much to understand you, but I can't ever . . .
   ever. I'll never understand anything of this world . . .

YOUNG MAN: But don't you hear the birds? Don't you hear the
   music in the air? —And don't you see how beautiful everything is? Look at the flowers! And the sun!
   Holds her tightly in his arms.
   Oh my darling, we shall live here on the earth you and I. You
   and I!

THE GIRL: No, no! . . .

YOUNG MAN: Listen, we shall live here happily, so happily! Love
   will make us happy. Dearest!

THE GIRL: No, no! I'm mad, I'm mad! Let me go! Let me go!

YOUNG MAN *clings to her in desperation*: Don't you hear, we shall live
   here on the earth! You and I! In the sun! I love you, do you
   hear me, *I love you!* And you shall love me too! Listen to me,
   listen to me! Love me, love me! . . .

THE GIRL *beside herself with bewilderment, tears herself from him*: No,
   no. I'm mad, I'm mad! Let me go, let me go!

THE DWARF *who has watched all of this intently, pokes him with his cane*:
   Listen here, my boy, calm down, rest yourself a bit.

THE GIRL *with both hands at her head*: Go away from me! Go! Go!

YOUNG MAN *gets up, despairingly. Tries to keep her hands in his, she pulls them away. Goes, with his face turned away.*

THE GIRL *staring around her, perplexed and frightened. Cries out*: Help me, help me, I'm mad!

THE DWARF *approaches obligingly, struts around.*

THE GIRL *not seeing him at first, or not recognizing him. —Then*: No, is that you, little mopsey, it is really you!

THE DWARF *swaggers.*

THE GIRL: Oh, I understand you! You're so nice! I understand you!
THE DWARF *flattered*: Miss Judith . . .
THE GIRL *in high spirits*: You're so funny. Your legs are so short. I can understand you!

THE DWARF *struts.*

THE GIRL: And you have such a fine vest.
THE DWARF: Do you think so, Miss?
THE GIRL: Yes, it's handsome. — —
With a sidelong glance up toward the YOUNG MAN: You see him up there, he . . .
Whispers in THE DWARF'S *ear.*
THE DWARF *covers his mouth, giggles. Looks askance at the* YOUNG MAN.
THE GIRL *whispers again.*
THE DWARF *bursts out in a loud guffaw, crude and indecent.*
THE GIRL *laughs with him, crazily and unnaturally*: Yes, my dear, you're handsome! —And I'm crazy as a loon. Hehehe! — —
Seizes the guitar: Now I'll play, and you shall dance. Dance, little mopsey! Dance, do you hear!
She plays wildly and discordantly.
THE DWARF *dances around, gaily and self-importantly, kicking up his heels, swaying absurdly.*
YOUNG MAN *desperately, disconcertedly. —Springs forward to her, throws himself down on his knees, cries out in anguish*: Save me! Save me!

THE GIRL *in a fit of laughter, while she plays more wildly than before.*

THE DWARF *waves him off with a movement of his hand, while he whirls around.*

YOUNG MAN *darts up again.* —*To the* MAN IN THE SKULL-CAP: What is the meaning of it, what is the meaning . . . ?

MAN IN THE SKULL-CAP: The *meaning* my young friend, it's this, that everything must whirl around, must whirl around . . .

YOUNG MAN *dashes over to the* MAN ON CRUTCHES: Help me! Help me!

MAN ON CRUTCHES *slowly takes his measure from head to toe. Turns his back.*

YOUNG MAN *to the* MAN WITH THE IRON HOOK, *grabs his arm*: What is the meaning of it, what is the meaning?

MAN WITH THE IRON HOOK *roughly pushes him away*: Oh, go to hell.

The music and the dancing continue more wildly and madly.

YOUNG MAN *screams*: Save me! Save me!
Rushes forward and back. Finally, far down to the right on the sphere. Stands hesitantly. Then flings himself out into the darkness.
A piercing scream is heard from down there.
The dancing and playing stop abruptly. Wonderment, and a stir of excitement. Silence.

THE DWARF *goes down to the right. Looks down*: Jeezus, he jumped off!

MAN ON CRUTCHES *joins him*: Jumped off! —My god!

THE DWARF: Bless my soul, he must have gone to the bottom.

MAN IN THE SKULL-CAP *to himself, in satisfaction*: Hehe, they think there's a bottom . . . hehehe, they think there's a bottom . . .

MAN ON CRUTCHES *thoughtfully*: Jumped off! — —

THE DWARF: Yes, damned if he didn't. Why, it would never enter my head.

MAN ON CRUTCHES: Mmm, maybe he didn't fit in here?

THE DWARF: Fit in! —Imagine!

That's the end of that. They return to their tasks. The WOODSMAN *saws. The* MAN IN TIGHTS *lops off a head.*

MAN IN THE SKULL-CAP: The bottom, hehe . . . The bottom . . .

The King:

A Play in Three Acts
(1932)

Characters

KING AMAR-AZU
KING IREAM-AZU
SIBILE, *Amar-Azu's favorite wife*
NADUR, *a young man at the court*
THE CAPTAIN OF THE BODYGUARD
THE HIGH PRIEST
THE FOOL
THREE COUNCILLORS
THE MASTER OF THE HOUSEHOLD
THE ROYAL CUP-BEARER

Courtiers, noblemen, priests, dancers, servants at the court, people, beggars, rabble.

Act One

The enclosed courtyard in AMAR-AZU'S *royal palace.*

THE KING *sits on his throne under a baldachin of heavy, barbaric splendor, clothed in all the symbols of his power, surrounded by his bodyguard and his entire court.*

Below the throne stand the priests headed by THE HIGH PRIEST.

Downstage, a throng of people, beggars, artisans, freemen, rabble.

THE HIGH PRIEST: Behold it is the god's, the great Azu's, will that, on this day in the eighth year, when the light of heaven has run its course and the fate of the people is hidden from every eye, our almighty Lord and King shall be divested of all his power and glory and shall become as a beggar, the meanest and lowliest of his people. That he may be brought low before the god and before us, that his splendor may be as dust, as an ash without fire, cast upon barren ground. That he may become unclean, one whom none will touch until he has cleansed himself. And upon his throne shall be set another who shall reign over us while the feast shall last, until the sun's setting on the third day, when the sacrifice shall be fulfilled which is pleasing in the sight of the god.

Amar-Azu, Azu's divine son, I bid thee descend from thy throne!

THE KING *comes slowly down from the throne.*

THE HIGH PRIEST *reverently, with measured ritual solemnity, takes from him the symbols of power, sword and chain and finally the serpentine-adorned tiara.*

ONE OF THE PRIESTS *carries forth a cushion before* THE KING.

THE HIGH PRIEST: Almighty Lord and King, I bid thee return to the god his ring and staff which only thou, divine one, may touch.

THE KING *takes off his ring. Places it and the staff on the cushion.*

95

THE HIGH PRIEST *cries out*: The great Azu, mightiest of gods, rules over us! *He alone!*

A muted ripple of voices and mumbling goes through the crowd.
THE HIGH PRIEST *rips the ornaments from* THE KING, *the needlework of gold and the jewels sewn into his coat. —Hurls him down the steps.*
THE MOB *surges forward. Uncertainly approaches* THE KING. *One of them tears a bit of gold knit from his clothes. Others likewise pull off whatever is left. Subdued mumbling. Suppressed laughter. One of them pushes him. Another does. The hum of voices rises. They push in upon him, tear off his clothes. — —Beat him to the ground. Throw themselves over him.*
Clamor, suppressed excitement, confused tumult.
THE KING *finally rising, bloody and in shreds. Looks at the crowd around him. — —Mumbling they give way for him, he goes away slowly, alone.*
Cries and merriment. Confusion. Laughter. Pranks. Costumed figures come out of the multitude. Hop about, dance. Make noise. The court and the people are mixed together. THE FOOL, *a hunchbacked dwarf, skips about with his rattle.*

A MAN *to those around him*: They rejoice! I tell you, this is a dangerous moment! Azu reigns over us, Azu himself, the terrible one! The heavens are upon us and filled with fire!

ANOTHER: Do you think it's not good that the god himself rules over us! Ask the priests.

THE FIRST: No, it is not good. For the priests perhaps, but not for us. The ruler may be cruel. But the god! The god is more cruel than any man! He is fire! —And heaven, it is filled with fire! I tell you that . . .!

THE FOOL *jostles* THE FIRST MAN: Ha! —Do you suppose all's not well because things are turned upside down! Isn't it a blessing that for once there is some order in the world! Well?
Everything turned upside down! And the heavens filled with fire!

Jumps into the midst of the mob, swinging his rattle. He cries out in a hoarse, high-pitched voice.

The heavens are filled with fire! — —The heavens are filled with fire!

SOMEONE *uneasily*: What are they waiting for?

ANOTHER: Hurry, hurry!

AN ARTISAN'S APPRENTICE *out to the right*: Aren't they coming? Do you see them?

ANOTHER: No.

THE FIRST: Mmm. They should be here by now.

A THIRD: There! Do you see them! *They are coming! — —They are coming!*

EVERYONE: *They are coming!*

Shouting and yelling, laughter, joy and clatter. The court and the bodyguard take their places. The priests have remained standing.

The din suddenly diminishes. The multitude to the right gives way.

It becomes completely silent.

A CRIMINAL *is brought in, with hands and feet chained. Emaciated, half-naked. Blinded by the light.*

Everyone falls far back. They come to a halt with him, in the middle of the courtyard.

THE CRIMINAL *stands where they have placed him, does not move. — — Rubs his eyes. Looks around without moving, but turns his head almost imperceptibly. Then completely still, stands and is silent, looking at them with his hollow eyes. — — —Finally*: What do you want with me?

THE PRIESTS *advance slowly down to him.*

HIGH PRIEST: Behold, it is Azu's holy will that you shall be our ruler and king, almighty before all the people and appointed by the god in the infinite wisdom of his choice. That you shall bear his ring and staff and be his anointed in which he has pleasure. That you shall be crowned and consecrated and be invested with the royal robe and that your power shall be great on earth and all the people shall fall down and worship you. And as long as the feast shall last your body will be holy and

will stand under the protection of the god. And those injunctions on the purification of everything in your presence and of that which shall go through your mouth and that which your hand shall touch shall be observed, as with the hallowed and enshrined, that in everything he does he may remain pure and his power shall not turn from him. And on the third day when the sun sets you shall be offered to the god by fire.
As Azu's holy law bids you and us.

THE CRIMINAL'S *fetters are loosened.*
The royal robe is brought forward. The HIGH PRIEST *invests him. Adornments and a golden chain, the sword ornamented with jewels. Anoints him with oil.*

HIGH PRIEST: In Azu's holy name I anoint you our Lord and King, whose power shall cause the earth to tremble, for whom the people shall fall down. And the name you bear shall be Iream-Azu, as one consecrated to Azu, in which the god has pleasure. *Places the tiara on his head.*

THE PRIEST *bears forth a cushion with the god's ring and staff.*

HIGH PRIEST: I bid you receive the god's ring and staff, which only you, his appointed, may touch.

THE CRIMINAL *hesitates. — —Looks about him, trembling and with hostility. —Waits.*
Puts on the ring. Takes the staff.

HIGH PRIEST *calls out:* The god dwells within you, divine one!

A whisper goes through the multitude, a muffled hum and murmur of voices. THE PRIESTS *lead him up to the throne, and he is seated.*

HIGH PRIEST: Hail to thee, Lord King! Hail to thee, Iream-Azu, Azu's divine son!

He and THE PRIESTS *bow down to the earth.*

EVERYONE: Hail to thee! Hail to thee!
Throw themselves to the ground.
Hail to thee! Hail to thee!

THE PRIESTS *retire in procession, out to the right.*

THE MULTITUDE *pushes forward*: Hail to thee! Hail to thee!

They do homage to THE KING *wildly and in disorder. Throngs in confusion. Also laughter and mocking. Those who are costumed for the festival mix among the crowed and make a game of it.*

POOR MEN AND THE MOB *push up to the throne*: Hail to thee, our King, our Lord! Pardon us! Be merciful to us!

IREAM-AZU *looks at them—follows them with his gaze.*

There is more and more of a jumble. Pranks and jesting.

Food and drink are carried in and offered around to everyone. They throw themselves over the plates, clutch greedily at the food, stuff themselves, drink until they are near choking.

BEGGARS AND WRETCHES *standing downstage in a group.*

ONE OF THEM *with a hoarse voice, wheezes when he speaks*: He's ours! He comes from the dungeons!

ANOTHER: Now it's our turn!

A YOUNGER MAN: Rot! What are you babbling about!

AN OLD MAN: He gives us food and wine, he does, that's more than the other one did!

THE YOUNGER MAN: This is the Azu feast when everything's turned on its head. Don't you know that, at your age!

THE OLD MAN: Maybe so! But anyway he gives us bread!

THE YOUNGER MAN: It isn't him! It's the others.

THE OLD MAN: It's all the same. Food is food. I say let's eat, drink, and be merry!

A PALE YOUNG MAN: No, grandpa! Let me tell you. Let's eat—but not be merry. You can save that happy day awhile.

THE OLD MAN: Way I see it, we'd better get some while we can.

THE YOUNG MAN: It's better to *wait*, I say. You hear me!

THE FOOL *jumping around*: Today you can do as you please! Come on, don't wait! Soon enough you'll have the whip on your backs again, you dogs! Get your hand in while you dare! Get your share, you cowards!

A POOR MAN: That fool speaks strangely.

AN OLDER MAN: Yes, it's a time for fools.

THE YOUNG MAN: Listen you, not only for fools!

More and more unbridled merrymaking and delirium and drunkenness. The court mingles with the people, every tie is loosened. Whores press through the swarms, allowing advances, asking to be fondled, appraised, and led away by the revelers.

IREAM-AZU *sitting throughout motionless on his throne, staring straight ahead.*

Wonderful foods are carried to the interior of the palace. Great serving dishes with whole roasted animals, magnificent drinking-vessels of gold and silver. Enormous pastries. Everything carried within by a steady stream of servants, by an indirect route in front of the throne. —THE KING *doesn't see it.*

MASTER OF THE HOUSEHOLD: May it please our Lord and King graciously to descend to the circle of the unworthy, to allow his royal mouth to partake of some food? My menial service has brought forth those things which I in my simplicity have thought might please a ruler and a prince, and in the festival hall a meal has been prepared which my Lord and King may deign to judge with all his royal mercy. No animal has been considered worthy of my Sovereign's table which has seen the new moon rise twice into the heavens. The priests have blessed and purified all, after which, by the master chef's imperfect art, it has been prepared in the way which we, my Lord's incapable servants, have believed to be the best, that our Lord and King may have a pleasing fare.

IREAM-AZU *sits motionless, without seeing him.*

CUP-BEARER: Lord King! The most insignificant of your servants in his ignorance of your will has allowed to be brought to the table, which only awaits the approach of its sovereign, drinks which among men are called priceless, more costly than pearls and precious stones—which fill our bodies with sensual pleasure and our souls with a bliss which passes all understanding, spiced drinks, more ardent than women, opening our senses to all of the world's glory, and drinks redolent of herbs which give men dreams sweeter than those of love, golden wine which loosens words of jest from the tongue of the unhappy

man, and that wine from mountains in the west whose color is
dark as purple in the night and in whose fire the ruby at the
bottom of our Lord's cup pales and loses its glow. Graciously
deign to let your lips be moistened by these spirits which your
trifling servant has been able to search out in the darkness of
the cellars, and your soul be raised to the heights which we
poor wretches call the realm of the blessed.

IREAM-AZU *motionless.*

MASTER OF CEREMONIES: Most gracious Sovereign and Lord! All is
in readiness to receive our Lord and to be cast into darkness by
the light of his Glory.
Does it please your Magnificence that the festival shall have its
beginning?

IREAM-AZU *motionless.*

A COURTIER *downstage, to another in his company*: They won't get any
life into that one.

THE SECOND COURTIER: He doesn't care about anything.

THE FIRST COURTIER: He ought to be hungry I should think. What
do they get in prison? Quail and roast lamb? Who knows?

They laugh.

THE SECOND: He probably thinks that time is too short.

THE FIRST: Oh, life isn't so long. It goes on for awhile and then it's
over. Just about everybody has to put up with that. You have
to make good use of the little time you have. Right? I'm beginning to get hungry—how about you?

THE SECOND: I could eat a bite if they ever get started.

THE FIRST: He seems to be completely dull-witted.

THE SECOND: Oh no, I wouldn't say that. I think he's observing
everyone very carefully.

THE FIRST: He's a bore. —
Usually they eat and gorge themselves as much as they possibly
can. Doesn't seem unreasonable. Life's worth living after all.
Remember the last one—whatever it was he was called, I've
forgotten our holy list of kings—he ate enough to split. And

lay with women around the clock, until his strength gave out. Even tried to get at the ones that weren't purified.

This one just sits there and stares.

ONE OF THE PEOPLE: Why not eat, drink, and make happy days. Some day we'll die, anyway.

ANOTHER: He doesn't care a bit about it, not at all.

A THIRD: Didn't they starve him down there in the dungeons the way they usually do?

A FOURTH: Don't you worry yourself about that.

> DANCERS *in. They dance for* THE KING. *Music. Kettledrums and cymbals.*
>
> IREAM-AZU *sits motionless.*
>
> OTHER DANCERS *in. The music becomes more abandoned. The multitude sways with the music; raw, groaning calls from the men to the dancers. Rising excitement.*
>
> *Still more of them, their naked bodies rubbed with oils. They dance by themselves below the throne. They glide into the swarm of women and then reappear in front of the throne. People sway and moan. The music becomes more and more deafening in its barbaric monotony. A feeling of torpor prevails. A strange, sharp cry from* THE DANCERS *is heard now and then—first from one, then from many of them, and finally from all. The men answer, excite them further. The dance becomes more and more enticing. At a fever pitch, they all move as a drunken mass, benumbed by intoxication.*
>
> IREAM-AZU *arises from the throne. Totters down among* THE DANCERS. *Takes hold of one of the women. But releases her. Looks at her—the others have bowed down to the ground. Lifts his hand to touch her, but does not do it. Stands there with his eyes on her.*
>
> *Holds her by the wrist and takes her with him. Into the palace, with great, faltering steps—pulling her after him.*
>
> *Howls, exultation.*
>
> *The court, the bodyguard, and* THE DANCERS *follow* THE KING.

ONE OF THE COURTIERS *in the foreground*: Well, that's better!

> *They follow the others.*

How long has he been in prison?

THE SECOND: About two years I've heard.

THE FIRST: Ho. — —I'd like to be in his shoes. For tonight anyway.

> THE SECOND *nods in agreement.* —*They disappear into the palace.*

> *The crowd thins out. The stage is almost empty.*

> BEGGARS *remain. Servants put up flaming torches on the palace walls. From within is heard the hum of festivities, subdued music.*

> *The tattered figures from out of the mob stand together in a knot and talk in whispers.*

AN OLD MAN *coming in*: Aren't they going to give us more bread?

ONE OF THE RABBLE: No.

OLD MAN: They're not?

THE FIRST: Ask him there!

> *Points at one of the servants still remaining; he has climbed up to fasten his torch.*

OLD MAN: You! Won't there be any more today?

SERVANT: Haven't you stuffed yourself enough!

OLD MAN: It's for my son who can't come.

SERVANT *steps down*: If he can't manage that, he won't get any, that's all.

OLD MAN: I know, but he couldn't. He's a leper. Or maybe you don't allow that either?

SERVANT: Must we receive lepers too! Isn't this dirty rabble quite enough!

> *The pack of beggars slowly surround the* SERVANT.

OLD MAN: Rabble? You can be proud, I'd say, with a criminal as your lord.

SERVANT: He is not our lord!

ONE OF THE CROWD *hotly*: Who then?

SERVANT: Amar-Azu, the king, of course.

OLD MAN: No, sir! The one that's put on the throne is king! You're wrong! You don't preach like the priests do! Maybe you don't think the one the god lives in is king!

SERVANT: Talk! That's just something we pretend! Day after

tomorrow he'll be roasted like a pig, might even be burned to
the pan, who knows. And you think he's our sovereign.
Goes.

The crowd follows him.

OLD MAN *calls after them*: Yes! Yes, you . . .

THE SERVANT *to the crowd*: Out of the way here!

OLD MAN: Maybe you don't think the one the god . . .

SERVANT: Out of the way, I say!

They stab him.

Uneasy whispers.

OLD MAN: What are you doing! —Are you mad! Completely out of
your senses! I don't want to be mixed up in this . . . !

ONE OF THE MEN: You hold your tongue!

OLD MAN: All right, all right!

Hurries away.

ONE OF THE MEN: What'll we do with him?

ANOTHER: Throw him in the river! There's plenty of room!

They take him with them.

The stage is empty.

AMAR-AZU *in, in rags, with ashes in his hair, followed by Nadur with a rough
cloak over him instead of his court dress*: Why do you follow me?
You shouldn't do it, I tell you.

NADUR: Lord, I cannot be parted from you.

AMAR-AZU: But they will say you are unclean, and the priests will
call down a curse on you, and you'll never again be allowed to
come near me. Don't you know that?

NADUR: Lord, when you are king I can be apart from you, but not
now.

AMAR-AZU: Not now?

NADUR: No, Lord.

AMAR-AZU goes toward him and presses his hands.

NADUR: Let me be your shadow, nothing more—one who follows you.

AMAR-AZU: And then? Then, Nadur?

NADUR: The King, the great king, has no shadow.

AMAR-AZU: No . . .

He sits down in the foreground.

He has nothing, only himself.

NADUR: And the power and the glory, and man's adoration, and women rubbed with scented oils who wait for him, and a palace filled with treasures of gold and silver . . .

AMAR-AZU: Yes. You are right. He owns all of the world's emptiness. He is the poorest of all.

NADUR: Yes, Lord, this is what you've taught me—to understand the vanity of all things. And I believe in you.

AMAR-AZU *hesitating*: Perhaps you shouldn't believe me, Nadur.

NADUR: But it is the truth.

AMAR-AZU: It is not always easy to believe the truth.

NADUR: But you teach it and seek it yourself, don't you?

AMAR-AZU *silent. Then*: To seek the truth is like looking for a grain of sand by the sea. There are so many.

NADUR: I know it's not that you are looking for, but rather the costly pearls which perhaps are there.

AMAR-AZU: In each pearl there is only one grain of sand.

After a moment.

What shall become of you?

NADUR: I don't know, Lord.

AMAR-AZU: And of me? . . .

NADUR: You. You shall become King again!

AMAR-AZU *thinking*: Nadur—I've been through the great feast of Azu once before, this old custom that the sovereign shall debase himself and become as a beggar. It is the happiest time in my life—if one can talk about happiness at all. I am a man—and men insult me as they please. Scorn and spit on me—as they wish. It is not mere show as everything else. It is reality, Nadur, reality!

Rises.

And the sacrifice to the god, the cruel sacrifice of the poor victim in there—that too is reality! And depravity and shame, passions and lewdness, and the loosening of every band! We become equals—as we are. All of us like animals, full of desire and thirst for cruelty and blood and madness! — —For a short time we become real people. For three days.

And the lie begins again, as if nothing had happened.

NADUR *silent.*

AMAR-AZU: Isn't it a relief when everything is real!
When people are themselves! — — —
Walks back and forth. — —Stops.
And I, I become more nearly human than any other . . . the least of the least . . . defiled and despised . . . in rags that cannot hide meanness.
They let me be the poor man who owns nothing. Who thought he was a king but found he was a beggar.
But that's reality too! No lies and deceit like all the rest!
Stands, looks into the distance, thinking. — — —Returns and sits down beside him.
I will tell you, Nadur . . . before, many years ago, it was the king himself who was sacrificed. When his time ran out, he sacrificed himself for his people. That was the old custom as it was in the beginning. And last time . . . the first time . . . I felt as if I wanted to be sacrificed . . . yes, for these poor wretched people who I couldn't do anything else for . . . I felt as if I should be sacrificed, sacrificed for them . . .
He falls silent.

NADUR: You don't now?

AMAR-AZU *does not answer. — —After a moment*: Then, in later times they took someone else instead, someone they thought was of less value, one of those criminals. That seemed a more comfortable way to do it. Manners had become gentler. One couldn't sacrifice a king.
That's the world's way of progress and how men change.
— — —
You say nothing?

NADUR: No . . .

AMAR-AZU: Why not?

NADUR: I don't know.

AMAR-AZU *rises, walks back and forth. — — —Stops in front of him*: Do
  you think it is worth it to sacrifice yourself for mankind? Do
  you?

NADUR: Yes, Lord.

AMAR-AZU *looks at him. —Walks again. More intensely, back and forth.
  Then he stops and looks up at the festively lighted palace*: Looks as if
  they are having fun in there.
  Stands listening to the noise and laughter from the palace.
  Isn't happiness strange. It doesn't need a cause.
  And the great, profound happiness which a man can feel . . .
  which comes from the depths of the soul and gives him the
  power . . . to do so much . . . — —It doesn't need a cause either.
  Walks again. — — —Stands in front of NADUR.
  I tell you I don't think men are worth sacrificing oneself for!
  But it's not that which . . . — —After all it doesn't matter so
  much. That's not the question really . . .
  Silent.
  He sits down beside the young man.
  It's only a cruel custom. It's of no use. Everything remains the
  same as it was before.
  All it does is satisfy men's thirst for cruelty and blood. That's
  all, it can't be anything else. Sacrifice, sacrifice to quench all
  that thirst for blood, blood and atrocities! That is the significance of the old custom. — —
  Before, a very long time ago, it was believed that the great Azu
  was the god of fire, not the sun god as people think now and
  have been taught for many years. You know as I do that another doctrine is preached today.
  But for the great masses he is still the god of fire. And always
  will be. For most people god is always a fire god! Fire, blood,
  cruelty, and destruction . . . That is man's god, no matter
  what other god he learns to worship!

  — — —

  Isn't it true what I say? Maybe you don't believe it even now!

NADUR: Yes, Lord, it's true. How can it be that we cannot help
  ourselves out of such distress, how is it possible?

AMAR-AZU *sits silently.* *Then*: For me, the great Azu was always the
   god of light . . . The light which would show men the way,
   raise them and purify them. Make them see.
   That's what I have believed.

NADUR: Have? Don't you believe it anymore?

AMAR-AZU *doesn't answer.*

NADUR: But that's how you've taught me! And that's what I want
   always to believe! And I can, I feel it!

AMAR-AZU: Yes, yes, my friend. You shall believe it, nothing else.

NADUR: But you?

AMAR-AZU: Well . . . I believe it too. If someone rules, it must be
   the god of light. It must be.

NADUR: But you doubt? . . . — —Doubt everything!
   How can you speak this way . . . I don't understand. It's sacri-
   lege, and maybe not to be forgiven . . .

AMAR-AZU *silent.*

NADUR: *"If someone rules . . ."* — — —It's blasphemy! I don't want
   to hear you when you blaspheme! When you do I feel you have
   nothing to tell me.

AMAR-AZU *silent.*

NADUR: What do you believe in! If not in him, he who is the
   Light! What do you have then! Nothing!

AMAR-AZU: My friend, — —who has *believed* as I? Believed in the
   god, believed in men, in his people.
   When I ascended my throne as the young king, who believed
   as I . . . Who could have felt the wonder, the magnificence and
   purity. Yes! I felt that I was Azu's son, the son of light. And
   my eyes were full of His light, as a sign that He loved me, and
   that I belonged to Him.
   But then—when I looked around me I saw that the world
   wasn't made for light, and perhaps not even the struggle for
   light. That it was full of hollows and thickets, of dark holes
   where the light can't find its way in. Never find the way in.
   There can never be light where men live—because that's not

the way they live. Man's world is not a world for light. It can
never get in. Because the light is straight, too straight for that
world.

Sits silently. —NADUR *doesn't answer.*

But that's not the way *you* should think. And you don't either.

NADUR: Yes, Lord, I can think as you do. But not *believe* as you do.

AMAR-AZU *puts his hand on his head*: My young friend . . .

— — —

You have the soul of youth.

The young souls are heaven's flowers on the earth. Maybe it is
Eia, the gentle mother of god who sows them in the ground.
The sun cares for them and men tramp them down. But new
ones come, new ones always come . . . She comes back every
spring, she never tires . . .

And men are made happy, and they tramp them down. But the
great mother never tires.

NADUR *looks up at him, inspired*: You can say that, and you're such a
doubter!

AMAR-AZU: Doubter? — —He who believes much doubts much.
His heart is so full of doubt it could burst. But it doesn't. Because he *believes*. He holds fast—a little longer. Because he
believes.

NADUR: Oh Lord, when you speak I think I understand you so well.
This is the way you should always talk.

AMAR-AZU: My dear son . . .

Puts his hand on NADUR'S *head.*

You are my own youth—as if I had seen it again.

Puts his arm around him and goes with him up to the front of the palace.
And when I saw the king's palace up on the crown of the hill,
lighted and festive, with the city below and all of this great
land, I was filled with joy of the sight of it and the call that
awaited me. I felt then that it was glorious to be born to rule on
earth. To have the power to do everything, and to change all
the things that were evil and must be changed—that were not
right! And I was the Sovereign. I could do so much for mankind, for my people. I relied on the god, my Father, I knew

that I was in his service.—And I entered the stronghold of
power, its ramparts radiant and shining out over the land . . .
Yes! I didn't want to be only a prince on earth, but a mediator
between the god and his people, as I am called, and knew that
I was appointed to be.

But I had no power on earth.

And my heavenly father left me.

I became the most impotent of all who have ruled. I could do
nothing.

I, who had wanted to do so much! . . . — — —

The stronghold of power! —I see now that it is fire, a burning
pyre, flames that reach out and spread fear and surrender
everywhere. Fire, violence, and terror—they are the only rulers
of the world:

Not *we*.

He stands in silence. Thinking.

No, not we . . .

NADUR —*listens, touches his arm*: I think someone's coming . . .
They go down. Move aside so that they are hidden in the darkness.

ONE OF THE GUESTS *coming out of the palace. Stops.*

ANOTHER *follows a short distance after. Walks slowly across the courtyard.*
Stops: Good evening, my good friend—out for a little air?

THE FIRST: There's such a crowd, it's good to cool off a bit.

They say there are more of the rabble invited this time than
usual.

THE SECOND: Yes, I wonder why that is. Does anyone know who
asked them?

The bastards are peeing on the steps so it smells like a pigsty.

THE FIRST: They could feed them in separate halls, but I suppose
that wouldn't do.

THE SECOND: No.

After a moment.

How do you like the festivities otherwise?

THE FIRST: Not bad. The dancers are young as flowers because they have a new master. I can understand they're happy to have a little change.

THE SECOND: Change? Amar-Azu never touched them, I hear, only his favorite wife.

THE FIRST: Is that right?

THE SECOND: That's what they say.

THE FIRST: He's no man.

THE SECOND: No, he's a deity.

THE FIRST: A strange god who has no desire for women. The great Azu in his temple must have a virgin every full moon.

THE SECOND: Amar-Azu is not like the god.

THE FIRST: No.

After a moment.

THE SECOND: Then how can he be divine?

THE FIRST: You'd have to ask the priests about that.

They are silent.

THE SECOND: The priests have no respect for the king.

THE FIRST *doesn't answer.*

THE SECOND: They have power.

THE FIRST *after a moment*: They're not the ones that have the power.

THE SECOND: No . . .

They are silent.

He might as well remain what he is now.

THE FIRST *doesn't answer.*

THE SECOND: There seem to be some people who think so.

THE FIRST: So?

THE SECOND: Probably the ones who would like to . . .

THE FIRST *carefully*: I don't know anything about that.

THE SECOND: No . . . — —of course . . .

THE FIRST: Shall we return to the festivities? Perhaps we are expected.

THE SECOND: Perhaps.

THE FIRST: One shouldn't drift away, it's not quite right.

They return to the palace.

NADUR: What was it? What did they mean?

AMAR-AZU: Oh, probably nothing.

NADUR: Yes . . . — — —Lord King, do you think . . . ?

AMAR-AZU: What did you say, my friend?

> *They are silent.* AMAR-AZU *leans on his staff and looks away.*

Have you been in the desert, Nadur? It's quiet, you hear nothing but your own steps. And when you stand still and look around, your footprints disappear in the sand, and you can't find your way back. But far away there's another country. And you walk endlessly to reach it, some day. You see a vision of it, not clearly, but what it must be like, and how blissful it must be to live there. And you break up and move on again and again, and wander endlessly in the burning sun, in the freezing night . . .

Wandering and wandering . . .

> *He is silent.*

NADUR: And then?

AMAR-AZU: Then?

Why do you ask that?

> SIBILE, *the king's favorite wife, comes out of the palace. Goes across the courtyard, looks around. Down to the left—out through the archway which leads toward the city. Looks down toward the road.*

AMAR-AZU *hidden at the right*: What are you looking for?

SIBILE: Is it you, my Lord!

> *Comes toward them.*

Who should I be looking for but you!

> *Stops a short distance from them.*

AMAR-AZU: Come.

SIBILE: Beloved . . .

AMAR-AZU *stretches out his hand toward her*: But you don't come . . .

SIBILE: Beloved, you know how much I want to! I want nothing more, but during the feast you are an outcast, and I'm not allowed to touch you.

> AMAR-AZU *his hands outstretched toward her.*

SIBILE: Lord . . . !

AMAR-AZU: For love all things are pure.

SIBILE: Yes, yes! But you know that we would be parted forever—would you want that?

AMAR-AZU *does not answer.*

SIBILE: You will be king again in a few days, and I love you, my love embraces you, and is stronger and more ardent than ever before, most beloved of all men.

AMAR-AZU: Sibile . . . I am happier now than before.

SIBILE: Happier now than when you're with me?

AMAR-AZU: But you are with me. You have come to me even though I am a beggar.

SIBILE: Yes, I felt so uneasy. Surely nothing can happen to you?

AMAR-AZU: Me?

Shakes his head.

SIBILE: And are you getting something to eat? Will you let me bring you something?

AMAR-AZU *shakes his head. Stands silently.*

SIBILE: Are you all right, beloved?

AMAR-AZU: Nothing is lacking, I have everything a man needs.

SIBILE: Then you ask little, Lord King.

AMAR-AZU: No. — —I ask much.

He stands and looks away.

SIBILE: What are you thinking about?

AMAR-AZU *doesn't answer.*

SIBILE: Lord . . . tell me . . .

AMAR-AZU *turns to her:* How is the festival?

SIBILE: I don't know because you're not there. I only heard the noise, and that there were many others who were not you . . .

AMAR-AZU *doesn't answer.*

SIBILE: Do you love me?

AMAR-AZU: I love you very much, Sibile.

SIBILE: I love you more!

AMAR-AZU: No!

SIBILE: My great king . . . soon you will rest by my side! I love you when you lie with your restless head on my knee and dream the dreams I see in your face. Then nothing can surpass my love.

AMAR-AZU: They are not dreams, Sibile. But I love to rest like that with you.

SIBILE: My darling . . .

AMAR-AZU *stretches out his hand, looks at her.* — —: You must go back to the festival now, perhaps they miss you there.

SIBILE *goes slowly, smiling, nods farewell.*
In, to the palace.
NADUR *stands absent-mindedly, watches her leave.*

AMAR-AZU *puts his hand on his shoulder*: My friend . . . ?

NADUR: I'm thinking how great love can be . . .

AMAR-AZU: Yes. — — —
We love without meeting, without understanding—it's strange. And often it is then that we seem to love each other most.

NADUR: I don't think there is anything greater than love, and without it man is nothing.

AMAR-AZU: Love is one thing—man is another.
He is silent for a long time. Then:
There are many who have loved each other—deeply and truly— but if their souls were to meet in the great void after death, they wouldn't recognize each other or know that they were near.

NADUR: No, Lord . . . I don't think so! And I don't understand why you say so. And now—when you have just had such evidence of love?

AMAR-AZU: Why not now? — —It is just as true now as always, Nadur.

IREAM-AZU *out from the palace. A woman with him, holds her by the hand.*

THE WOMAN: My Lord King, you needn't flee out into the darkness to hide. The bed chambers are ready for us, if you wish— if I please you.

IREAM-AZU: Yes, of course . . . you're right . . .

Pulls her close to him in a strong embrace. — —Then, breaks away.
Can't we get out of here! Come with me, we'll escape from
this place!
THE WOMAN: I'll follow wherever you wish, my Lord! I belong to
you, do what you wish with me!
Embraces him. —Then:
But why should we flee, my Lord. Here we have everything we
can ask for. The silver lamps are lighted, and the slave girl has
prepared our couch, as soft as dreams, and the room is filled
with the most inviting incense of love.
We lack nothing here.
Men from the bodyguard have come out behind them, unnoticed.
And, my Lord . . . I don't think it's possible to flee . . .
IREAM-AZU *notices. Looks wildly at the guard. And at her. — — Embraces
her. Roughly, excitedly. Twists her neck while he pulls her close to him,
caresses her:* You shall love me through this long, long night.
And tomorrow you shall die.

THE WOMAN *pulls herself away from him.*

IREAM-AZU: Well, come on. — — — — — — Come.
THE WOMAN: Almighty Lord, be merciful to me . . .!
IREAM-AZU: Come on then.

THE WOMAN *hesitates.*
IREAM-AZU *makes a sign to the guard.*
They bring her to him.

IREAM-AZU: Why leave? Why? —Everything awaits and is as it
should be.
It's wonderful to live.
In, to the palace. The guard follows them.
The two figures in the foreground stand silently a moment.
AMAR-AZU: Let's find a place out in the field where we can go to
sleep. The heavens are full of stars, it's good to rest under them.
Out.

Act Two

THE FOOL *lies sleeping on the stairway to the throne, grunts, breathes heavily. Settles down again. —Sentries are seen at the entrances to the courtyard.*

IREAM-AZU *out from the palace. Goes toward the archway—tries to look out. Takes a few turns across the courtyard, looks now and then at the road toward the city. —Goes up and sits on the throne.*

THE FOOL *after a moment, begins to awaken. Stretches, rubs his eyes:* Morning.

IREAM-AZU *answers with a nod.*

THE FOOL: Has my gracious Lord had a good night? —Good sleep?

IREAM-AZU *doesn't answer.*

THE FOOL: Yes, sir, that was a nice little party! Must be far into the day by now.
Yawns, stretches.
Oh ho . . .
Sits up with his legs crossed.
Well? How's life? Not bad, eh?

IREAM-AZU: No.

THE FOOL: On no, it's a pleasant diversion. Pity it's so short.

IREAM-AZU: Fools usually live rather long.

THE FOOL: Yes, no trouble for us. It's worse for the smart ones. To say nothing of those that are too wise. They very seldom live long at all.

IREAM-AZU *doesn't answer.*

THE FOOL: What did you think of those people last night? It was a little mixed of course. But that's not bad either, is it?

IREAM-AZU *silent.*

THE FOOL: One kind of riffraff is just as stylish as another, don't you think?

116

IREAM-AZU *silent.*

THE FOOL: The rabble are also people, I suppose.

IREAM-AZU: I belong among them myself.

THE FOOL: Yes. I can understand that.

> IREAM-AZU *down to the courtyard. Goes toward the archway, and as he passes, looks out through it.*

THE FOOL: What are you waiting for?

IREAM-AZU: Waiting for? —Nothing.
  Goes back and forth.

THE FOOL: Say listen . . . you were wise not to stay with that woman all night.

IREAM-AZU *looks at him for a moment*: I've no use for any wisdom.

THE FOOL: No, suppose not. Who has. But anyway. No use wasting time on that kind of thing when it can be used better for something else.
  There are other things than breasts and buttocks to think about— — —much more delicious things— —

IREAM-AZU *doesn't answer.*

THE FOOL: By the way, you have gotten rid of her haven't you, you haven't forgotten it have you?

IREAM-AZU: Ask the executioner.

THE FOOL: Yes. —He's my particular friend. But he probably won't have much time to see me for a while now, I guess. Too bad. Otherwise he's such a nice and pleasant person. You'll see that yourself if you happen to meet him sometime.

IREAM-AZU: I have met him.

THE FOOL: Really? You are already acquainted?

IREAM-AZU: Yes.

THE FOOL: Yes, I can well imagine that the executioner and the Sovereign must know each other. That's always been the custom. But we have had such strange manners here lately. Amar-Azu hardly knows that an executioner exists in this country.

IREAM-AZU: The people know it!

THE FOOL: That's what they say. And the council and the priests and that kind—they seem to know him.

IREAM-AZU *doesn't answer.*

THE FOOL: Although not as well as they should!

IREAM-AZU *looks at him. After a moment*: What do you mean by that?

THE FOOL: Nothing.

I'm not as stupid as I sound sometimes.

IREAM-AZU *goes back and forth. —Up to the archway, glances out.*

THE FOOL: What are you waiting for, actually?

IREAM-AZU *looks at him—without answering.*

In a moment, up on the throne again.

THE FOOL: Too bad you've come to power in such uncertain times. There'll be trouble while you're on the throne, you'll see.

IREAM-AZU: Uncertain?

THE FOOL: Yes.

IREAM-AZU: That's something I know nothing about.

THE FOOL: No, no. I'm just talking. No. I hope that during your reign everything will move as peacefully and quietly as possible. That would be best for you, don't you think?

Rises, goes toward the courtyard.

You're having luck with the weather. It'll probably last. Really fine weather . . . — —Calm and peaceful . . .

Approaches him and whispers in his hissing voice:

I'll tell you something . . . It's all a question of good, suitable weather conditions . . .!

Bursts out in crude, hoarse laughter.

Suitable weather . . . ! — — —

Sits on the step, grins, and looks up at the sky.

IREAM-AZU *after a moment*: Are you in Amar-Azu's service?

THE FOOL: Yes, but you know he just doesn't have much use for me.

IREAM-AZU: Why not?

THE FOOL: Well, he's a fool himself.

IREAM-AZU: Oh? — —

I don't believe it.

THE FOOL: Yes. Didn't you know that? He is a particularly remarkable and important person. He is one of the god's own fools down here.

Laughs dryly. — — —Sits grinning up at him.
You probably need a fool, don't you?

IREAM-AZU *doesn't answer.*

THE FOOL: Don't you think so? It varies quite a bit, you know.
Some of them are so far from being foolish they can't be with-
out a fool. They are much too terrifying for that. Their
power and glory here on earth is so great that—
IREAM-AZU *suddenly*: Silence! . . .
*Voices are heard outside the archway, as if from a disturbance. —He
listens intensely.*
THE SENTRY'S VOICE *clear and commanding*: No one enters here!

IREAM-AZU *down to the courtyard, goes back and forth in suppressed
rage.*
THE FOOL *bursts out laughing. — —Limps away, grinning.*

THE CAPTAIN OF THE GUARD *coming in*: At your service, my
Lord.

IREAM-AZU *walks back and forth without noticing him.*

CAPTAIN *bows*: I have the honor to be your humble servant, captain
of my Lord and King's bodyguard.

IREAM-AZU *doesn't answer him.*

CAPTAIN: In other words, I watch over you.
IREAM-AZU *stops, angrily. —Then*: I hope you carry out these im-
portant duties well.
CAPTAIN: That is also my hope, my Lord.

IREAM-AZU *walks on.*

CAPTAIN: Nor is it that which causes me any difficulty.
Regards him. —After a moment.
Who are these ragpickers howling in the streets?
IREAM-AZU: What? . . . — —
How should I know!
CAPTAIN: No, of course not.
Walks a bit across the courtyard.
During the festival there are always a few disorders. We don't

pay very much attention to it—it's even permitted to a certain extent. We let them break loose a bit . . .

Now that it's gone this far . . .

IREAM-AZU: This far? . . .

CAPTAIN *goes back and forth. —After a moment*:

What do the people have to do with who sits on the throne!

IREAM-AZU: On the throne . . . ? — — —No—they have nothing to say about it . . .

CAPTAIN: No.

They have the king that's given to them.

IREAM-AZU: Yes—of course.

Silent. —Then.

Right now it doesn't matter who sits on the throne!

CAPTAIN: No. It doesn't matter. They take anybody with a worthless life. There are many to choose from.

IREAM-AZU: You don't say. — —Then they could have taken somebody else.

CAPTAIN: Yes.

But you are the one they chose.

Observes him. —Then.

Nowadays there's no significance at all in who fate chooses.

It's nothing more than a joke.

Once—because of the god, I suppose—they took somebody who seemed to be somewhat worthy of the sacrifice. When they still thought that was important.

Now that we don't believe very much any more in gods or men, it doesn't matter.

IREAM-AZU: No . . .

CAPTAIN: Do you come from the people?

IREAM-AZU: Yes.

CAPTAIN: What is it they really want?

IREAM-AZU: What they want? — —How can I know that . . .

CAPTAIN: I hope it's something noble, since they're making such a racket. — — —

I hope that something will *happen* in this country, when our people awake!

IREAM-AZU *gives no answer.*

CAPTAIN: What is it? — — —What do they want? — —Where do they plan to go from here? —Can you tell me?

IREAM-AZU: Oh, they only mean to be fighting for life I suppose.

CAPTAIN: Life? — — —

Indifferently.

Is it worth so much?

IREAM-AZU: Yes. When you don't have it.

CAPTAIN *looks at him.* — — —*Walks up and down.*

People must be cowards when they fight for life.

IREAM-AZU: Could be.

CAPTAIN: Is it necessary?

IREAM-AZU: I don't know.

I guess people are cowards most of the time.

CAPTAIN: Do you think so?

IREAM-AZU: Yes. If they're ever something else, it's because then it's safer not to be a coward.

CAPTAIN *silent. Regards him closely for a rather long time. —Then:* But that's no reason for them to be assassins and bandits!

IREAM-AZU: What . . . ? — —

CAPTAIN: Cutting down defenseless people, plundering, stealing!

IREAM-AZU: Is that what they're doing?

CAPTAIN *silent. —Then:* What kind of a struggle is *that*?

IREAM-AZU *when the* CAPTAIN *has nothing more to say:* Oh, they don't think too much about the fine points.

CAPTAIN: What?

IREAM-AZU: No one's been very fussy about them.

CAPTAIN: They haven't?

In a moment.

No . . . — —I guess they haven't.

IREAM-AZU: Oh no.

CAPTAIN: You mean they can't be much different than they are.

IREAM-AZU: No.

CAPTAIN *after a moment*: Are they starving? . . .

IREAM-AZU: I don't know. They usually are.

CAPTAIN: I've heard talk about it.

IREAM-AZU: Really?

CAPTAIN *hesitantly toward him*: What were you sentenced for?
    For murder?

IREAM-AZU: Yes, somebody who deserved to die.

CAPTAIN: Why?

IREAM-AZU: Because he whipped his stable boy to death.

CAPTAIN: For good reason, maybe?

IREAM-AZU: Yes, he had. The boy had put his saddle on wrong.

> CAPTAIN *silent.*

IREAM-AZU: He didn't fasten the straps tightly enough, and the
    saddle was loose.

> CAPTAIN *silent.*

IREAM-AZU: Of course he had good reason, he wouldn't have done
    it otherwise, quite naturally.

CAPTAIN *goes up to him quickly.* —*Fiercely, in a low voice*: Are you sorry
    for that crime?

IREAM-AZU: No.

CAPTAIN: You have no reason to be!

IREAM-AZU: I know.

CAPTAIN: But I'm telling you that I know too!

> *Off right voices are heard, someone is approaching.* —*He leans toward
> him and whispers*:
> It was stupid of him to whip that boy to death!
> That's why we're living in a lawless land!

IREAM-AZU: Yes!

> *They are approaching.*
> CAPTAIN *motions* IREAM-AZU *into the palace.* —*Goes out through the
> archway.*
> *The* HIGH PRIEST *and two councillors in, agitated, followed by one of
> the Azu priests.*

HIGH PRIEST: This is frightful!

FIRST COUNCILLOR: Yes, it must be suppressed! Without mercy, cost what it may!

SECOND COUNCILLOR: No one counts the cost!

HIGH PRIEST: No! The god offers—

FIRST COUNCILLOR: Who knows what the god offers. But order must be restored!

SECOND COUNCILLOR: Yes!

HIGH PRIEST: How is it possible that things have gotten so far out of hand?

FIRST COUNCILLOR: It has spread like wildfire. And no one can say where this will end!

SECOND COUNCILLOR: We can be sure of nothing!

THIRD COUNCILLOR *rushes in*: Smoke has been sighted several places to the south!

SECOND COUNCILLOR: Can it be true!

THIRD COUNCILLOR: Yes! And they say there has been a battle somewhere down in the city and blood is flowing!

HIGH PRIEST: This is dreadful! A festival to honor the god!

PRIEST: Yes, is this the god's holy day!

HIGH PRIEST: I cannot understand—

PRIEST: No . . .

THIRD COUNCILLOR: They say it's being howled about among the people that now they have one of their own as king!

SECOND COUNCILLOR: Their own?

PRIEST: What do they mean by that?

HIGH PRIEST: They always have had during the feast, it's an ancient custom.

THIRD COUNCILLOR: Certainly. But this time they've put a different meaning in it!

HIGH PRIEST: A different meaning?

THIRD COUNCILLOR: Yes!

PRIEST: A different meaning . . .!

FIRST COUNCILLOR: What nonsense! He's to be sacrificed!

SECOND COUNCILLOR: Yes, the criminal is to be sacrificed!

PRIEST: Does he come from the people?

FIRST COUNCILLOR: Quite naturally. Criminals always come from the people.

SECOND COUNCILLOR: And he's merely to be sacrificed according to custom.

FIRST COUNCILLOR: Yes, of course!

A MESSENGER *in, breathless*: The rabble have broken through! — — —They're cutting down everyone they can get hold of! —everyone who's not on their side! — —

FIRST COUNCILLOR: Broken through! — — And the bodyguard?

MESSENGER: They couldn't keep them back!

FIRST COUNCILLOR: A pack of dirty rabble!

SECOND COUNCILLOR: It's incredible!

FIRST COUNCILLOR: Not at all! *He's* their leader! I told you . . . !

MESSENGER: There are dead and wounded everywhere in the street —trampled to death—strangled—because they haven't many weapons, the scum! — —

FIRST COUNCILLOR: This must be drowned in blood!

HIGH PRIEST: Yes, these misdeeds can only be purged with blood!

FIRST COUNCILLOR: Who are these devils? Where have they come from?

HIGH PRIEST: Are these the god's people?

FIRST COUNCILLOR: Hardly!

HIGH PRIEST: No, they oppose all that's holy!

SECOND COUNCILLOR: Against law and order!

HIGH PRIEST: Then they shall be crushed!

SECOND COUNCILLOR: Yes!

They go in toward the palace.

HIGH PRIEST: How can the god allow this to happen! — —I don't understand—

FIRST COUNCILLOR: Gods permit many things.

HIGH PRIEST: Yes, which are beyond us . . .

AMAR-AZU and NADUR come through the archway into the courtyard. In front of the servants' door to the palace stands a dish of food. They go toward it, sit down, and eat.

NADUR *after a moment. As* AMAR *sits looking into the distance*:
  What are you thinking about, my King?
AMAR-AZU: I'm thinking of the night under the stars.
NADUR: Yes . . .
AMAR-AZU: Isn't it strange that man lives this way.
NADUR: Yes . . . and they know so little about it. They don't care.
AMAR-AZU: No.
  There was no need to build this house, Nadur. Not for their
  sake. And I don't really think it was built for them.
NADUR: Yes, my Lord, I think it was!
AMAR-AZU: So that it wouldn't be empty, you mean?
NADUR: No . . .
  After a moment.
AMAR-AZU: What do you think the earth is intended for, Nadur?
  The earth and the stars, the sunrise and the sunset—a home
  which no prince could have dreamed of, and which is every-
  one's, each one, every moment he lives.
  And perhaps this is our only life and our only home. I often
  think it must be so.
  What do we do with this world, this lovely, precious world
  which we've been given.
  Do you think it was intended for *this*?
NADUR: No, my Lord. It can't have been.
  I've always thought that it was built as a temple. I remember I
  thought so even as a child.
AMAR-AZU: Where no service has ever been celebrated, or ever shall
  be.
NADUR: No—not yet.
AMAR-AZU: When?
  They sit silently.
NADUR: I don't know. Sometime perhaps.
AMAR-AZU *studies him for a long time*: I sat and looked at you when
  we were resting out there . . .
NADUR: Didn't you sleep?
AMAR-AZU: No . . . I couldn't sleep.
NADUR: And I, I . . . — — —

AMAR-AZU: Yes, you just went peacefully to sleep.

Arises, restless.

Let me tell you something. It's hardly any sort of temple, and that's why . . . — —Perhaps everything hangs on that. Perhaps that explains it all.

When I was young I dreamed that a springtime of life would come, a wonderful spring . . .

And last night, the scent of the violets just about to bloom made me remember . . . I remembered what I'd once thought . . .

Becomes silent.

There'll never be a springtime for mankind. Not as I believed . . . Those were childish dreams. — — —

The spring of mankind, it's happening now. It's the fresh blood-smell over the earth.

And anyway, it's better than dampness and decay. Spring is better than autumn. It doesn't smell.

NADUR: My Lord! . . . You speak as if . . . — —You lay waste everything with your doubt!

AMAR-AZU: Yes, I lay it waste, that nothing shall remain of lies and illusion.

NADUR: Perhaps nothing will remain! Maybe you'll see, in the end, that there's nothing at all left for you! That you stand there with empty hands. That even your soul will be a beggar—!

AMAR-AZU: It is better to be a beggar than to own things which don't exist.

NADUR: What do you know what exists and doesn't! Can you decide! What are the eternal dreams within us—and how we can live without them!

AMAR-AZU: I know lies, my son. I know the pretty world of illusion—know it better than most. Because I've lived there a long time.

That is why I long for another world, why I long for something within us which isn't deceitful sham. — — —If there's anything which isn't.

NADUR: Can you doubt it!

AMAR-AZU: I can doubt everything.

But then my longing becomes . . . — —is even greater still . . . *For a long time, stands and looks away, supported by his staff.* If we had vision . . . — —If our eyes could be opened . . . — —and we could see . . . — — — Then I could see into my country . . . — —my dearly beloved . . .

SIBILE *coming out of the palace*: Beloved, are you here . . .

AMAR-AZU *stretching out his hand toward her.* —*She takes a step closer. But stops*: Will you follow me . . . far, far away— —to my country . . .

SIBILE: I don't understand you, my King. Your country is here . . .

AMAR-AZU: Here? . . .

SIBILE: Yes.

But, my Lord King, what is it that is happening here!

AMAR-AZU: Happening? In my country nothing happens. Not now.

SIBILE: Not now!

AMAR-AZU *shakes his head.*

SIBILE: Don't you know then what's taking place, all the terrible things that are told! —They may want to do you harm! Maybe something will happen to you!

AMAR-AZU: Nothing can happen to me.

SIBILE: My King! . . . You dream . . . — —Wake up from your dreams, the time is past for that . . .

AMAR-AZU: Dream . . .

You are the ones who dream . . . And I who keep watch . . . It is time to awaken . . .

SIBILE: My Lord King . . .

AMAR-AZU: Why do you call me king? I am only a man. That call is great enough. And heavy enough.

The beggars of mankind must keep watch—stretch out their empty hands . . . to understand their own unutterable poverty . . .

SIBILE *goes closer*: Beloved . . . my beloved . . .

AMAR-AZU: Beloved?

SIBILE: Yes! . . .

AMAR-AZU: Why won't you come with me then?

SIBILE: Come with you? Where?

AMAR-AZU: To the country where all is not lies!

SIBILE: Lies?

AMAR-AZU: Yes!

SIBILE: I don't know what country you're talking about. But I will
wait for you in the land of our love, which is the most beautiful and precious I have.

AMAR-AZU: My country ís not beautiful. It's the poorest of all of
them.

Hardly a straw grows, and the ground is hard to rest upon, like
a rock in the desert.

But it is man's real country! Where all gather who want to
try to live. The poor and the miserable, the homeless and desperate, with nothing to cover themselves. The destitute who
have been deprived of everything.

And there the beggar is king! He who has nothing but his
nakedness and his unclean hand! There he rules over his lost
people! And he lashes them with the scourge of poverty until
they are bloody and sore . . . — — —And they are happy!

For this is not the land of dreams and lies! No, it is their true
land, their homeland in the desert. And those who have
reached it rest on the rock with gratitude and tears of joy because it's there. Because the soul had a country, a rock to cling
to, something that was true.

SIBILE: Lord, in my land too, everything is true.

AMAR-AZU: True!

SIBILE: Yes, I feel it without having to know it.

AMAR-AZU *stretches out his hand*: Come with me then.

SIBILE: I have followed you all my life. By loving you.

AMAR-AZU: Then it's strange that we're so far apart.

SIBILE: Yes, Lord. It is strange . . .

AMAR-AZU: The lovely masquerade of souls which we call love . . .

SIBILE: No!

AMAR-AZU: Where illusions meet . . .

SIBILE: No, my Lord! . . .

AMAR-AZU: Believing that their world is exalted and fair!
But the soul's world is not fair! And souls that really meet
would not love! — —Lies are needed for that!

NADUR: Lord, you—!

AMAR-AZU: Lies are needed for everything! For everything of
which man is capable! For all greatness and nobility and—

SIBILE: It's not true! I know it isn't . . . !

Turns to NADUR.

Is it?

NADUR: No! He doesn't know what he's saying.

AMAR-AZU: It would be well if I didn't know. To know more than
is necessary is madness. The happy medium—man travels best
with the happy medium. His soul has its noble stature. We
can meet with dignity, exalted as we wish and our feast need
not be disturbed by anything.

But if we doubt more than need be, the masks are torn off—
and our faces shine, ghost-like and slack in the festive light—
and all are strangers—and we must fumble about among the
masks to find out who we were—we have no heart for the search
and we leave the hall infinitely sick to death of it . . .

To wander in the desert . . . the vast and empty desert . . .
— — — —And my land of dreams . . . my poor, dear land . . .
— —I hardly know if it exists . . .

SIBILE: Then I know more than you, wise King. The land of my
love exists. And it's not poor and destitute like yours.

It has made me richer than anyone else on earth.

NADUR: Yes! . . . Richer than any other . . .

Such is love! Love that's real!

SIBILE: Yes.

NADUR: The noblest and holiest we have within us!

AMAR-AZU: We like best the lies that slip most easily over our
tongues.

They come from our holiest place which we hardly dare enter.
Because we might regret it.

NADUR: Defiler! — —Blasphemer! . . .
   You cut yourself off from everything, from—
AMAR-AZU: Yes. —I am on the road that leads away . . . — —I've
   broken camp . . .
NADUR: Yes, broken away from mankind! From everything that
   has any value in life, from all that's noble!
AMAR-AZU: Yes, from all of that.
   I've left the festive hall . . .

   NADUR *troubled, walks back and forth.*

AMAR-AZU: . . . and will soon leave all behind.
SIBILE *goes toward the palace entrance. Turns toward him*: You have
   drawn apart from me, but I . . . I am always with you.
   In.
NADUR: You are inhuman! You are as far from all humanity as you
   can be!

   AMAR-AZU *doesn't answer.*

NADUR: You ravage and destroy and want nothing else! With your
   absurd demands! They're hostile to mankind! You don't love
   men! You hate them!
AMAR-AZU: I've broken camp . . .
NADUR: Broken camp! — —You're rootless, nothing else!
AMAR-AZU: Yes! Pull up my roots from this world where I have
   nothing more to do . . .
NADUR: We all belong to this world, all of us have a task here—and
   yours is a great and glorious one, if you will help men instead
   of degrading them!
AMAR-AZU: They degrade themselves as they've always done.
NADUR: Yes, and they don't need any help to do that!
   Inhuman— — !
AMAR-AZU: Why shouldn't I be! It is all I can be! To be inhuman!
   Walks about in agitation.
   I can't bear to be among men any longer, I choke! Can't you
   feel the stench!
NADUR: The leper stinks too, but only because he's a leper!

AMAR-AZU *doesn't answer.*

NADUR: You are like a wild beast!

AMAR-AZU: No. — —You don't understand me . . .

NADUR: I understand that you want evil, want to do evil!

AMAR-AZU: I do myself the most harm . . .

NADUR: By your lack of love and humanity!

AMAR-AZU: Yes. By that lack.

The breast that bursts no longer has a human voice . . . And the blood loses its way . . . — —And the bared heart fares badly . . .

NADUR: But she . . . ! — —She! . . .

She is the loveliest person you could find! . . . — —Her soul, untouched . . . and defenseless . . . her . . . — — —

Have you found anything more sublime, anything more precious on earth . . .

And she must suffer . . . —she must . . .

Didn't you see . . . — —didn't you see the light around her . . . on her brow . . . her head . . . surrounding *her* . . .

What would life be worth if nothing reached perfection, were transfigured and beautiful . . . as she . . . What is life worth without . . . without— —

She . . . she who . . . !

Collapses.

AMAR-AZU *lays a hand on his shoulder— —he turns away*: My son . . .

Tries to look at him.

NADUR *hides his face.*

AMAR-AZU *goes away from him.* — — —*After a moment*: Have you loved her a long time?

NADUR: Yes.

Pardon me— —

AMAR-AZU: Pardon . . .

NADUR: I never thought I'd show it.

AMAR-AZU *silent.*

NADUR: And that is why I went with you.

AMAR-AZU: Because of that? —And then to be driven off as an outcast?

NADUR: Yes, I didn't want to be here any longer . . .

AMAR-AZU *goes to him. Lays his hand gently on his shoulder*: Nadur . . .?
Perhaps it's right like this . . .
After a moment.
Maybe it's you she loves . . . — —That part of me which was
like you . . . once.

NADUR: Me? . . . — —She loves me? . . .

AMAR-AZU *nods his head in affirmation.*

NADUR: Me? . . . — — —

AMAR-AZU: Something which was like you.

NADUR *looks shyly up at him—turns away again from his gaze.*
Stands silently. — —*Slowly out toward the archway.*

AMAR-AZU: You go?

NADUR *looks back.*
Goes out.

HIGH PRIEST *coming in*: My King.

AMAR-AZU *doesn't answer.*

HIGH PRIEST: What great words do you have today?

AMAR-AZU *doesn't answer.*

HIGH PRIEST: What do you believe in?

AMAR-AZU: Nothing.

HIGH PRIEST: Nothing. — —
Finally you speak the truth. I have waited a long time for it.
Finally an end to your phrases. No more now that you see the
work fulfilled which you have had such a great part in. The
work of unbelief. The work of doubt in the world.
Nothing . . . — — —
I've known it. —He who begins to doubt, begins to slip away
from firm ground, he is already lost.
And already he has the great void within him.

AMAR-AZU *doesn't answer.*

HIGH PRIEST: Is it better this way?

AMAR-AZU: Yes.

HIGH PRIEST: Happier?

AMAR-AZU *doesn't answer.*

HIGH PRIEST: Is this a happier state?

AMAR-AZU: Happier? . . .

HIGH PRIEST *after a moment*: He whom the god holds in his iron hand has peace. The people whom he holds in his chains of iron are safe in them.

You have no peace. And your people have none either.

AMAR-AZU *makes no answer.*

HIGH PRIEST: The laws and the customs may be cruel. But a people without law and custom will meet a crueler fate, they will crumble and fall.

AMAR-AZU: Perhaps we need to crumble, deeply within, so that we can be made clean.

HIGH PRIEST: Clean?

AMAR-AZU: Yes.

HIGH PRIEST: I fear we might succeed only too well with our crumbling. But the cleansing, I think we'll have to let wait awhile.

AMAR-AZU: I fear so too.

HIGH PRIEST: And still you do not shrink from the thought!

AMAR-AZU: Where man is concerned there is no reason to shrink from anything. Nothing can make him worse than he is. But his taint can be revealed to him—and he can long for purity of heart.

HIGH PRIEST: Folly! —Only God the almighty can make us clean.

AMAR-AZU: He has succeeded badly, it seems.

HIGH PRIEST: Shall men have any better success!

AMAR-AZU: It doesn't seem so!

HIGH PRIEST: Fool! —— —

This is how you talk when everything is about to collapse around you! When the ground is giving way under you!

Do you dread nothing! — —Don't you know—don't you see
what threatens!

Your country is in danger!

AMAR-AZU: *My* country is always in danger!

HIGH PRIEST: And who shall save it?

AMAR-AZU: I can't see that anyone is trying to do it.

HIGH PRIEST: Until now it has been up to us to save it from destruction. And with the Almighty's help it will be done again.
We don't hazard law and order. We're not as fearless as you
are!

AMAR-AZU: My fear is much greater than yours!

HIGH PRIEST: Yes! The fear of the ungodly man who's lost his
footing! He who has forsaken his god, and whom the god has
forsaken!

AMAR-AZU: I believe that all of us are forsaken, and that it's well
we are.

HIGH PRIEST: Well? —Verily, the Lord our God has forsaken us!
When one of his chosen speaks so. He has turned his face from
us and sees us no more.

AMAR-AZU: I don't think he sees anything. I think his eye is
shattered as the likeness in the temple.

HIGH PRIEST: Yes! His eye is shattered like a dead man's! And if
you wish you can see through the cracks into empty nothingness! If it does not strike you with terror!

AMAR-AZU: That's not what terrifies me. It is you and all men who
frighten me!

HIGH PRIEST: We are not worthy. None of us. And the fear of
man's bestiality fills me too.

And that is why I do not rely on anything but the god, upon
his hard hand of iron which holds us in its grasp and never lets
go. —If man gets loose the world's fate is sealed. And his
own.

AMAR-AZU: He won't get loose. You can be sure of that. Yes, maybe from your mighty god. But never from his own chains. He
who says otherwise, dreams. And you needn't fear dreamers.
They're not dangerous, nor is their innocent play.

Let the children play. They'll soon grow up and no longer believe what they believed—not in anything.

HIGH PRIEST: No. Not in anything . . .

So it is. —The thought that soars free, who knows where it
will strike. Now it rides toward heaven as if to visit a star.
Now it sinks in weariness and desperation to the deepest pit,
trying to find a refuge there. It is imprisoned in its longing and
its doubt—its jail is only greater and more desolate than any
other.

AMAR-AZU: Yes . . .

HIGH PRIEST: This is my belief. And therefore I believe in our
fetters, those the god has bound us with.

Only in them does man have peace. But not when he wanders
about without a home, not when he strives for a goal he can't
reach. *He* sets a goal for us, for our life. And our helpless
dreams and visions which comprehend nothing, he counts for
naught.

It is well that we all are worthless before god.

AMAR-AZU: He can't complain about our worthlessness! He can be
satisfied with us! Our souls are dwarfed, and we live in the
same hovels we've always lived in. If we have dreams and visions,
we use them only for burning and murdering those who didn't
see the same vision we did. If we creep out of our holes, it's to
hate because we thirst after blood like the beast of prey in the
mountains!

HIGH PRIEST: The beast should be tamed!

I know the world as well as you do! But I'm not floating in
space because of it, I don't forsake it.

I know the god needs his stewards to help him down here on
earth. He can take care of the movement of the stars himself.

AMAR-AZU: Lead them then—but not as livestock to be offered to
your god.

HIGH PRIEST: They are not sacrificed in vain, but for their own advantage.

Although they no longer understand it.

Nor do you understand it. You think the world can be ruled

by love and goodness. But it's ruled badly by them. It suffers
more harm from them than from violence and fear.

You think that the god can be Love. But he can't. To help men,
he must subdue them, hold them in the strength of his hand.
I am old and have tested my faith during a long life. And I de-
plore unbelief and error, doubt which spreads more and more,
and that his name no longer strikes terror in the heart as once
it did. I mourn my god, that he hides himself from us. For
only he can save us.

AMAR-AZU: Only violence! As always!

HIGH PRIEST: Only he can subdue us! And can link the chains and
close the doors on us so that we may have peace!

AMAR-AZU: Grieve men and not their gods. They'll find gods
enough again, and more besides.

But when shall men live here on earth!

Goes toward the exit.

HIGH PRIEST: You betray him . . . As you have always done.

Watches him as he leaves.

And it looks as if He himself has betrayed his people.

But I'll never betray him! I am old and I stand at the edge of
the grave. I might be indifferent to everything in this world.
But I'll not betray! He has given me this task. And his work
shall be fulfilled until again he turns his face toward us and
strikes down all doubt, all unbelief and blindness with his
avenging arm. And then he'll find that we, his servants, have
managed his inheritance well.

AMAR-AZU *looks sorrowfully at him*: That inheritance has always been
well managed, better than any other.

HIGH PRIEST: Yes! And shall be still. Even if all should fail and the
god no longer has mercy on his people! It may be the work of
man, until it again is god's work. Until he seizes the reins
again and compels us to follow him.

AMAR-AZU: Man's work is all.

Aren't you aware of that, old man that you are?

Goes.

HIGH PRIEST *out to the left.*

IREAM-AZU *coming from the palace.* —*Down to the archway toward the city. Tries to peer out.*
Up and down across the courtyard. Back again to the archway sometimes, watching.
SERVANTS *coming out of the palace carrying large baskets of bread on their heads.*

IREAM-AZU: Where are you going with that!

ONE OF THEM: To give bread to the populace . . .

IREAM-AZU: We're not giving out any bread!

SERVANTS: What . . . !

ONE OF THEM: But my Lord . . . we always do during the festival . . .

AN OLDER SERVANT: My Lord King . . . This is ancient custom and usage.

IREAM-AZU: Now there's a new custom!
Beckons them back.

SERVANTS *uneasy, wondering*: No bread . . . ? — —No bread . . . ?
In.

IREAM-AZU *again, up and down.*

AN OLD BEGGAR *comes in, faltering, supported by his crutches. Stretches out his hand*: Mighty lord . . . — — —mighty lord . . .

IREAM-AZU *pays no attention to him.*

BEGGAR: Mighty lord . . . — —I am so poor . . .
Have mercy . . . — —have mercy . . .

IREAM-AZU: I'm not waiting for beggars!
Goes away from him, toward the palace entrance.

BEGGAR: No, not for beggars!
Throws off his hood. Flings his crutches to the ground. A young man, excited.

IREAM-AZU *turns about violently—hurries up to him*: Is it you! . . . Are you bringing . . . !

BEGGAR: Yes!
We have weapons! . . . — —Some of the troops have gone over to us! . . .
All the lower part of the city will soon be in our hands! . . .

IREAM-AZU *seizes his hand. Exhales in relief.*

Act Three

Cries, noises of battle. Wild yelling below the walls.
IREAM-AZU *walks alone about the courtyard.*
Empty. Only a few frightened servants are seen in passing; they disappear again inside the palace. The yelling becomes wilder and wilder.
CAPTAIN *in through the archway. Excitedly*: Who are these swine!
IREAM-AZU: Swine!
CAPTAIN: They're not men— —they're animals!
IREAM-AZU: Really?

> CAPTAIN *walks about in agitation.*

IREAM-AZU: Don't you recognize your own people!
CAPTAIN: No! . . .
IREAM-AZU: You've never looked them in the face before! Then it's time you did!
CAPTAIN: They are burning the city! — —All the houses near the palace are in flames!
IREAM-AZU: Let them burn!
CAPTAIN: They captured two of the councillors when some of the troops went over to them, and have crucified them down there—high up, for all to see!
IREAM-AZU: What about it!
CAPTAIN: What about it!
> *Goes up close to him.*
> Do you approve it!

> IREAM-AZU *shrugs his shoulders.*

CAPTAIN: It's horrible!
IREAM-AZU: Who the devil has said that your people are angels! Neither are soldiers!
CAPTAIN: No.
IREAM-AZU: Did you think a host of noble heroes would come to occupy the palace?

CAPTAIN: Not heroes, that would be asking too much . . .
But at least . . . at least fighting men! —Not this kind, they
behave like animals, they haven't a shred of honor.

IREAM-AZU: We care nothing for your virtues, you can keep them!
We need others! And we have them!

CAPTAIN: What are they? What virtues do they have?
They are nothing more than animals turned loose . . .

IREAM-AZU: They are as they are! They have their own nobility!
It's worth more than yours!

CAPTAIN *walks up and down, in agitation.*

IREAM-AZU: Recall the troops!

CAPTAIN *does not answer.*

IREAM-AZU: Recall your troops, I say! — — —They have no place
in this battle!

CAPTAIN *walks continuously.*

IREAM-AZU: You know you have the power to do it! They obey
you! Like the bastards they are!

CAPTAIN *no answer.*

IREAM-AZU: Don't you understand . . . now's the time! — — —
Do you call yourself a warrior!

CAPTAIN: I have been. —Once, long ago—in the day of a great
sovereign.
That was a time for *action.*

IREAM-AZU: And it's time again!

CAPTAIN *walking back and forth.*

IREAM-AZU: Do you hear me!

CAPTAIN: My men are not at the center of resistance. It's the mer-
cenaries—but even they aren't fighting as they should.
But the law-abiding people are there—citizens—nobles—all
are there—all!

IREAM-AZU: Yes, they have something to defend!

CAPTAIN: Yes.
Something to fight for. And all of them are there . . .

Cries and wailing are heard outside as people in the struggle are cut down or give way.

IREAM-AZU *listens intently*: Are they my people! — — —Are my people falling back! —

Toward the exit. —The CAPTAIN *stops him.*

Let me through! — — —Do you hear! —

CAPTAIN: You are not going outside the palace!

IREAM-AZU: Let me through! Do you hear me! They'll be taken down from the crosses—I promise you, if you . . .

CAPTAIN: No.

The guard is here to protect you. But if you try to get out . . . !

Goes out through the archway.

IREAM-AZU *alone. —Back and forth, excitedly. —Stops. Listens. The noises of battle are heard above the cries. Shouting and roars which sound like cries of victory. He listens breathlessly.*

CAPTAIN *finally returns. —In a low voice*: It's not your side that wavers . . .

IREAM-AZU *lights up.*

CAPTAIN: But they defend themselves bravely . . . with the High Priest in the forefront.

IREAM-AZU *scornfully*: The High Priest! —Yes, he has something to defend!

CAPTAIN: Yes.

The shouting is heard closer by.

IREAM-AZU: We're winning!

CAPTAIN: Winning . . . — —

What does your victory bring. What is it that you want.

IREAM-AZU: We want to live! We shall not be sacrificed! Not this time! Now we shall live instead—finally!

CAPTAIN: Live? . . . — — —

And for *what*!

The noise of the mob rises in violence. Piercing cries of terror are heard.

What do you want!

IREAM-AZU: We shall avenge the stable boy who was whipped to death! — —for the sake of a saddle strap! — —Now he's learned to saddle, and so he's riding the horse himself!

Goes up to the CAPTAIN.

And what do *you* really want?

CAPTAIN *silent.*

IREAM-AZU: What is it *you* want?

CAPTAIN: I? . . .

IREAM-AZU: Yes! And I'd like to know soon. What do you have to do with the people! Can you tell me!

CAPTAIN: I thought that they could save my country . . .

IREAM-AZU: Aha! — —

CAPTAIN: That they were called to do it.

IREAM-AZU: They need to save themslves first of all!

CAPTAIN: Themselves . . .

IREAM-AZU: We are talking about men not about the country!

CAPTAIN: Men . . .

What is a man without a country. What is a man without something to sacrifice himself for . . .

IREAM-AZU: No . . .

Looks at him. —The CAPTAIN *stands silently.*

We have! We are used to sacrifice! But today we offer up others instead! As you do!

You ought to understand this, you talk so easily of sacrifice.

CAPTAIN: Yes.

IREAM-AZU: Maybe it's time for you to be sacrificed!

CAPTAIN *thoughtfully. Then*: For what?

IREAM-AZU: For the people! If you know who they are!

For those who shall live!

CAPTAIN *silently. Then*: It makes sense only when we are sacrificed for something greater than ourselves.

IREAM-AZU: Yes! Here men are sacrificed for mankind. That makes good sense!

Even though you lack the wit to understand it!

CAPTAIN: No . . . I don't understand it.

I don't think I have a people to offer myself for . . .

IREAM-AZU: No! Perhaps not!

CAPTAIN: Only my country . . .

IREAM-AZU: How will you fight for it! I'd like to know!
I think people like you are more dangerous than our real ad-
versaries.
How will you fight for it! For or against us!

CAPTAIN *doesn't answer.*

IREAM-AZU: I say withdraw the troops!

CAPTAIN *silent.*

IREAM-AZU: Order them back, I tell you! They have nothing to do
with this!

CAPTAIN: No. It's true . . . This is no battle for soldiers.

IREAM-AZU: No, it is a battle between noble lords and the mob!
The roar of the mob, cries of horror are heard.
Do you hear that!

CAPTAIN: Yes. — — —
But who will fight against his own people.

IREAM-AZU: There are many who will!

CAPTAIN: Yes. When they are forced to it.
Goes heavily toward the exit.

IREAM-AZU *screams at him in rage*: What do you want of us! Tell me!

CAPTAIN *turns quietly toward him*: I want to serve a king once more in
my life. And you are a king.
But not *my* king.

IREAM-AZU *looks silently at him. Then*: Are you going to your people?

CAPTAIN: I am going to my *soldiers.*

IREAM-AZU: The hour has come!

CAPTAIN: Yes. It's about time!
Goes.
*Battle alarms. Horns blow shrilly. The sound of drums is heard. Com-
mand calls which are relayed farther and farther away. Noise of a more
violent struggle.*
IREAM-AZU *unbearably restless. His tension rises—to the point of
anxiety.*

THE FOOL *steals out of the palace. Sits on the steps leading to the throne. Observes his uneasiness, grins*: Do you need a fool, dear king? —Are you the kind who can't be without one? Eh?

IREAM-AZU *pretends not to notice him.*

THE FOOL *after a moment*: How do you like the weather. Calm and peaceful, eh? If it only holds . . .
A cry that cannot be understood is heard through the archway. More and more of the same cries.

IREAM-AZU: What's that? . . .

THE FOOL *shrugs his shoulders.*

IREAM-AZU: What are they saying out there . . . ?

THE FOOL: I don't know.

IREAM-AZU: I can't hear it . . .

THE FOOL: No, I can't hear anything. Nothing at all. Except the frogs croaking down there in the swamp, but they always do that when there's going to be a change in the weather.
Yawns. Stretches out, with his head on the step.

THE GUARD *into the archway*: The Captain has fallen! — — — Our captain! — —

IREAM-AZU: He's fallen . . .!

THE GUARD: Yes! — — —Our lord . . .
Stands staring in front of him.

IREAM-AZU *stands, as he does—silent.*
After a moment.
Was your lord a good man?

GUARD: Yes, my king.

IREAM-AZU: Did you know him . . . know anything about him?

GUARD: No, my king.

IREAM-AZU: Why did you follow him then—how could that be?

GUARD: He was worth following. We would have gladly died for him.
The people are heard continuing the assault, wild cries.

IREAM-AZU *nods his head in affirmation*: It's good to have something to die for.

GUARD: Yes. It's something a soldier needs.

Cries of victory are heard, wilder, closer.

IREAM-AZU: What do you think he died for?

GUARD: *He?* . . . — — —

He fell in battle, my king.

IREAM-AZU: Yes.

Fell in battle. — —

An outcry that outdoes all the others. Increases in violence. Comes closer and closer, up toward the palace. A wave of people, sweeping away everything in its path.

Finally the people enter. Torn, many wounded.

THE LEADER *in the foreground*: We've won!

THE CROWD *in endless jubilation*: We've won! We've won!

Wild joy. Some are crying, others pale from the excitement, others still in battle. All of them in violent agitation.

They gather around IREAM.

Our king! — —You're our king!

They do homage, a confusion of cries and joy.

IREAM-AZU *when he can be heard*: We are the masters now and no one else! — —Our own masters!

THE CROWD: Yes, yes!

IREAM-AZU: And have avenged ourselves! Finally!

CRIES: Yes! —Avenged ourselves!

CRIES: Now we'll have revenge! — — —Revenge!

IREAM-AZU: We have fought! — —Against oppression! — —No more oppressed!

CRIES: No! No! — —We've won! — —We have won the victory!

IREAM-AZU: Never again.

THE CROWD *a chaos of shrieking, impossible to understand.*

IREAM-AZU *in the midst of the confusion*: Put out the fires!

CRIES: Let them burn!

IREAM-AZU: Give orders that the fires be put out! It is *our* city which is burning now!

CRIES: Yes! Yes! It's ours!

SOMEONE *goes out to give the command.*

THE LEADER: We threw them back! — —they ran away or they joined us! — —except the leaders—
Bring in the prisoners!

CRIES: Yes! Yes!

THE LEADER: They shall pay for their crimes—finally!

CRIES: Yes! — —They shall be punished by death! —The executioner!
The executioner!

IREAM-AZU: They shall be brought in to honor a new king!

THE LEADER: Do you want their homage!

IREAM-AZU: Yes!

CRIES: No, no! Their blood! — —We want to see their blood!

OTHERS: The tyrants' blood!

OTHERS: Death to them and theirs! Death to them!

IREAM-AZU: They shall do honor before their king!

VOICES: Do honor?

OTHERS: Yes, yes! They shall honor our king! *Our king!*

IREAM-AZU *commands*: Bring them in!
The HIGH PRIEST *and some of the* COUNCILLORS *are brought in.*
The crowd shrieks and flings insults at them. The HIGH PRIEST *is in his robe, torn to shreds, with a sword at his side.*
They stand in a group at the right.

IREAM-AZU *calmly*: You shall pay honor to the king!
They are silent. They stand there, teeth clenched in hate.
The people's king!
They look at him with hostility.

CRIES: Do honor to our king! — —Our king! — — —
Do you hear!

A MAN *to the* HIGH PRIEST: The god has given you a new king!
Are you blind!

HIGH PRIEST: We do not know him or his people.

VOICE: Don't know him! —You crowned him yourself! — —
Don't you know your own people!
They go toward him, shouting and threatening.

HIGH PRIEST: You are wild animals escaped from your cages!

CRIES: Yes! Yes! We are wild animals!

OTHERS: And the god has given us power now! —Now we have the power here!

HIGH PRIEST: You are damned! — — —The way of the Most High is so hidden from you that . . . !

CRIES: Yes, it is hidden from us!

ONE OF THEM: Go that way yourself, you know it so well! Send him to the god!

CRIES: Burn him! Offer him to the god!

THE CROWD *shouting*: Offer him to the god! Offer him to the god!

HIGH PRIEST *steps out in front of them*: Yes! Sacrifice me to my God! If there is still any mercy on this earth, sacrifice me to my God. That I may go before him and ask what he has meant with his world. And close accounts with him.

VOICE: You can square accounts with us!

HIGH PRIEST: No. Not before men. Before Him alone! As you yourselves will have to do one day.

I am prepared. You who have yet to manage your own affairs, sacrifice me to my God!

VOICE: You think you can give a good account of yourself!

HIGH PRIEST: Yes! Yes, I can!

I shall stand before him and speak of his own work which he has allowed to go to ruin. Of his world which we built with his help, and which now lies ravaged.

Clenches his fist against the sky.

Why do you smash your world to bits, you demented God! Why do you make men homeless and let them roam like jackals around the smouldering walls which you yourself told them to raise! Why have you let this happen! Why do you betray us!

A hum of voices, from THE PEOPLE, *some shouting at him.*

HIGH PRIEST: Why do you betray your old servant who has never broken faith!

VOICE: Yes, he has deserted you, old man!

Outcries and abuse.

HIGH PRIEST: You are lost! Homeless race—without god, without a world to live in! Damnation shall rest upon you and all your deeds until vengeance is exacted one day!

May you be forever damned!

THE PEOPLE *in wild agitation*: Burn him! — —Leave him to the executioner!

— —Send them to the executioner! —Their blood! — —We want to see their blood!

There is a movement over by the archway, those standing there look out—become silent, make way for someone. The silence spreads more and more—over the whole courtyard.

AMAR-AZU *is carried in. Followed by* NADUR. *They carefully lay him down in the foreground.*

NADUR *leaning over him*: Dear Lord . . . do you live . . . ?

AMAR-AZU *in a weak voice*: My son . . . — —I see visions so fair . . . — — —am I here? . . .

NADUR: Yes, my Lord . . . — — —And I am with you again . . . as it was before . . . as always . . .

AMAR-AZU: Yes . . . you . . .

It is as if I dreamed . . . —as then . . . — —as then . . .

NADUR: Yes! — —

AMAR-AZU: You are really with me . . . — —You won't leave me . . .

NADUR: No, no . . .

AMAR-AZU: No, it was I who left you . . . — —But now I'm with you again . . .

NADUR *his hand on* AMAR'S *forehead.*

AMAR-AZU: I went away from . . . from all men . . .

But you must return to them again . . . — —and believe again . . .

You must believe again . . . you who can . . .

NADUR *grips his hand and holds it hard in his own*: Yes! . . .

AMAR-AZU: . . . you who can believe . . . — —

NADUR: Yes, yes . . .

SIBILE *comes out of the palace*: My beloved! — —What have you done
to him, my dearest! —
Goes to him and embraces him.
What have they done . . . — — —what have they done to
you . . . — —god's chosen . . .

NADUR: It was his own people . . . they did not recognize him because he was dressed as a beggar . . .

SIBILE *caresses and kisses him.*

NADUR: I couldn't get to him before it happened . . .

SIBILE: Beloved . . . —my beloved . . . — —You must not die . . .
You must not die . . . I can't be parted from you . . .

AMAR-AZU: No, I shall not die . . .
Don't you see . . . — — —I live . . . I'm close beside you . . .
—and shall not die . . .

SIBILE *caresses him, cries.*

AMAR-AZU: Don't mourn for what lies here so poor and burnt . . .
unable to do any more . . .
I stand beside you . . . — —don't you see me . . . —that I
live . . .
Don't you recognize me . . . because I've been away so long . . .
— —Don't you remember me as I once was . . .
Touches her head.
My dear, my dearest . . .
I give you to my youth . . . to what I was.
Places her hand in NADUR'S. —*Then, in a lifeless voice.*
And you shall believe again . . . — —you who can . . .

NADUR: Yes, yes . . .

AMAR-AZU: — —believe again . . . — — —believe again . . . — —
Collapses in exhaustion.

NADUR *leans over him and sees that he no longer lives.*

Silence.

IREAM-AZU *finally. —in a subdued voice, and in a different tone*:

Skåne-Reportage

The King
Malmö stadsteater, 1950
Director: Lars-Levi Laestadius
Design: Härje Ekman

Hariette Garellick (Sibile), Folke Sundquist (Nadur), and Arnold
Sjöstrand (Amar-Azu) in *The King*
Malmö stadsteater, 1950
Director: Lars-Levi Laestadius
Design: Härje Ekman

Has your god revealed his will to you?

The prisoners are silent.

Has his will been made clear to you?

HIGH PRIEST *finally*: We can see that he has allowed a man to die.

IREAM-AZU: Who was your king.

HIGH PRIEST *after a moment*: We have only the Lord our God.

IREAM-AZU: And not even him, because you cannot understand his will.

HIGH PRIEST: No, not even him. — — —

No longer can we divine his meaning in what he has allowed to happen.

IREAM-AZU: Others can divine it.

THE PEOPLE *mumbling in agreement.*

IREAM-AZU *goes slowly down to* AMAR'S *deathbed—stands and regards him for a long time in silence. Then turns to* NADUR: Who are you?

A VOICE: He's not one of us, he's only dressed that way.

OTHERS: He's not one of ours!

IREAM-AZU: You have followed him—the other king?

NADUR: Yes!

A VOICE: Yes, he always has! He doesn't belong to us!

IREAM-AZU *turning to the* HIGH PRIEST: Does he belong to you?

HIGH PRIEST: No.

By the god's law he should be banished.

IREAM-AZU: Banished? Why?

HIGH PRIEST: He has become unclean.

IREAM-AZU: Unclean?

HIGH PRIEST: Yes.

IREAM-AZU: So, perhaps, have many of us.

To NADUR.

Why have you followed him?

NADUR: For me there is no one else to follow.

THE PEOPLE: Hear! Hear us! —Banish him! — —Banish him!

IREAM-AZU: Why?

THE PEOPLE: Because he followed the king!

IREAM-AZU: Is it a crime to follow one's king?

THE PEOPLE: He followed the other one! The other one!

IREAM-AZU: He has followed *his* king. They say that he was the only one who did.

A VOICE: No, no one followed him! And now he's dead!

ANOTHER VOICE: He is dead!

THE CROWD *a confusion of voices*: The king is dead! — —Hail the king! — —Hail our king!

IREAM-AZU *when the voices have subsided*: I don't know you. Nor do I know your king. I don't know who he really was.
Who was he?

NADUR: My king was a beggar.

IREAM-AZU: Beggar?
Can a king be a beggar?

NADUR: Yes. In *his* kingdom.
In that country all of us are beggars. But he was our King. For he was the poorest of us all. He knew our unspeakable poverty better than any of us.

IREAM-AZU: Beggars . . . — —

NADUR: Yes.
All of us are beggars, Lord.

IREAM-AZU *after a moment*: We have never owned anything. Now is our time to inherit the earth.

NADUR: Yes. In new poverty—and with a new faith.

IREAM-AZU: New faith? . . .

NADUR: Yes!

HIGH PRIEST: There is only one faith! And it is dead in this world, you have let it fall bloody in the dirt!

NADUR: Yes. There is only *one* faith. One which never dies.

IREAM-AZU: I don't quite understand you. — —
But shall this man be condemned!

THE PEOPLE *mumbling, whispering among themselves*.

IREAM-AZU: I have nothing to condemn you for.
You are free among your new people. —Why should you be banished?

HIGH PRIEST: He has broken the divine laws! Therefore his word is blasphemy and error!

Hum of voices, scornful mumbling in the crowd.

IREAM-AZU: There are no longer any divine laws. And therefore he shall not be banished.

Not if he will serve us.

NADUR: I will serve mankind.

IREAM-AZU: That is right.

Takes his hand.

And all of us are men.

THE PEOPLE: Hail! Hail to thee! — —Our king!

IREAM-AZU *is taken up to the throne.*

THE PEOPLE *joyfully*: Hail to thee! — —Our king! —Hail to thee!

The Hangman:

A Play in One Act
(1933)

Characters

THE HANGMAN
THE OLD SHOEMAKER
A COOPER
SKINNER-JACK
A BUTCHER'S HELPER
AN APPRENTICE
A CARPENTER
GALLOWS-LASSE
GALLOWS-LASSE'S BOY
A PEASANT
NIGHT CLUB GUESTS
NEGROES IN A JAZZ BAND
THE WOMAN WITH THE HALO

In the tableaux:
A HANGMAN
THE HANGMAN'S WIFE
A YOUNG HANGMAN
A BOY
THE BOY'S MOTHER
THE CONDEMNED WOMAN
THE JUDGE
THE FIGURE OF CHRIST

A mediaeval tavern.

THE HANGMAN *sits at a long, narrow table close to the back wall. He is a great and awesome figure in a blood-red robe, a dominating presence at the table, lighted by the flicker of smoking candles. The hangman's brand has been burned into his forehead.*

Half-drunken craftsmen, people from the quarter nearby, hot and flushed, sit hunched over their stoups at the same table—but none of them sit near him. The girl who fills their flagons steals quietly and timidly over the stone floor.

A BUTCHER'S HELPER *shouts*: It's good ale, master! I guess you know the old mother's been out on the gallows hill and pinched a poacher's finger from you and she's hung it by a thread down in the barrel. She serves no better than she drinks herself, and looks to her guests, she does. There's nothing like a finger from the gallows to give the ale a musty smack, y'know!

AN OLD SHOEMAKER *thoughtfully wipes the ale from his withered beard*: Aye, it's strange, all that comes from up there, what a remarkable power it has.

AN APPRENTICE: That's god's truth! I remember once they hung a countryman for poaching in my home parish, though he said he didn't do it. When master kicked him off the step, and the loop pulled tight, he cut loose a fart that reeked all round the hillside, and the flowers drooped, and the meadow to the east lay faded and withered, for there was a westerly wind I'd say, and it was a bad harvest in the parish that summer.

They laugh, lean over the table.

BUTCHER'S HELPER: Yes, my father told me that once when he was young, a tanner screwed his sister-in-law, and the same thing happened to him when he went up, it's easy enough to do when you leave this earthly life in such a haste. When they stood back for the blast, they saw a cloud rise to the sky, so black it was horrible, and the devil himself sat in the stern with a poker, driving off his sinful soul and grinning happily at the stink.

155

OLD SHOEMAKER: That's enough of your drivel. I don't jest about
   the power these things have, it's true and certain as can be.
   Looks sideways at THE HANGMAN.
   — —Take Kristen, Anna's boy, he fell in a fit and was frothing
   at the mouth for the spell that came over him! I was there
   myself and helped to hold him many times, to open up his
   mouth, it was frightful how it rode him, worse than anything
   I've seen. But when his mother brought him up there the time
   Jerker the Smith lost his life, and he drank some of the blood,
   he was better. He hasn't fallen down once since then.
SKINNER-JACK: Mmm . . .
OLD SHOEMAKER: You know as well as I do, you live next door.
A COOPER: Yes, no one doubts it's true.
APPRENTICE: No, everyone knows that's the way it is.
BUTCHER'S HELPER: But a murderer's blood it must be, and while
   the heat's still there, otherwise it's no use.
APPRENTICE: That has to be.
SKINNER-JACK: Yes, it's strange, it is . . .
OLD SHOEMAKER: Just like a child suffering from the pain of
   rickets can be well again if he's given the blood scraped from
   the headsman's sword, I know that from my childhood. Every-
   one about the village knew it, the midwife used to get it
   from the headsman's house.
   Isn't that right, master?

THE HANGMAN *does not see him. He is motionless. His face is impassive,
impenetrable in the flickering light.*

OLD SHOEMAKER: Aye. Evil has a healing power, that's certain.
COOPER: Yes, it's horrible the way people hunger for it. When I go
   home past the gallows hill at night there's a clamor and cry up
   there to make your heart stop for the dread of it. You don't
   have to guess where the apothecaries and sorcerers and other
   godless magic makers get their mischief from, that the poor
   and oppressed have to pay dearly for in the sweat of their brow.
   They say there are corpses up there that have been stripped to
   the bare bone, and which you can't even tell have been people

walking the earth once upon a time. I know as well as you do
that it has power, and is nothing to shrink from when the need
is great, I've tried it myself as far as that goes, and on my old
woman too—but I say, shame! Shame! It's not only the swine
and birds of the heaven that live on rotting flesh, we do too!

APPRENTICE: Phew! Why don't you shut up! It makes me sick to
listen to you. —

What was it you swallowed, did you say?

COOPER: I didn't say and I won't either. I say the devil's shame!
For he's in everything that comes from up there! I tell you!

BUTCHER'S HELPER: Rot! — —All you talk is filth tonight. I've
no mind to hear any more like that.

APPRENTICE: Why don't you drain your ale?

BUTCHER'S HELPER: I drink. Drink yourself, you drunken cur.

SKINNER-JACK: But it's strange, isn't it, that it can help and have
such power.

COOPER: And just the same it has.

OLD SHOEMAKER: Yes, it has power over one thing and another.
You're always in danger when it's near.
*They become silent, sit and push their stoups—move slightly. Some of
them turn away furtively and cross themselves.*

OLD SHOEMAKER *looking askance at the great, silent figure*: They say
that neither sword nor knife can bite the headsman. —I have
no idea if it's true.

BUTCHER'S HELPER: It's a lie!

OLD SHOEMAKER: There's always the kind that's "hard." I heard
tell of one when I was young, he was hard. When they were to
take off his head with the sword for his inhuman way of life,
the edge wouldn't cut into him. Then they took an axe to him
but it was thrown out of the hands of the one that held it, and
then they were scared and let him be, for they knew then there
were powers in him.

APPRENTICE: Talk!

OLD SHOEMAKER: It's as true as I'm sitting here telling it!

BUTCHER'S HELPER: Eh, babble, babble. Everybody knows that
master headsmen have been smited with both sword and axe

like any other beggar's wretch. And master Jens that got it
with his own axe, remember that!

OLD SHOEMAKER: Yes, Jens, that was something else again, he
wasn't really one of them. Poor man, he fell into bad luck
without knowing why, and had to beg to stay alive because he
couldn't leave his old woman and their children. That's not the
same thing. He couldn't bear the work and was more frightened than the poor sinner himself up there on the gallows hill.
He was afraid of the evil, he was. And he came to a sorry end
because he was so hellish frightened of it, he couldn't hold himself together anymore, that's what I think, that's why he got
hold of Staffan and struck him dead, his best friend too, you
know. —If you want to know, the axe was much stronger than
he was, and it sucked him in, he couldn't get away, and sure
enough one fine day, there he lay, just as he knew he would.
No, he hadn't any powers in him. But for them that has,
there's nothing that'll bite.

SKINNER-JACK: Yes, it's sure the hangman has a power that no
other has, as close as he is to evil. And that his axe and all
that has a power in itself, that's certain too. That's why no one
dares lay hand to it or anything the headsman's clan has
touched.

COOPER: Yes, that's right.

OLD SHOEMAKER: There are forces abroad which no man can divine,
that's certain. And the evil won't let go once it's taken
hold.

A CARPENTER *who throughout has been sitting silently and a little apart*:
You have no idea. Evil's not easy to really get to know, and if
you do, it may happen you'll be filled with wonder. Not that I
know so much about it either, but one time it somehow let me
come quite near so I could see its face, you might say. That's
something you remember all your life, if it lets you into its
secrets that way. And it's strange but afterwards it seems you're
never afraid again.

SKINNER-JACK: Mmm . . .

OLD SHOEMAKER: Is that right. I wonder . . .

CARPENTER: Yes. I'll tell you why I'm not afraid if you want to hear.

It happened to me in my childhood, I don't remember just how old I was—we lived on a little farm my father had, and I was their only child. I had a happy home and the best and dearest parents—they are dead now, both of them, may God give their souls peace. The farm lay a little far off, and I was used to being alone with mother and father there at home. But one day during the summer when everyone was out harvesting, there was nothing to do and I went off into the forest—farther than I had ever been before. As I went along the wild path, I suddenly saw something rise up and run off—two children running. I went after them and thought, I'll catch up with you! But it wasn't so easy, again and again they disappeared into the thickets. I wanted to meet them so that we could play together for a while, and I ran harder and came closer and closer to them. Finally I noticed that one of them crept in and hid under a fallen spruce. I hurried after him—and there he lay huddled among the branches! Laughing and sweaty, I threw myself over him and held onto him. He tried to tear himself away from me and put up his head; his eyes were wild and frightened, and his mouth twisted in an evil grin. He had short red hair, and his face was full of small, dirty scars. He was almost naked, he had only a ragged woolen shirt, and he lay there trembling, it felt like holding on to an animal.

COOPER: So? . . . What kind of a brat was it?

CARPENTER: Well, I thought he looked a little odd, but I wouldn't let him go—because I didn't think badly of him at all. He lay still looking at me and didn't say a word. But soon I could see we'd become friends. Then I let him go and we got up together—but he watched me all the time, I could see. The other one came out of its hiding place, with eyes wide open in a little face, pale and frightened, it was his sister.

They were glad to play when we once got started, they hid in places they surely knew about before, and when I found them they ran without a sound to another one. I have never seen children play so quietly. They were excited and raced around like little weasels, but hardly made a sound. They didn't say much to me either. But we had a good time anyway, at least I thought so. Sometimes while we were playing they would stand beside each other and just look at me.

When I got home I didn't say anything about where I'd been and what I had done. I don't know—it seemed to be my secret somehow.

OLD SHOEMAKER: Hmm . . .

CARPENTER: Every day after that I would sneak out and play with them. They were so busy at home with the harvesting that I could easily leave. We played so hard that we were drenched with sweat from our silent running about—for I didn't yell and shout either as I certainly would have done otherwise, because they didn't. I felt as if we had known each other always. They lived somewhere there in the forest—I saw a little gray house in the distance once, it lay close to a mountain wall which hung out over it.

I really wanted to see how it looked over by their house, but it seemed as if they didn't want me to. They thought we ought to stay where we usually were. But one day I took off by myself toward the house, because I wanted to see it, and they followed a little way behind. It was a usual sort of place, but the yard was bare and uncared for and gave a dreary impression. The door was ajar and we went carefully through it—they behind me.

Slowly.

It was dim and smelled musty.

More slowly.

A woman came toward us, but without a word of greeting.

It has become darker at the table where he sits telling the story. —It gradually becomes entirely dark.

A tableau is seen up to the left: a wall of rough-hewn logs. On it hangs a large double-edged sword, broad and straight, covered with signs and inscriptions.

—HANGMAN'S WIFE. THE BOY. *He looks around him in wonder.*

CARPENTER *continues the story from the darkness*: Her eyes were hard and she looked at me continuously without saying a word, I don't know, it seemed there was something evil about her. The tufts of her hair hung down to her cheeks and her large, bloodless mouth was somehow scornful and wicked . . . — — —

HANGMAN'S WIFE *in the tableau, to her own children—who cannot be seen in the darkness*: How did he come here?

CHILD'S VOICE *anxiously*: He's been playing with us in the forest.

HANGMAN'S WIFE: Playing with *you*?

CHILDREN *anxiously*: Yes.

> HANGMAN'S WIFE *looks questioningly at the* BOY—*seems somewhat gentler.*

BOY *walks around and looks at things curiously*: It's so strange here— —
It's not like this at home.

HANGMAN'S WIFE *curtly*: So that's it.

BOY: Isn't there a strange smell?
Goes to the sword.
What's that? —A sword . . .
Closer. Looks at the engraved figures.
Look, there's the Christ child!
Very close, as if he were drawn toward it. —*Touches it.*
A deep sigh is heard, as if someone gave a sob.

BOY *looks about, goes back to them*: Who is crying?

HANGMAN'S WIFE: Crying? — —
Fiercely.
There's no one crying!
Stares at him. Her eyes change—she becomes frightened.
Come!
Takes him roughly by the hand, and goes with him to the sword. Lets him touch it as before.
The deep sigh is heard again, and the sound of someone sobbing is heard clearly.

HANGMAN'S WIFE *cries out. Pulls him away*: The sword! — —It is in the sword!
Lets him go and turns away.

After a moment—Touches her mouth with her hand; it has a look of evil about it.
Who's brat are you?

BOY: Christopher's in Våla—that's my father's name.

HANGMAN'S WIFE: Uh-huh.
After a moment.
Let me look at you.
Sits down on a stool and draws him closer. Strokes his hair a little.
Poor child . . .
Looks at him carefully for a long time.
I'd better take you home to your family.
Gets ready. Puts on the red hood, a mark of the outcast.
The tableau fades.

CARPENTER *narrates in the darkness*: . . . and a peculiar hood which I'd never seen a woman wear before. And we went on our way. "Is this where you play?" she said when we had come into the forest. And while we walked she talked a little with me. When she noticed that I was worried, she took my hand.
I didn't understand anything, and didn't dare to ask.
When we came up the hill at home, mother hurried to the front steps, her face was white, I'd never seen her like that before . . .
Tableau up to the right: A front porch step. The HANGMAN'S WIFE *holding* THE BOY'S *hand.* THE BOY'S MOTHER.

MOTHER: What are you doing with my child! Let the boy go, I tell you! Let him go, you dirty scum!

HANGMAN'S WIFE *quickly releases him. Her face is twisted, she is like a hunted animal.*

MOTHER: What have you done with my child!

HANGMAN'S WIFE: He came into our house . . .

MOTHER: Did you coax him into your filthy nest!

HANGMAN'S WIFE: I did not. He came to us himself, I can tell you. And when he came near the sword and happened to touch it, there was a sigh and a sobbing there inside it.

MOTHER *looks uncertainly and anxiously at the boy, her eyes show her agitation.*

HANGMAN'S WIFE: I suppose you know what that means.

MOTHER: No . . . I don't.

HANGMAN'S WIFE: That he'll die by the headsman's sword one day.

MOTHER *gives a half-suppressed scream and stares at the* BOY. *She is deathly white and her lips tremble—but she does not answer with even a word.*

HANGMAN'S WIFE: I thought it would be wise for you to know, but I see you're angry instead.
Here's your brat, and you won't hear from us until that time comes, since that's the way you want it!
Turns angrily and leaves.

MOTHER *reaches uncertainly for the child, as if she can't find him. Takes him close to her and kisses him—but her gaze is hard and distant. Hurries off. — — —Calls far away:*
Christopher! . . . — —Christopher! . . .
The BOY *stands there alone.*
The tableau fades.

CARPENTER *narrates in the darkness:* . . . I saw her run across the field, calling.
She and father came back, and they were silent and depressed. I remember I stood by the window and watched them coming along by the ditch.
The light comes up slowly over the table where they are sitting.

CARPENTER: That was a sad and gloomy time. They left me alone in the daytime, nobody paid any attention to me. And nothing was the same, not even the slopes of the meadow, even though it was sunny and beautiful as ever. I tried to play a little, but it was no use. When they came near, they'd pass by without saying a word. As if they didn't know me. But in the evenings mother would hold me so close and tight that I could hardly breathe.
I didn't understand why everything was so sorrowful and

changed. Or what I had done, but only that it was something
terrible, and that it hurt them to look at me. I tried to find
something to do and to keep out of the way as much as I could
because I knew that was what they wanted.

Finally one day mother called me. She took me by the hand
and started to walk into the forest and father stood there and
watched us go. When I noticed that she was turning in on the
path where I'd been before, I was really frightened for the first
time. But everything was so miserable anyway that I'd begun
to think that nothing worse could happen, and so I just
followed along. I crept close to her and tried to walk along as
best I could over the stones and roots, so that it would be easier
for her. Her face seemed so small that I could hardly recognize
her.

When we got there and went up toward the house, she shud-
dered.

I pressed her hand as tightly as I could so that she wouldn't be
so unhappy.

More slowly.

Besides the children and the woman there was a man in the
house this time. He looked rough and powerful . . .

It becomes darker at the table.

. . . and his face, with thick protruding and wrinkled lips, was
full of great scars, and he had a raw and wild expression, his
eyes were heavy, bloodshot, and yellowish. I had never seen
anything which filled me with so much dread . . .

It has become entirely dark.

*Tableau up to the left: The wall with the headsman's sword—as before.
The* MOTHER *and the* BOY *a little apart. The* HANGMAN *and the*
HANGMAN'S WIFE—*both with their backs toward them.*

MOTHER *pleading:* Won't you please help us? . . .

No answer.

You know you can if you only will . . .

No answer.

There is a way which is sure . . .

They are still motionless.

MOTHER *going toward the* HANGMAN: You can free him from it!
— — —and make me so eternally grateful . . .
Only you can free him!
No answer.
MOTHER *stands silently.* —*Then begins again:* It wasn't right of me . . .
— —No, I know it . . . But . . . — — —
They are still silent.
MOTHER *beside herself with desperation:* Be merciful to me!

HANGMAN *looks sideways at her.*

MOTHER: He is my only child . . . ! — — —the dearest thing I
have . . . !
Bursts into tears.

BOY *takes her arm to keep her from crying so much. It is no help, she
continues. And then she sobs in hopeless despair.*

VOICES OF THE HANGMAN'S CHILDREN *are heard whispering from the
darkness:* Father . . . ! — — — — —Father . . . !

HANGMAN *turns around, looks toward them. Looks at the* BOY.
After a moment. —*He goes to a pail of water standing there in the room.
Beckons the* BOY *toward him.*

BOY *uneasily toward him.*

HANGMAN *while all the others are silent, he takes a handful of water:*
Drink!

BOY *drinks out of his hand. He does so three times.*
The others have been watching tensely.

HANGMAN: The curse is lifted—now that you have drunk from my
hand. You needn't be afraid anymore.
Strokes his head lightly.
It is as if a miracle had occurred.
MOTHER *her face shining with happiness.* —*The birds are heard singing
outside the house.* —*She goes to the* BOY *and takes him in her arms,
kisses him.* — — —*With tears of joy in her eyes she goes to the* HANG-
MAN *and stretches out her hand to him:*
God bless you!

HANGMAN *merely turns away.*

MOTHER *and the* BOY *leave, after stopping a moment at the door.*

HANGMAN'S WIFE *spits after them:* Scum!

Bird song is heard more jubilantly, while the tableau fades.

CARPENTER'S VOICE *is heard from the darkness:* We went happily home. — —

The light up slowly over the table. They sit silently a moment.

OLD SHOEMAKER: Ah, ha . . .

COOPER: So, you see . . .

SKINNER-JACK: Evil has strange ways, no one can deny it.

COOPER: It's as if it had some good in it too.

OLD SHOEMAKER: Yes.

COOPER: And what power it has. It can both kill and set free, it seems.

SKINNER-JACK: Yes sir.

COOPER: It's strange, I must say.

OLD SHOEMAKER: Yes, and that was surely a worthy tale.

APPRENTICE: I think your mother should have asked forgiveness of the gallows hag, she gave her such a rap.

COOPER: That's what I thought, but anyway she didn't.

APPRENTICE: Uh-huh.

They sit thinking a while. Drink and wipe their mouths.

SKINNER-JACK: Sure the headsman's good sometimes, too. I've heard that he's helped the sick and the poor, and folk that's down and out, when every other remedy has failed.

OLD SHOEMAKER: Yes, and that he can suffer like the rest of us, that's true enough. He feels the ill of what he does. And it's well known that he always asks the victim's pardon before he takes off his head.

APPRENTICE: No, he doesn't hate them he kills! He can be a good friend, I've seen that happen.

BUTCHER'S HELPER: Good friend! Yes, one time I saw them hanging around each other's necks on the way to the gibbet.

COOPER: No, no . . .

BUTCHER'S HELPER: Yes, the both of them were so drunk they

could hardly stand, and had drained all there was and more, so that they wobbled up to the block. There wasn't much difference mind you, but I'd say the headsman was the tighter of the two. Wham! he said when he chopped the head off 'im.
They laugh. Sit and drink a moment.

APPRENTICE: Ah ha, so you were meant for the gallows once. Well, that can happen to any of us.

SKINNER-JACK: Yes, that's sure as can be.

COOPER: But that he can have such *power*, after all! That was nothing more nor less than a miracle you told us about. If he hadn't lifted the curse then you'd been lost for good.

BUTCHER'S HELPER: Yes, he does miracles, he does! Worse than a flock of saints when it comes to that!

COOPER: Oh, no, saints and the holy virgin can have the better of him there.

SKINNER-JACK: And Jesus Christ, who delivered us from all our sins!

APPRENTICE: Oh, that may be, you fool, but what's that got to do with it. We're talking about the headsman!

OLD SHOEMAKER: Yes, he's got a power in him. The evil has a power, no doubting that.

COOPER: But where does that power come from? I tell you, from the devil! And that's why people are so mad for it, more than for anything else in this world, even God's word and the sacrament.

OLD SHOEMAKER: But it helped him.

APPRENTICE: It did all the same!

COOPER: That may be.

BUTCHER'S HELPER: And a priest, maybe he couldn't have done a thing.

OLD SHOEMAKER: No, never, it was the evil that had the say. He was under *its* spell!

COOPER: Yes, it's all the devil's work and stinks the more!

BUTCHER'S HELPER: Mm . . . ?

COOPER: You heard yourself that when his mother said "God bless you," the headsman turned away.

APPRENTICE: Ooh . . .

BUTCHER'S HELPER: No, to hell with it, let's drink! Don't talk about such vile stuff!

APPRENTICE: Yes, more ale! — —More ale, I say! And strong!

SKINNER-JACK: Take it out of the right barrel! — —No . . . not out of the one with the finger . . . — —Is it true you have thieves' fingers in your ale here?

THE GIRL *becomes pale, shakes her head.*

APPRENTICE: Yes, the whole town knows you have! Well, bring it on! Makes no difference if it's strong! — —Wham! as he said!

COOPER: Wham bam yourself! Watch out or you'll have no throat to swill yourself tight with!

APPRENTICE: May as well drink while we can then!

BUTCHER'S HELPER: The devil himself has brewed this, you can tell by the taste!

APPRENTICE: Yes this is a hellish nest, but their ale's best!
They drink. Spread themselves, with elbows on the table's edge.

OLD SHOEMAKER: I wonder if there's to be an execution on the gallows hill tomorrow morning or when it is? . . .

COOPER: Perhaps . . .

SKINNER-JACK: It could be . . .

OLD SHOEMAKER: I mean because the master's here, and all turned out in that fine red pomp.

COOPER: Yes, it's likely so . . .

OLD SHOEMAKER: But who's heard there'll be an execution, anyone?

COOPER: No . . .

OLD SHOEMAKER: Ah ha. We'll hear when the drums start rolling.

BUTCHER'S HELPER: Drink up, old man! Don't sit and babble!
They drink.

A YOUNG MAN *coming in with a couple of women in tow.*

APPRENTICE: Well, have a look, here come the whores!

COOPER: Yes, where the master is, his people gather.

SKINNER-JACK: Turn up the light so we can see your sluts, my boy!

COOPER: They've pretty snouts; do they come from the bawdy house?

APPRENTICE: You can see well enough.

OLD SHOEMAKER: Won't you sit with master here? Or don't you dare?

SKINNER-JACK: No, no . . . You know him only too well, I guess.

BUTCHER'S HELPER: Listen to me, young virgins, have you been out to the gallows hill? One's hanging there they've stole the clothes off so he hasn't a living thread to hide him, and all the Lord's work and wonders are there to see. Womenfolk have trudged from far off since morning to see the splendor. — — What are you grinning at? But you watch out for master, that's all I say!

COOPER: Hasn't he clapped you in the stocks yet?

APPRENTICE: Be sure of that. They'd be as cozy in the irons as fingers in a glove.

SKINNER-JACK: One fine day he'll lash you out of town, and you'll jump smartly if you want to keep your pretty rumps!

ONE OF THE WOMEN *turns toward them*: Hold your tongue, Skinner-Jack, and go home to your old woman. She is not a bit better than we. Only last night again she was with us in the house and gave out for all because she was so poorly served at home, she said!

SKINNER-JACK: Don't be so cheeky. That's no news to me, I know all about her running around! But I'll skin her while she's still kicking, promise you that.

BUTCHER'S HELPER: You think that'll help!

SKINNER-JACK: I'll have to put an end to her yet!

BUTCHER'S HELPER: That'll make her happy—then she can lay with the devil himself!

SKINNER-JACK *sits there, muttering. They laugh at him.*

COOPER: No, there's no getting the best of women either in this world or the next.

APPRENTICE: Oh, they'll be burned and drowned and heads chopped off like the rest of us, I expect.

BUTCHER'S HELPER: No, master surely has no mercy on them.

APPRENTICE: Oh, no.

BUTCHER'S HELPER: You've seen, as I have, that many a headsman likes best of all to take the heads of womenfolk.

APPRENTICE: Now that might well be!

COOPER: They're sweeter than those grubby males, that's clear.

BUTCHER'S HELPER: Yes, I'd say that's true.

OLD SHOEMAKER: Not that they like it. Not always. I was there once when he couldn't carry it through at all.

COOPER: Oh?

OLD SHOEMAKER: No, he didn't have it in him. He fell for her right there by the block.

APPRENTICE: So?

COOPER: Oh no?

OLD SHOEMAKER: Everyone around saw how he went soft for her. He just stood looking at her and couldn't even raise the axe!

APPRENTICE: No. —Did he know her?

OLD SHOEMAKER: No. She was from outside, just come to town. No one knew her really. And he'd never seen her before.

APPRENTICE: Think of that . . .

OLD SHOEMAKER: It happened while they stood there together—he felt a love for her.

And she was a beauty too . . .

More slowly.

— — —I remember well, she had long, black hair, dangerous eyes, gentle and moist like an animal's. I can see her face in front of me now, so strange and fair . . .

It has gradually become dark at the table.

A tableau can be seen up to the left: The projecting part of a gallows. HANGMAN *in his red attire. The* CONDEMNED WOMAN. *The* JUDGE. *Other members of the Court. The* PRIEST. *—Some onlookers may be seen.*

OLD SHOEMAKER'S VOICE *continues in the dark*: No, it was no wonder he went for her. He was quite pale, I remember, and his hand trembled . . .

YOUNG HANGMAN *in the tableau—in a low voice*: I cannot do it . . .

PEOPLE *whispering among themselves.*

SOMEONE *after a moment*: What's the matter, master!

THE JUDGE *after a long pause*: Do your duty, headsman! Justice must take its course.

HANGMAN *motionless, does not answer.*

VOICE *in the crowd, whispering*: That's odd . . .

ANOTHER: Very odd, I'd say . . .

HANGMAN *lays down his axe. —Goes forward, gives the* WOMAN *his hand.*
The people stand silently.

SOMEONE: Remarkable . . .

ANOTHER *whispers*: He loves her . . .

HANGMAN *after a moment—comes forward, holding the* WOMAN *by the hand*: Most honorable judge and court, and all who witness here!
Before God and the law I make known that I wish to marry this woman and love her as a Christian with all my heart as long as I live.
So help me God and grant me, a sinner, a blessed journey from this life.
Hum of voices and movement. They are moved.
After a moment.
You have the power to pardon, if you wish—it is allowed by ancient custom.
Whispering and mumbling among the people.

SOMEONE: The gallows must be fed!

THE OTHERS *speak against him. Stir of voices and mumbling. Then*: Mercy! — —Mercy!
She must be pardoned! — —She must be pardoned!
They are moved, swept away by their feelings.

JUDGE: You are right, headsman, it has happened before, and there is the seal of ancient usage. But pardon cannot always be granted even then . . .

THE PEOPLE: Mercy!! —Mercy! — —Let her be pardoned! —Pardoned!

THE JUDGE: Silentium! —The court will decide this matter.
The court confers.

VOICE *in the crowd, whispers*: You have eyes to see that she too . . .!

ANOTHER: Yes! There are tears in her eyes! —Can't you see!
After a moment one of the members of the court beckons silence.

JUDGE: With God's help and the law's we have reached a decision. Considering your good Christian turn of mind, and deeply moved by the great power of the love we see, which is most edifying in this place and a comfort and solace to many gathered here, we have determined, inasmuch as you wish to enter with this woman the holy state of matrimony sanctified by the church, to free the sinner from her rightful punishment.

THE PEOPLE *express their loud approval.*

For the sake of our Lord Jesus Christ and his grace—that he may grant us his forgiveness on the day of judgment.

THE PEOPLE *become silent, stand in reverence.*

But she shall be branded with the gallows mark, as the law prescribes.

SOMEONE: Yes, that's right!

ANOTHER: Yes, the gallows must have its due.

JUDGE: And may the church then sanctify their union and join them as lawful man and wife.

HANGMAN *takes her hand in both of his.*
It becomes quiet. They stand watching them, moved by what has happened.

PRIEST: May Jesus Christ, who was hanged upon the gallows-cross, be merciful unto us. Amen.

HANGMAN *and the* WOMAN *go quietly hand in hand across the stage and out to the right.*
The tableau fades.
The light comes up slowly over the table.

COOPER: That was remarkable indeed.

OLD SHOEMAKER: Yes, so it was . . .

COOPER: And how did it go for them after that? Were they really happy?

OLD SHOEMAKER: Yes. They lived as the happiest of people there in the headsman's house, that's what their neighbors said. They'd never had the like of such a headsman, they said, I guess he was changed by this love or whatever it was. He wasn't the same man he'd been, and it was a different way of life he lived there in that house than it was before, when every kind of hellhound hung about as they'll do. I saw them together many times when she carried the child. They were like any other pair of lovers, and she was a lovely sight to see, though she had to wear the red cowl as the headsman's wife, and then that ugly mark on her forehead, of course. But no matter, she was fair.

When she was to give birth they tried to get the midwife to come, like the others, for they felt a joy in that child just like ordinary folk, at least that's what they say. But they didn't get one, of course.

COOPER: That's unchristian, I think, when they deny them even that.

SKINNER-JACK: But there's an evil pox about it, you understand, and then maybe she'd go and deliver a decent woman afterwards!

COOPER: Yes, I suppose.

OLD SHOEMAKER: No, and so she had to lie there alone it seems, because he didn't happen to be there when it happened. And then suddenly it came, and maybe all wasn't as it should be; anyway no one knows for sure or how it really happened, but she confessed to the court that she'd strangled the child.

COOPER: No . . . ? Did she?

APPRENTICE: How could that be?

OLD SHOEMAKER: Well, they say she said that when the child was born and she got enough of her strength back so she could take care of him a bit and wipe the blood from his face, she saw that he had a birthmark on his forehead, and it was like a gallows.

They'd branded her about the time the child began to grow in
her, you see, and it gnawed and ached so bad, she said. She
didn't want the child to live in this world, she said, and
that they'd already put the mark on him, and she loved him so
much, that's how she went on. There was no sense in what she
said, I heard, and of course she was born for misdeeds, poor
creature, that's clear enough.

APPRENTICE: That was hard on her, it was.

BUTCHER'S HELPER: Damned hard, I'd say.

OLD SHOEMAKER: Well, she was condemned to be buried alive, for
it wasn't any little crime she had to answer for when all was
done, and he had to wield the shovel himself. I was there and
saw it for myself that time, and it wasn't so easy for him, as
you can guess, for he really had loved her, no doubt of that,
even if he couldn't anymore after the horrible thing she'd done.
He stood there looking at her fine body as it disappeared be-
neath the shovelsful, and then her face—he waited with that as
long as he could. And all the time she never said a word, they'd
said goodbye I guess. She just lay there and looked at him with
her loving eyes. Finally, when he had to cover her face too, he
turned away. No, it wasn't easy for him. But he had to do it,
that's how the sentence read.

They say he went up there late at night and tried to dig her up
again, as if maybe she'd still be alive, but that was prattle,
nothing else, for he must have known she couldn't live.

Soon after, he wandered away from these parts and no one
knew what became of him.

They are silent.

COOPER: God save us all. Poor creatures.

SKINNER-JACK: But they must have known it'd never work and that
the child would be like them.

BUTCHER'S HELPER: Yes, no wonder it had the gallows mark!

OLD SHOEMAKER: No, it sticks fast, it does.

SKINNER-JACK: Sure enough, it does.

OLD SHOEMAKER: There's no getting away from it, that's certain.

COOPER: So finally he became her executioner after all.

OLD SHOEMAKER: He did.

COOPER: Mm . . . and I suppose that's the way it was meant to be. *Noise and shouting heard outside, a man comes jostling in, yells at someone following after him in the darkness, threatens him with an arm that is maimed.*

GALLOWS-LASSE: It's a lie, you dirty yokel! You counted 'em yourself and they tallied, huh!

PEASANT: But there was lead in your dice, you thief!

GALLOWS-LASSE: The hell there was! Was there, Jackie boy?

A YOUNG BOY *who follows close behind him*: No, no, never on your life!

PEASANT: Oh sure, that hellion's with you in all your sharper's tricks, and cheats for you, you crippled scum that can't hold the cards or anything else! They were marked, they were, otherwise you couldn't have done me out of every penny!

GALLOWS-LASSE: Hold your chops, bog-trotter!

He sits down at a table and looks furtively around him. When he sees the HANGMAN *his face twitches. It is thin and hollowed, and his eyes are glistening. —The* BOY *creeps close to him on the bench.*

BUTCHER'S HELPER: Ah ha, so Gallows-Lasse is out again!

OLD SHOEMAKER: Listen, aren't you a little nervous to be sitting near master, Lasse?

GALLOWS-LASSE: Eh, don't talk such crap to me!

Dawdling, comes closer to them—sits at the farthest end of the table. The BOY *sneaks after him.*

PEASANT: Yes, that would be right for you, you devil's spawn. He'll soon have hold of all of you!

BUTCHER'S HELPER: Yes, next time it'll be the gallows, Lasse lad. They've nothing more to take off of you, boy.

GALLOWS-LASSE: You're spouting dirt, you've no sense for anything else. There's no gallows will get me!

COOPER: No no . . .

SKINNER-JACK: You don't say . . . ?

GALLOWS-LASSE *sits up closer with a jerk of his shoulders. Calls to the* GIRL: Ale!

She hurries over with it.

BOY *holds the stoup up to his mouth and he heaves down a big gulp.*

When he has to draw a breath the BOY *waits and then gives it to him again.*

GALLOWS-LASSE *turns slowly toward the* PEASANT, *who is sitting somewhere down by the door*: Cheat, you said! . . .

PEASANT: Yes, cheat I said! You!

GALLOWS-LASSE: Do you think I have to cheat to do you out of your lousy ploughman's money! It rolls right into my bag, can't stand the smell in your silly breeches!

PEASANT: Hold your tongue!

They laugh at the PEASANT, *who cannot find any very strong words of abuse.*

OLD SHOEMAKER: No sir. Gallows-Lasse doesn't need to mark the cards or weight the trumps, not unless he wants to.

SKINNER-JACK: No, he's got better tricks than that to cut your oats, peasant.

COOPER: I'd say they are the same thieving snares the others use. I can't see how you get by, Lasse, the way you do.

GALLOWS-LASSE: Eh. Don't worry your head. Lasse'll come through!

OLD SHOEMAKER: No doubt of that . . .

GALLOWS-LASSE: I remember when they had the fingers off of me when I was about like him (*indicates the* BOY), and nailed 'em to the stock. Ha. And I was there myself, and had me a good snigger at the sight of 'em! —Aha, there's your thieving fingers, they was thinking when they looked at me. But I just laughed, I did, and told 'em that it didn't do me no harm. Lasse'll always get along, I said! And he did!

He blinks hard and his face twitches. —Pokes the BOY *with the stump of his arm to get more beer.*

BOY *eagerly hurries to get the stoup. He has a small, sharp face and his eyes move quickly. He is very much aware of everything that happens.*

SKINNER-JACK: Oh yes, but when they began to take off your hands, that was something else again!

GALLOWS-LASSE: Eh, what's it matter to me, d'ya think. No . . .

He wipes the ale from his mouth with his sleeve.

OLD SHOEMAKER *leans toward the others—he whispers, his voice hissing with excitement*: Do you know he has the mandrake root!

GALLOWS-LASSE *loudly and clearly*: No, it's all the same to me. I've got no trouble. And I've got the boy here. He's got the flair.

SKINNER-JACK: Yes, I guess so!

BOY *blinks his eyes, pleased with the praise.*

COOPER: Is the boy your son, Lasse?

GALLOWS-LASSE: Well, I don't know for sure, but I think he damn near is, he seems to take after me, y'know.

COOPER: Aha, so you don't know.

GALLOWS-LASSE: No. Hanna is his mother, but he's left her. Beatings and not a bite to eat was all he got there. He sticks with me now so that I can teach him a bit about what's needed in the world. He's quick to learn, you've never seen the like. — —Am I your father, Jocke?

BOY *grins*: Eh, it makes no difference.

GALLOWS-LASSE: Yes, you're right. The hell with it! But he's well off with me, he is. How about it, Jocke?

BOY *grins*: Right!

SKINNER-JACK: Don't tell me you get along with no one else besides that snot-nose. I don't believe it.

GALLOWS-LASSE: No? . . .

SKINNER-JACK: Not on your life . . .

OLD SHOEMAKER: No, you've got mightier powers than that to help you out.

GALLOWS-LASSE: And what are they, hmm?

OLD SHOEMAKER: I don't know . . .

GALLOWS-LASSE: No, that's what I thought. — —Then why do you talk such crap?

They are silent for a moment. Sit there moving and fingering the stoups.

APPRENTICE: But I don't suppose it's true you have the mandrake?

GALLOWS-LASSE: Eh, blabber . . .

APPRENTICE: No, how could you pull it up the way you are.

GALLOWS-LASSE *does not answer, but there is a sudden change in his glistening eyes, and his thin face contracts.*

BUTCHER'S HELPER: Oh, if need be Lasse'd find a way for worse than that.

SKINNER-JACK: That's true enough.

COOPER: But to drag it up out of the gallows hill is not an easy thing. And without even a hand to help.

OLD SHOEMAKER: No, and more than that, you're dead if you hear it scream!

They look sideways at him. His head jerks violently for a moment and he twitches repeatedly.

BUTCHER'S HELPER: He's got it and much more besides, be sure of that! I'd say you were sold to hell long since, Lasse boy!

GALLOWS-LASSE: Damned right I am!

BUTCHER'S HELPER: See, didn't I tell you!

APPRENTICE: Listen to that!

COOPER: But don't the demons take hold of you at night?

GALLOWS-LASSE: Eh . . . Not when your best friend is the devil himself. Then you sleep as sweet as a suckling brat.

BUTCHER'S HELPER: Uh, now you're bragging, Lasse!

SKINNER-JACK: Oho, Lasse! Now you're laying it on! Then you wouldn't have to go round in this world so crippled up like that!

APPRENTICE: Master's taken care of you as if he thought you're his and not the devil's.

They laugh.

GALLOWS-LASSE—*his feverish eyes shining with hate*: What do you think that matters to me!

APPRENTICE: Nothing, nothing at all!

SKINNER-JACK: They've treated you like common gallows fodder, seems to me!

GALLOWS-LASSE: Even so! They won't put an end to Gallows-Lasse, you'll see!

He is near to screaming, and he glares at them.

On no they won't! That's not as easy as you think, I'll tell you!

SKINNER-JACK: Aha! But they're well on the way!

GALLOWS-LASSE *stands up, screams*: They haven't had the power to take anything away from me! No, sir! They haven't! There's no human power that can touch me, if you want to know!

SKINNER-JACK: What are you saying, Lasse boy, I've never heard such gabble!

GALLOWS-LASSE: Never in this life, never! What I have no power in the world can take from me! And the boy here will get it after me, he will!

BUTCHER'S HELPER: What? Now Lasse, have you something for your heirs, too? Listen here to Lasse!

GALLOWS-LASSE: Yes, I have! Much more than any of you! He's going to get both the mandrake and all of hell when I'm gone!

COOPER: Do you have the mandrake?

GALLOWS-LASSE: Yes, you can have the devil's word on it! You want to see her, do you!

COOPER: No no . . . !

GALLOWS-LASSE: She's here on my chest! She's grown like a little human, she has, and with her you can both thieve and a bit of all the rest, and everything prospers in your hands—even if you don't have any!

They stare at him in astonishment and fright.

COOPER: How could you get hold of one, you poor wretch! On the gallows hill?

GALLOWS-LASSE: Where else? Right under the gibbet itself, where they bury the corpses once they've blown down!

SKINNER-JACK: Did you dare to go up there! At night!

GALLOWS-LASSE: Yes I did! But it wasn't like being home with mother, reading Our Father in bed, not a bit! You wouldn't have dared, not you!

SKINNER-JACK: No, no! . . .

GALLOWS-LASSE: They groan and they wail, it's terrible . . .

APPRENTICE: Who?

GALLOWS-LASSE: The dead, of course! And they went for me and grabbed at me while I searched for it! They did! And I had to bash them with all my might, and they howled and moaned like the madmen in the fool's pen when the gallows boy gives them a kick to quiet them down! There was a wailing and howling like in the other world; I thought I'd lose my senses—and I couldn't drive them off! —They had hideous faces, and

I yelled at them. Get out, be off with you, you spooks! I'm not dead yet, I'm alive and I need it! And finally I kept them off a ways. And then I saw that she grew right under the gallows, where Peter the Butcher and several others hung. I pushed away the dirt around her with one of my arm stumps, and then I lay down and cut her loose with my teeth! —

APPRENTICE: No! You didn't!

GALLOWS-LASSE: Yes, I did! Them that hasn't guts enough themselves use the dogs!

His eyes are feverish and wild.

But then she screamed! Screamed, screamed! Enough to freeze your blood! — —But I didn't have anything in my ears! like the other poor cowards! —I could stand it! —and pulled and ripped at the root! —it smelled of death and blood to hell and destruction—and roared and shrieked from the lower world! —but I didn't stop my ears—I just tore and ripped—*because I wanted to have her!*

He rages like someone possessed. They shrink back from him.

And when I got her up it crashed around me, and roared and trembled! —and the pit opened up and blood and corpses flowed out! —the darkness split open, and fire poured out over the world—and horror and cries! —and everything burned! —as if hell'd gone loose on earth! — —

I've got 'er! I've got 'er! I yelled!

He stands up and shakes both of his arm stumps above his head, like a horrid maimed phantom. It is as if his crazed countenance had burst and his voi e had lost all semblance of human expression.

I've riches for my heirs, I have! Riches for my heirs! You can have the devil's word on that!

He collapses and at the same time the light fades to darkness around him and the figures at the table.

But the light remains on the HANGMAN. *He sits there motionless, staring heavily and timelessly out into the darkness.*

More people have come in; there is a buzz and stir, voices and laughter are heard, and the clinking of glasses off in the dimly lighted room. A

Gösta Ekman in *The Hangman*
Vasateatern, 1935
Director: Per Lindberg

globe of light up near the ceiling turns slowly, casting a vague blue-violet and greenish light, dancers glide over the floor in the center of the stage, and music is heard softly. The interior seems larger, without any definite limit. Groups are seen sitting and drinking at the tables. The dance extends into the aisles between the tables and throughout the room; women in light-colored evening dresses hang on the shoulders of men with half-closed eyes; the jazz music throbs.

A PLUMP ATTRACTIVE WOMAN *glides past the* HANGMAN, *who still sits at the center of things—turns her head toward him, over her escort's shoulder*: But look at that, the hangman's here. How interesting!

The glow of the light wanders over the crowd, waiters hurry, perspiring, through the muffled noise of voices and cries. They arrange new tables down by the footlights where new arrivals sit down. The beat of the music continues. Part of the platform where the Negro orchestra is playing is seen to the left.

A FAT GENTLEMAN *with a buckled shirt front comes forward and bows courteously to the* HANGMAN: It is a great honor to see the hangman here among us!

Bows again, rubs his hands obligingly.

The dance ends and the couples go to their tables and sit down, smiling.

YOUNG GENTLEMAN *in a group at one of the tables*: Did you know the hangman is here?

ONE OF THE LADIES: No, is he!

GENTLEMAN: Yes, he's sitting over there.

ANOTHER OF THE LADIES: Oh, that's just marvellous, don't you think?

A YOUNG MAN *with an energetically childish face steps up to the* HANGMAN, *salutes with his arm extended in front of him*: Heil!

Stands there stiffly a moment. Turns around, clicks his heels, and returns to his table.

A SHABBILY DRESSED MAN *comes in, walks among the tables whispering something as he holds out his thin hand. He is shown out by a waiter.*

HARLOTS *sit, sipping from their glasses.*

ONE: He's quite elegant in that red outfit, isn't he?

ANOTHER: Oh, he is!

THE FIRST: And he looks so brutal!

THE THIRD: I think he looks like a pimp.

THE FIRST: Oh, no not at all, are you mad? He's a very handsome man.

THE SECOND: Why does he sit there with his hand on his forehead all the time?

THE FIRST: Oh, how should I know.

THE THIRD: He is *handsome*.

THE FIRST: Yes . . .

THE SECOND: What do you think it's like with a hangman, hmm?

THE FIRST: Luscious, can't you imagine.

> *The music begins again, languishing this time; another orchestra is playing—offstage somewhere, seemingly in the distance. Couples dance into the hovering blue light. Slender arms hang over the men's shoulders. Their eyes are nearly closed, as if they were half asleep.*

VOICE AT A TABLE: Anything special tomorrow?

ANOTHER VOICE: I don't know, but I hear they have plenty of people to liquidate. Okay by me.

THE FIRST: No, no harm in that. After all, there are lots of people in the world, decent and proper people. It's always the best ones that are left, they're careful about that.

THE SECOND: Quite right.

AN ELDERLY MILITARY GENTLEMAN *who smacks his lips and has a firm, strutting step, passes the* HANGMAN's *table*: Order is an excellent thing, sir! Damn me if people musn't learn their manners!

VOICE AT A TABLE: What's this! We ordered dry and you've given us medium dry! What sort of place is this?

WAITER: Pardon, pardon . . .

VOICE: Yes, I hope so. Such poor service . . . and after sitting here waiting half the night.

ANOTHER: And he's already opened it too!

THE FIRST: Well, you'll have to change it. We don't drink anything but dry.

A WELL-FED MIDDLE-CLASS LADY *who has been to the powder room*

passes by, swaying as she walks. When she sees the HANGMAN *she claps her hands*: But my heavens look at this! Is the hangman here! Really, I must tell Herbert!
Goes up to the HANGMAN *and lays her hand on his arm familiarly.*
My son wants so much to meet you! He so admires bloodshed, dear child!
She looks around for her table in a motherly way, goes back to it.

GUTTERSNIPE *who has managed to sneak in, goes around to the tables opening the rags he has on to show that he is naked underneath. Finally the waiters discover him and throw him out.*

VOICE *at a table near the footlights*: On the contrary, sir! Violence is the highest expression of humanity's physical and spiritual powers! That is a fact which, thanks to us, has finally become quite obvious. And those who believe otherwise shall be convinced precisely through the use of violence, and then they will surely believe in it, don't you think?

ANOTHER VOICE: Yes, of course, certainly.

THE FIRST: Yes. We hope so too!
Their voices are lost for a moment because the Negro band has begun to play once more. —Then the voices are heard again.

THE FIRST: As I was saying. We shall demand absolutely that those who think in any other way shall be castrated! This is a simple necessity to ensure the victory of our ideas. You cannot ask that we should allow this disease to spread to coming generations. No sir! We know our responsibilities!

THE SECOND: Yes, of course.
Their voices are lost again. —Then.

THE FIRST: But my dear sir, you are still so absurdly trapped in the idiotic ideas of the past! You understand there will never be any other philosophy than ours! That's all finished now, you see!

THE SECOND: Oh yes, I see. Now I understand you! Yes, of course, quite naturally!

THE FIRST: Yes, isn't that true, when you've shaken off the old ways of thinking you begin to see our new way of looking at reality. It's a little hard in the beginning, but actually it's really quite simple.

THE SECOND: Quite.

Two people down by the footlights talking.

THE FIRST: Have you seen how we beat up the rebels down where we live? It is really one of the most inspiring performances you can imagine, I assure you. You feel as if you were training men for a new life, on a higher plane, ennobling them.

THE SECOND: Yes, I'd really like to see that.

THE FIRST: We have even succeeded in converting old men in their eighties, if we keep it up long enough.

THE SECOND: Unbelievable. And imagine how difficult it is otherwise to get people to believe anything at all.

THE FIRST: Yes! You can be sure that we really have achieved some remarkable results.

The music drowns out their voices. —Then.

THE FIRST: But we feel a responsibility for every generation to come, you understand! We know that the critical time is now! If people think correctly now, there will never be any false doctrine in the future. We must not forget that we live in a great epoch! It is a decisive time for all of humanity and for man's future development on earth.

THE SECOND: Yes, certainly.

THE FIRST: We are responsible for it, you see.

At a table near the footlights.

A VOICE: Classes! There are no classes anymore! That's the most wonderful and remarkable thing that's happened! There are those who think as we do, and then the others who are locked up and being taught to think as we do. The ones that survive will have learned the lesson well, be sure of that.

ANOTHER VOICE: Quite so.

FIRST VOICE: You can see it for yourself—we sit here drinking champagne or just a glass of beer as most of them do, of course, white collar people, workers, and those a little better off, all of us together, all alike. And everyone thinks exactly alike—as we do! Everyone on the outside thinks as we do!

SECOND VOICE: Aha.

FIRST VOICE: You see before you the glorious, incomparable view of a collected and united people! And those in doubt will soon be a part of us, no doubt of that. And we'll manage the stubborn ones! A people united in confidence, waiting outside their prisons to hear the cries from within of someone who has seen the light.

THE SECOND: What a moving thought. And what spirit!

THE FIRST: Yes, the world has never seen anything like it! It's like a devotional for all men, and many stand at attention, waiting for the groaning of the converts. It shows the reverence they feel for what is happening in secret to their people. A grand and touching spectacle that could take place nowhere else. We are like no other people on earth! None other!

A GENTLEMAN *in a group at another table*: Yes, it is absolutely necessary that we have a god for ourselves, and soon. We cannot expect that our people shall worship a god used by other, inferior races. Ours is a very religious people, but we need a god of our own! The notion of one god is openly scornful of our philosophy and shall be punished as all crimes are nowadays.

ANOTHER VOICE: True, true!

A POOR WRETCH *roams through the room, with an insolent grin, begging, lurches against the tables so that the glasses spill, when he's not given anything.*
At a dimly lit table off to the right.

A MAN: Now what the hell! We ordered beer and sausage and you bring champagne. What the devil's the idea! You think we're millionaires, like those damned swine there!

WAITER: Oh, pardon me, I thought you belonged to the upper class . . .

MAN: Damned if we do! Have a better look next time or you'll get one between the eyes so you'll wake up!
The music stops, an intermission. There is a certain calm on the stage during the following.

A SOLDIER *comes staggering in, sits down by the* HANGMAN *and begins to chatter at him*: Eh, what kind of a getup is that! . . . How come you're not in field grays? Huh? . . . Look at him! . . .

A MAN *at a table nearby—whispers to him*: Be quiet . . . Don't you see it's the hangman? . . .

THE SOLDIER: Yes, I can see! But just the same I think he looks so damned silly! Is that supposed to be a hangman? Ha! What's he good for? No, give me machine guns and hand grenades! That's the real stuff, I'll tell you! You don't know the craft, I can see it all over you!

THE MAN: Don't talk such nonsense! You can bet he does—better than you. No heckling, boy. You two belong together, you ought to know that.

THE SOLDIER: Yeah, but he ought to use machine guns, I say! . . . Shiny modern stuff! You get me? . . . So it moves faster! Field grays are better, old boy!

THE MAN: Go ahead and brag, youngster! You haven't seen any more of war than my night pot, anyone can hear that!

SOLDIER: But I will! Damned if I won't! And then you'll see some blood and smoke!

MAN: Yes, when you get up front!

SOLDIER: Yeah, me and the other guys! They're boys who call their shots, believe me! And don't scare easy, that's for damn sure!

AN OLD GENTLEMAN: Well spoken, boy!
    The boy's all right. Maybe just a little too much beer in his young blood, but all right. It's glorious to have such young people in our land! I'm moved, an old man like me . . .

SOLDIER: You're muddled, old gaffer . . . you don't understand anything anymore . . .
    Stands up.
    Your health, hangman! I like you! You and I'll keep things straight here in the world! — — — — —Why don't you drink? What a sorry devil. — —You sad maybe?
    The talk and laughter begins again. The jazz band starts to play.
    A gentleman comes up to a table near the footlights, stands talking with the people there.

THE MAN STANDING: It's obvious that we must have war! War is health!

A people which doesn't want war is a sick people!

ONE AT THE TABLE: Yes, peace is something for infants and the sick, they need to have peace. But not a healthy full-grown man!

ANOTHER: A trench is the only place for a real man. We ought to live in trenches in times of peace, too, instead of houses . . . they make people soft.

An unexpected crash from the band disturbs them.

THE MAN STANDING: No, the war's bath of steel must be!

A sound people can't avoid it more than a decade at the most. Then they begin to degenerate—if they're healthy to begin with, of course.

ANOTHER AT THE TABLE: Yes. And whoever ends a war is a traitor!

MAN STANDING: Quite true!

EVERYONE AT THE TABLE: Down with the traitors! Down with the traitors!

MAN STANDING: Death to them!

ONE AT THE TABLE *conversing with his neighbor*: Yes, even if he wins, because without a shred of conscience he thrusts his people into the uncertainties of peace. We know what war is, but a people at peace are threatened by all kinds of unknown dangers.

HIS NEIGHBOR: Yes, you're right.

MAN STANDING: No, we must rid ourselves of this fateful milk-soppery! Children must be brought up for war. When they learn to walk, they must learn the military way, and not their mothers'!

ONE OF THEM: Yes, we can manage that. We'll take care of the children and not leave them to irresponsible parents.

MAN STANDING: No, naturally not.

THE FORMER SPEAKER: Then our future can be assured.

MAN STANDING: Yes!

A BLIND MAN *at a nearby table arises uncertainly from his chair, lays his groping hand on the back rest*: I hear you talking about war, comrades! That gladdens my heart! I hope it will be given to me to experience the day when our people march out again on the proud old battlefields! And that modern science will have advanced so far that even I can be with them! They have read me a new book that says they think we shall be able to see and take aim with the soul, directly. And in that case you'll find me in the front lines, and with a sure eye, for my soul, comrades, is strong as ever!

THOSE AT THE TABLES AND OTHERS AROUND THEM: Bravo! Bravo!

A VOICE: Proud words!

MAN STANDING: Magnificent!

ANOTHER: Men are like that only in the great epochs!

MAN STANDING: Yes, war puts its noble stamp on a man's forehead, as they say. Everyone can see that!

A THIRD: Superb!

A FOURTH: What a people! They're unconquerable!

ONE AT THE TABLE: Obviously we must spread our teachings throughout the world! It would be outrageous to keep this only for ourselves, and if any people fail to accept it we'll exterminate them.

MAN STANDING: Naturally. For their own sake. It would be happier for them to be exterminated than to live without experiencing this!

ONE AT THE TABLE: Naturally!

MAN STANDING: The world will thank us once it understands what we mean.

A MAN IN ANOTHER GROUP: Yes, isn't it true. And the most inspiring sight of all is to see youth in our ranks! We build on youth! The courageous, unsentimental modern youth! Everywhere they stand on our side, on the side of those in power. The young heroes . . .!

VOICE *from the sausage table far out to the right*: Do they even dare!

THE FORMER SPEAKER: Did somebody say something? . . . — — Eh, I must be hearing things.

There is a disturbance at the entrance, people are whispering and begin to stand up, stretch out their hands in salute, all eyes are turned in the same direction.

A SURGE OF VOICES *beginning at the entrance—spreads through the hall*: Hail to the murderers! Hail to the murderers!

TWO WELL-DRESSED YOUNG MEN *with a pleasant, ordinary appearance go along the aisle between the rows of hands, obligingly thank everyone to right and left. Everyone in the hall is standing. The jazz music stops and the more proper orchestra intones a hymn instead, while everyone stands still. While this is happening, two waiters hurry silently up to the new arrivals, and a head waiter follows, turning over a table with beer mugs on it, spilling on several women, who quietly and intensely ward off his hasty pardon—he rushes on. The place is filled to capacity, but the waiters come up to a group of people at the footlights and whisper to them.*

PEOPLE AT THE TABLE *arise and bow. This is heard*: Of course, naturally . . . We are quite happy to move . . . yes, we must go . . . delighted, delighted . . . naturally . . .
Bow deeply to the new arrivals, and then withdraw.
A new tablecloth is placed on the table, the young men take the table and sit down.

FIRST YOUNG MAN: Damned if we can ever go into a place without being recognized.

THE SECOND *blowing smoke from his cigarette, stretches his legs*: My god, yes. This is getting to be a bit of a strain.

THE FIRST: Yes, if I'd known how much trouble it is to be a murderer, I don't think I'd ever have shot that fellow. He was supposed to be a decent sort, too.

THE SECOND: Yes, but it was clear enough from the look of his body that he wasn't one of us.

THE FIRST: Yeah. It was horrible.
The Negro band begins playing its jazz music again.
A STARVED WOMAN *with a child in a shawl goes through without even the staff taking notice of her— —after a moment she leaves.*

YOUNG PEOPLE *at a table. One of them*: Are you going out to help move corpses tonight?

ANOTHER: Move corpses?

FIRST: Yes, we're going to move the corpses of some of the traitors to the new philosophy, from the churchyard out to a peatbog, better place for 'em out there.

SECOND: Uh . . .

FIRST: Uh? Don't you want to?

THE SECOND: I don't know . . . What's the idea of that?

FIRST: Idea? The idea of our organization, comrade!

SECOND: Eh . . . they were dead before we started.

FIRST: And so what!

SECOND: No, I think that's damned disgusting.

FIRST:—What are you saying? You don't want to! You refuse!

SECOND: Refuse? I just said that I think it's a little harsh.

FIRST: Harsh! Maybe you think it's foolish too?

SECOND: No, not exactly.

FIRST: Listen, you, what do you really mean! Sing out with it!

SECOND: What I mean? . . . — —What the hell do you think I am!

FIRST: Do you refuse to obey orders! You bringing your own little thoughts into this!

SECOND: Let me go, I tell you!

FIRST: No sir, we don't let go that easily!

SECOND: Let me go, you bastards!

FIRST: Did you hear what he called us! — — —Mongrel! Do you refuse! . . . You thinking about deserting! . . .

SECOND: I haven't refused!

FIRST: Yes you have!

A THIRD: Don't stand there and bicker with a deserter! Enough talk!

A shot is heard, and then a heavy thud.

Carry out the cadaver.

FIRST: No, let him lay, he's not bothering anybody.

THIRD: No. Carry him out.

A YOUNG GIRL *with a slender neck dances by, turns her head*: What was it?

HER ESCORT: Seems they shot somebody.

GIRL: Oh.

At the sausage table in the corner to the right.

ONE OF THEM: You know what I think's going to happen tomorrow, what they are talking so much about?

ANOTHER: No, what?

FIRST: Something entirely different than these snot-noses imagine.

SECOND: What?

FIRST: Uh . . .

Rolls a cigarette, lights it on one of the others, spits out the bits of tobacco.

We know how to pull a trigger too when the time's ripe. God knows if we weren't the ones who taught them a few tricks—if they needed to be taught.

SECOND: Oh, everyone has a knack for that nowadays.

FIRST: Sure. — — —

Be nice to purify humanity a little while longer, hmm? They need it.

SECOND: No, I wouldn't mind having a little chance at it.

Pause in the music.

A WOMAN comes in, goes quietly through the hall and sits down beside the HANGMAN. She is dressed as a beggar, but it is as if there were a halo of light around her, her face is radiant. When she enters, a stillness settles on the stage, although no one notices her in any way. She slowly lays her hands on the HANGMAN's—and he turns toward her, looks at her. She sits there during all that follows with the halo of light around her.

The music begins again—the invisible orchestra plays a sultry tango, after an old classical melody. It is quiet and the feeling of the music is in the air, but a gentleman feels the need to go out to the urinal. When he comes back, he sees the Negroes sitting at a table just below the bandstand, hurriedly eating a few sandwiches during the intermission. His face becomes blood-red and he goes up to them.

GENTLEMAN: How do you dare, you swine! Sitting here eating among white people!

THE NEGROES *turn around in surprise. The one closest rises part way from his chair:* What? What do you mean sir? . . .

GENTLEMAN: What I mean! Do you have the audacity to sit here and eat, you dirty ape!

THE NEGRO *springs to his feet, his eyes glisten, but he doesn't dare do anything.*

GENTLEMAN *calls out to everyone in the hall*: Listen to this, gentlemen! Just listen! —Have you seen the like of this! It's incredible. These apes sit here eating among *us*!
People quickly gather around him and the NEGROES. *Violent commotion.*

VOICE: Such insolence! — —Unheard of! — —Do you think this is a monkey cage! — —Does it look like one?

A NEGRO: We have to eat like everybody else!

GENTLEMAN: But not among people, you dog!

ANOTHER GENTLEMAN: Eat! You're here to *play*! Not to eat!

THIRD GENTLEMAN: You have the honor of playing for us because we are pleased to listen to your music! But you'd better behave or you'll be lynched! Understand!

FIRST GENTLEMAN: Up on your stand!

SECOND GENTLEMAN: Well! What are you waiting for!

THE NEGROES *make no sign of obeying the order.*

A STATELY GENTLEMAN *with a distinguished appearance*: This is non-violence at its best, gentlemen!

FIRST GENTLEMAN: Well! You going to move!

STATELY GENTLEMAN: Go on! Get up on the platform!

A NEGRO: We're hungry! We must have food if we're going to play!

FIRST GENTLEMAN: Hungry! The very idea!

A GIANT OF A NEGRO *steps forward—glares threateningly*: Yes, we must eat! We have a right to!

FIRST GENTLEMAN: Right! Have you any rights! Learn your place!

THE NEGRO: Yes, I have!

FIRST GENTLEMAN: What! Do you answer a white man that way, you blackguard!
He strikes him in the face.

THE NEGRO *cowers, stands trembling like an animal. Then like*

*lightning he springs at him and gives him a blow with his fist so that he
falls backwards, full length on the floor.*
*There is an indescribable melee. People rush to the center of the struggle.
The whole place is in the wildest excitement.*

VOICE: What's happened! — —What did he do! — —Hit a white
man! — —Incredible!

*The whites are in a wild rage. Yelling excitedly, they go toward them
threateningly.*
THE NEGROES *gather themselves in a knot, crouching and ready, with
bloodshot eyes and white teeth showing. They are like strange new
animals in a human jungle.*
A shot is fired.

SOMEONE *shrieking*: Are you shooting!
VOICES *here and there*: Who is shooting! — — —Who fired! — —
A NEGRO *in the group, howling and bloody, charges out among the whites*:
    It was you, you devils!
    He strikes furiously at everything around him.

*The other Negroes follow after him, yelling, but are held back by the
white men's revolvers. There is a crackle of more shots, and the blacks
creep down behind chairs and tables, some of them bleeding.*

PLEASANT BLOND GENTLEMAN: Well, are you going to play?
    Discharges his Browning at their hiding place.
ANOTHER: Will you give up!
THE NEGROES *yelling*: No! — —No!
A WHITE MAN: They dare to set themselves against us!
ANOTHER: Against *us*!
A THIRD: They're rebels!
THE BLOND: Now will you play?
THE NEGROES: No!
A WHITE MAN: Well I'll be damned! —Drive 'em out of there!
    *They begin to try to drive them out of their hiding place. The shots
    fly.*
VOICE *trying to calm things a bit*: We have another band! — —There's
another one!

THE BLOND: The hell with that sentimental slop! We want them to play! Get up there you apes!

ANOTHER: Up you go! —They're creeping away like rats, the sorry devils!

A THIRD: Come out of there! Don't you have guts enough to fight!

They are driven out; THE NEGROES run for it and are chased through the hall. The tumult is worse than before, everything in mad confusion. Women stand on their chairs and scream: Shoot them! —Shoot! Other women simply shriek at the top of their voices.

ONE OF THE WHITE MEN: No, damn it to hell! After all we're civilized . . . !

ANOTHER: What! Say that word once more and I'll shoot you down!

Civilization be damned!

Jumps over a table and throws himself into the fight again.

THE NEGROES *defend themselves with anything they can find. Objects fly through the air.*

THE BIG NEGRO *charges like a berserk, kicks away everything in his path, delivers murderous knockout blows to right and left—until he is hit by a well-aimed shot. —Grabs at his chest:*

Devils! . . .

Falls.

A WHITE MAN: That's what you needed!

The rest of THE NEGROES gather their forces and fight in blind rage, with hate gleaming in the whites of their eyes. They give strange and horrible war cries, as if they were in the wilds, but the whites aren't frightened by them and manage with their weapons alone. There is a continuous rain of shots from the revolvers. A furious, thronging battle.

CRIES FROM THE WHITES: This is open rebellion! — —They strike against our race! — —Hold them!

A UNIFORMED WHITE MAN *in the foreground—roars at a nearly dead Negro lying at his feet, his jaws at the white man's ankle:* You bite, you bloody coward!

Points his gun at him and fires.

THE TWO YOUNG MURDERERS *far down in front, do not take part in all of this. They simply sit and watch in amusement; they've done their job.*

ONE OF THEM: I like a little variety.

THE OTHER *knocks the ashes from his cigarette*: Yeah. It's always nice when there's something happening.

Two sweaty whites meet in the fray.

ONE OF THEM: We're holding 'em, friend!

THE OTHER: You bet we are!

THE NEGROES *are pressed all the harder—toward one end of the hall.*

A WHITE MAN: Drive them into the corner!

ANOTHER: Surround them!

A THIRD: Surround them!

They succeed. The whites are too much for them, they have to yield.

CRY OF TRIUMPH: They're surrounded!

THE BLOND MAN: You can't hold out against us!

ANOTHER: Give up, you beasts!

A THIRD: Give yourselves up, and no conditions!

THE NEGROES *put up their hands.*

THE BLOND MAN: Now that's better!

ANOTHER: They've knuckled under!

The whites catch their breath.

SOMEONE: That stuff doesn't work around here.

ANOTHER: You won't try that again, I'll tell you!

A THIRD: Oh no, you can be damn sure they won't!

THE BLOND MAN: Well! Up on your boxes now!

The blacks are driven back up on the bandstand and forced to pick up their instruments.

THE BLOND MAN *sits astride a chair in front of them with his revolver pointed at them*: Play, and if you don't you'll get it! Understand!

THE NEGROES *play. Wildly, hideously, with bloodshot eyes and bloody hands and faces, play as if possessed. Music that has never been heard before, furious, frightening, like nocturnal howls from the jungle and the boom of the death drums when the tribes gather in the bush at sunset. A huge Negro stands up front, his teeth clenched, madly beating frantic rolls on the drum; the blood is running from a sore on his head, his shirt is torn and stained red. He beats and beats with his great bleeding fists, and the other instruments blend in. It is like an inarticulate bellow.*

THE WHITES *dance—hop and leap to the music*: Wonderful! Wonderful! — —That's the spirit! — —That's the way it should sound!
Dancing everywhere in the hall—like a boiling witches' cauldron with bobbing waves. The lighted globe twirls from the ceiling and sweeps its light in all colors over the pungent brew. The women are radiant with lust and beauty; they gaze feverishly at the big bleeding Negro, and some of them push a knee between their escort's legs. The men squeeze hard upon their bellies, excited by their glances and the warm revolvers dangling on their backs like an extra, smoldering prick. It is a monstrous orgy.
A MAN IN FIERY-RED ECSTASY *his collar slit open in the fight, jumps up on a table by the* HANGMAN *and swings his Browning in the air. He tries to make himself heard, to make them listen to him. No luck. And the jazz band continues its wild serenade. —He shouts at them:*
Quiet over there!
The music dies away. The dancing stops. But even then it's not quiet. His yelling is heard:
Victory is ours, comrades! — —No use for anyone to oppose us! — —Order! —Discipline! — —Under their sign we'll win! — —On them we'll build our new empire in the world!
He waves his arms and yells. They gather around him to listen.
And on this proud day when we have asserted our race's superiority over all others we have the joy and pleasure to see among us the representative of the things we value most of all in life! The Hangman is here with us. We are proud to have him here because it shows, if we didn't know it before, that we live in a great era! That the time of dishonor and weakness is past and a new day is about to dawn for mankind! His mighty figure fills us with confidence and courage! It shall lead us—the only one we intend to follow!

We greet you, our leader, with the holy images, the symbols of the most holy and most precious things in life for us. We shall introduce a new epoch in the history of mankind! Blood is man's color! And we know that we are worthy of you! We know that you can rely on us when we joyously cry unto you our:

Hail! Hail!

He jumps down from the table, red and panting, and goes up to the HANGMAN.

THE HANGMAN *looks at him.* —*Doesn't move, nor does he answer.*

THE FIERY MAN *seems a little confused by this, doesn't know quite how he should continue.*—Hail! *he cries once more, a little hesitantly, with his arm up in salute, and all the others around him do likewise.*

THE HANGMAN *looks at them without a word.*

SOME OF THEM *uncertainly*: But . . . but aren't you the hangman?

THE HANGMAN *rises. Stands there, mighty and dreadful in his blood-red attire—a murmur of exaltation goes through the crowd*: Yes, I am the hangman!

Everyone's gaze is fixed on him. It becomes so quiet in the hall, where just a moment before there had been screaming and crashing, that you can hear the sound of his breathing.

Since the beginning of time I have looked to my task, and it seems I shall not have finished with it yet a while. Thousands of years go by, people arise and people disappear again into the night, but I remain after them, spattered with blood, watching them go, the only one who doesn't grow old. Faithfully I follow man's path, and no path they wander is so hidden that I have not raised a smoking pyre beside it and dampened the earth there with blood. I was with you from the beginning and shall follow you until your time runs out.

I have uprooted people from the earth, I have ravaged and laid waste kingdoms. Done everything you have asked of me. I have followed the ages to the grave and have rested there a while on my dripping sword until new generations have called me with young, impatient voices. I have scourged oceans of men till they bled and I have stilled their anxious sighs forever. For seers and saviors I have raised the burning-stake. I have plunged man's life in shadow and darkness. I have done everything for you.

They call me still, and I come. I look out over the lands—the earth lies febrile and hot, and the cries of sick birds are heard in the empty air. Then the rutting-time of evil is at hand! That is the hangman's hour!

Becomes silent. —Then.

When I stand at the gray window of the hangman's house, and outside the meadows lie still and calm in the evening, in strange and magnificent peace—then it is I feel as if my fate would choke me. I would sink down to the ground if she did not stand by my side.

He looks at the woman with the light about her, she who is like a beggar—he meets her gaze.

I turn my back because I cannot stand to see the earth so fair. But she stays on, looking out until it's dusk.

She is a prisoner, as I am, in our common home, but she can look at the earth's sweetness and still live.

When night has fallen, she strokes my forehead and tells me that the hangman's mark is gone. She isn't like anyone else; she can love me.

I have asked men who she is, but no one seems to know her. No one knows either why there is also such a boundless love in the world—not only I.

When she has quietly gone to sleep in my arms, I rise and lay a blanket over her, make ready—without a sound, so that she won't wake up. I steal away to my tasks in the night— —

It's well that she's not wakened, and well, too, that I'm alone with my thoughts, with what I must bear. — — —

But I know that she waits for me when I turn back from my deeds, that she will meet me when I come back borne down and soiled with blood.

Cries out.

Why must I bear all of this! Why must I be burdened with it

all! All of the anguish and guilt, everything that you have
done. Why should all the blood you have shed cry out of me
so that I never have peace!

Your destiny I must bear, and your road I must travel and not
tire, while you, long ago, have gone to rest from your deeds, in
your grave!

Who digs a grave deep enough to hide *me*! To give me peace!
Who lifts the weight of damnation from my shoulders and
gives me the peace of death!

No one! For no one can carry my burden!

Silent. He thinks. —Then.

I remember one time I sat keeping watch by a man who said he
was your savior. He wanted to save you by suffering and dying
for you. He wanted to take my burden from me.

I didn't understand what he meant, because he was a weakling
who didn't even have the strength of an ordinary man, that I
could see. He called himself Messiah and had preached peace
on earth and was condemned for it.

CHRIST *is not seen, his voice is heard in the distance*: Peace on earth.

HANGMAN: Peace? . . .

CHRIST: Yes . . .

Only . . . peace on earth . . .

HANGMAN: I don't understand why you should have to die so that
they can have peace.

CHRIST: No . . . I don't understand either . . . perhaps . . .

But this is what my Father told me. It is *his* secret.

HANGMAN: Yes . . . So . . .

CHRIST: There are many things my Father knows that he cannot
explain to me. —Not yet.

Silent. — —Then in a low voice, to himself.

That is why it is so difficult . . .

After a moment.

What hour is it?

HANGMAN: Soon the third hour.

CHRIST: When do you think . . .? — — —

Will it be . . . soon now? . . .

HANGMAN: I believe we must leave now . . .

Forgive me! . . .

CHRIST: I forgive you, brother.

HANGMAN: I don't know why he called me that! But because he did, it was as if I had crucified my brother. It was much harder than with any other I have had to do with.

I can't forget his eyes when he looked at me! When he said it! I remember it so well! I, the hangman, who has all the voices and the blood that's been shed within me, all of that which you have forgotten so long ago!

Why must I suffer! Why must I carry the burden for all of you! Why should your guilt be thrust upon me!

And earlier in the prison courtyard I had to scourge him, as if he couldn't die without it. I was so sick to death of it all that I could hardly raise the cross.

But the people were happy when I had it up. They shrieked for joy when they finally saw that he hanged there. I have never seen such delight at a place of execution as when I'd hung him on the cross! They mocked and scorned and reviled the poor man because he believed he was their Messiah and Christ and all the rest they said. They spit at him and laughed at it, and at his suffering. He closed his eyes to be spared the sight of them while he was about saving them. And maybe he tried to think that anyway he was their king and God's anointed. A crown of thorns which they had made for him hung crookedly and absurdly on his bloody head. I turned my back on all of it in disgust.

But before he gave up the ghost the whole earth darkened and I heard him call up there in a loud voice: —My God, my God, why hast thou forsaken me!

I could hardly stand it any longer.

The entire stage and the figure of the HANGMAN *darkens.*

Soon after that he was dead, as luck would have it. And we got him down in a hurry, for the sabbath was near and he couldn't be hanging there that day.

A height is seen in the background. An empty cross against the sky. Only the upper part of the cross is seen.

HANGMAN *while he goes up toward the height*: When everyone had gone to prepare for the sabbath and I was finally alone, I sat down there on death's hill with its carrion stench of rotting flesh and filth, as it always is in a place like that. I remember I sat there far into the night, under the stars.

The light has spread farther down and the HANGMAN *is seen sitting at the foot of the cross.*

Arises, clenches his fists against the sky.

Hear me, God! I have had enough of my hangman's work now! I can't bear it any longer! I can't live in blood and horror, and in all that you have allowed to happen! And what is the meaning of it, can you tell me! — —I have served faithfully and done all I could. Now I can do no more! . . . — — —Do you hear me!

Silence.

When he receives no answer—he shouts, wildly, furiously.

Today I have crucified your own son!

Silence. — —There is no answer.

Sits down again with his head in his hands.

No, it couldn't have been his son. He belonged to mankind, and it is not strange that he was treated the way they usually treat their own kind. It is only one of themselves they've crucified, as usual. — — —

He's gone, like all the others, and he's at peace. But I, unblest by God, shall be driven on and on forever. I shall go out into the world again to seek out the path of sorrow.

— —No one helps me!

No . . . He was no savior. How could he be capable of that? —How could someone like him save mankind? . . .

When I pierced his side to see if he could be taken down, he was already dead, much sooner than they usually are.

With greater feeling.

What good was a poor devil like that! — — —
More violently.
How could he help *you*! And take my burden from me! What
sort of Christ was that for men!
I understand why it must be I who serves you! Why you call
for *me*!
*Rises. With his back to the cross, he clenches his fist at the crowd
below.*
I am your Christ, with the hangman's mark on my forehead!
Sent down to you!
To bring war on earth, and to men an evil will!
He is silent. Bursts out again.
Your God gives no answer! He is dead and turned to stone!
He doesn't hear! He is long since dead!
But I, I am your Christ, I live! I am his mighty thought, his
son which he conceived and allowed to be born among you
when he was still powerful and alive and knew what he
wanted! — — —I, your Christ, I live! That you may have life!
I get out on my high road through the world and save you
every day in blood!
And me you'll not crucify, not me! — — —
In another voice.
I long for a death of sacrifice—like my poor helpless brother
did. To be nailed to my cross and to give up the ghost in the
great, merciful darkness.
But I know that hour shall never come. Again and again I must
return to my task as long as you abide.
My cross shall never be raised!
Goes down from the height, from which the light slowly fades.
My cross shall never be raised. — — —
And when you are no more, I shall go out into the eternal dark-
ness with my broadax thrown down on the barren earth in
memory of the breed that lived here!
*The light spreads over the crowd— but so that the individual figures can
hardly be distinguished.*

The HANGMAN *stands looking about him, with a hard and fiery look.*
He pushes the table aside, moves away, and starts to go out. —
But he pauses, and turns around. He sees THE WOMAN *who looks like a*
beggar, veiled in light.

THE WOMAN *rises—speaks to him in a quiet voice, her face radiant with a*
secret and painful happiness:

You know that I wait for you! That you are not alone—that I,
too, live in this world you think calls only for you. I wait for
you to come, borne down and soiled with blood. And you may
lay your head on my breast—and the hangman's mark will not
be seen any more. I kiss your burning forehead and wipe the
blood from your hand.

You know that I wait for you!

THE HANGMAN *looks at her and smiles in stillness and sorrow.*

The muffled roll of drums is heard outside. — — —He stands, listen-
ing. He adjusts his belt and goes out into the raw light of dawn.

The Philosopher's Stone:

A Play in Four Acts
(1947)

Characters

ALBERTUS, *alchemist*
MARIA, *his wife*
CATHERINE, *their daughter*
SIMONIDES, *rabbi*
JACOB, *his son*
THE "NIGHTCOCK," *a déclassé nobleman*
CLEMENS, *a wandering student*
TILDA TROOPTUB ⎱
MALENA SACKSTRAW ⎰ *harlots*
LUCAS WHORERAKE, *town constable*
THE PRINCE
TWO COURTIERS
A VALET DE CHAMBRE
A COURT RECORDER
SISTER TERESIA, *a nun in the Order of St. Mary the Virgin*
A BLIND MAN
JEWS IN THE GHETTO

Act One

The alchemist's laboratory. In the center, a great oven with many openings where crucibles and retorts are placed over the coals, and where there is also a large distillation apparatus with long, curved pipes leading down to a collecting vessel on the floor. Near the oven is a roughly constructed work table cluttered with bowls, small stone mortars, bottles, glass plates with specimens, instruments of different kinds, and a couple of opened folios.

ALBERTUS, *a man of fifty-some years, is intensely occupied with his work.*

MARIA *in from the kitchen*: Why doesn't she come!

ALBERTUS *doesn't answer, completely absorbed in his work.*

MARIA *walks about restlessly*: I don't understand why she doesn't come!
Out in the city a bell strikes the hour slowly. She counts the hours.
It's late in the evening! What can be the matter—!
Violently:
How *could* you send her up there!
When he doesn't answer:
Don't you *hear*!

ALBERTUS *looks up absently*: What is it?

MARIA: I said, how could you send her up there!

ALBERTUS: Up there? —You mean Catherine?

MARIA: Yes, of course! Do you know how late it is? It will soon be four hours since she left home! It shouldn't have taken more than a few minutes, as fast as she runs.

ALBERTUS: She's had to wait, I suppose; that always happens. Do you suppose the prince stands ready to receive as soon as someone comes. It's not like running into a common tradesman's house, you know. You have no idea how it is up at the court.

MARIA: No, praise God—I don't know a thing about it.

ALBERTUS: No. You don't.
Continues his work.

207

MARIA: But I've asked a thing or two. And now that my child's started going up there, I've heard a few things about their habits. It's not like down here among us simple folk, not the way Catherine's been brought up.

They keep late hours, that much I know. And they're open-handed when it suits their purpose. Even beggars have been welcome there at times.

Maybe they've given her sweets and dainties like last time? Do you suppose? And sweet wine in fine odd-shaped glasses.

ALBERTUS: And suppose they have? That won't do her any harm!

MARIA: Harm! A child not harmed by that, you think! Harm!...
— —My own innocent child . . .

About to cry.

And I had to lay out the best dress she has for her to wear . . .

ALBERTUS: I suppose she should go up there foul and dirty, the way she runs in the alleys here! She has to be at least somewhat decently dressed when she goes up to the court, to His Grace. Surely you understand that!

MARIA: Yes, yes . . . I understand. Decently dressed . . .

ALBERTUS: Yes. That's clear enough. Those people pay a lot of attention to things like that.

MARIA: Yes. They do. I know that.
I'd rather she'd have gone in her shabbiest skirt.

ALBERTUS *throws a glance at her*: Shabbiest skirt! You don't really mean that! —And do you think she herself would want to do that?

MARIA *doesn't answer.*

ALBERTUS: Well? Would she?

MARIA: It's not strange that a girl of her age likes pretty clothes. I'll not deny that.
And it's not an especially nice dress anyway; most girls of her age have much better ones.

ALBERTUS: Well then.
Why do you go on about it then. Don't you suppose I have other things to think about!

Examines the contents of a retort, places it carefully over the coals again.

MARIA *walks about restlessly. Mumbling, mostly to herself:* Last time she came after a couple of hours. But tonight . . .
Stops abruptly in front of him.
Why don't you fetch that devil's coin yourself!

ALBERTUS *turns quickly toward her without answering.*

MARIA: Yes! You did before!

ALBERTUS: Devil's coin?

MARIA: Yes! That's what I said!
You did when the old prince lived. And if this young one won't help you, you may as well let it be.

ALBERTUS: Let it be?

MARIA: Yes, rather than send that poor child . . .

ALBERTUS: Can't she even do that! Doesn't she have time for it? All she does is idle away her time here all day.

MARIA: She has *time.*

ALBERTUS: Must I leave my work then? Do I have to fetch the money when I'm right in the middle of . . . of what I'm doing. I *can't* leave; it's impossible. And she can do the job just as well. It's not at all necessary that I go. —It doesn't make a bit of difference who fetches those miserable coppers.

MARIA: Oh, it makes a difference, all right.

ALBERTUS *mumbles to himself.*

MARIA: Yes it does. And not only that it seems very important who fetches them . . . and how they are dressed as well. —Have you ever cared how she was dressed! If she went around in rags you wouldn't carē! You wouldn't even take any notice! But when she's to go up there, then your eyes begin to open up. Then you're wide awake! Then you can *use* her!

ALBERTUS: Use!

MARIA: Yes! For what suits *you*. How it suits her doesn't matter. Expose a child to that!

ALBERTUS: To what? If she goes up to fetch that maundy money, what does it matter. And does she mind? Does she?

MARIA *is silent.*

ALBERTUS: She almost begs to go, doesn't she?

MARIA: Any girl would like to go up to the palace and be shown in to His Grace. There's nothing odd about that. But she does it because she's forced.

ALBERTUS: Forced! Have I forced her to it!

MARIA: Yes, she said so herself.

ALBERTUS: Has she said that? It's impossible.

MARIA: Yes, that's what she said today when she left. "I don't understand why father forces me to do something like that," she said.

ALBERTUS: That's odd. She hasn't talked that way to me. Not a word.

MARIA: I don't think she talks with you about anything.

ALBERTUS: No, that's true. She doesn't. But she asked yesterday if she couldn't go soon to get the money again.

MARIA *is silent. Then*: She knows that once you've made up your mind, she has to do as you say.

ALBERTUS: Yes.

MARIA: But she tells me what she thinks. She speaks openly to me and says what she really feels.

ALBERTUS: Yes.

Watches her a minute. Turns away from her, toward the oven, begins to work with his apparatus. Lifts a distillation tube from the collecting vessel on the floor, reaches for another empty one on the table.

Come here and give me a hand.

MARIA *doesn't move.*

ALBERTUS: Come and help me, I said!

MARIA *unwillingly approaches the oven. Crosses herself.*

ALBERTUS: Take this.

Gives her a retort filled with a dark-red liquid.

MARIA *takes it, after crossing herself again.*

ALBERTUS: Can't you ever stop that!

MARIA *doesn't answer. —Stands with the vessel in her hands:*
  Where shall I put it?
ALBERTUS: In the usual place, of course! Don't you know where it's
  supposed to be!
MARIA *carries it to a table in the dark corner of the room to the left, behind
  the oven.*
  Comes out in the light again:
  Do you believe it's for your sake he pays it out! —
  That nest! Where they live in ungodliness, lust, and shame! It
  is sin, sin! Everything you put your hand to is sin! And she
  doesn't want to do it! Doesn't want to! You force her, that
  innocent creature, so that you can get your money, your sinful
  money! —it's sin, sin! using her for evil! —but she's *my* child!
  mine! —I bore her and carried her—under my breast—and in
  my arms—and you, have you ever cared anything about her?
  Cared the least bit for her or for me, either of us! But now
  she'll serve, now you can use her for this! —Why did I ever
  bring her into this world, to this tainted house . . . !

  ALBERTUS *pays no attention to her outburst, just shrugs his shoulders.*

MARIA *calms herself. Goes about, at her wits' end. —Submissive, dully:*
  Don't you understand that I'm worried about her?
ALBERTUS: No. I don't.
MARIA: Don't you think . . . ?
  She is a beautiful child . . . And this world is not good.

  ALBERTUS *sits down and thumbs through a folio on the table, ignores
  her.*

MARIA: I have tried to bring her up in virtue and the fear of God,
  and she's a child with a pure heart . . . —But, Lord knows, we
  are all consigned to the devil.
  Goes about helplessly when he doesn't answer her. —Wrings her hands.
  Why doesn't she come! . . .

  ALBERTUS *reads, pays no attention to her at all.*

MARIA *desperately. —Comes a bit closer to him:* I can't help that I'm
  worried . . . — — —I'm just a simple woman . . .

ALBERTUS: I am greatly amazed that such wise and sensible words can come from your mouth.

MARIA: Oh well . . .

Perhaps it's not as risky as I imagine— — —Do you think so? . . .

ALBERTUS *doesn't answer.*

MARIA *stands disconcertedly. —Approaches him again*: You know that I really want you to have what you need, I always have . . . You shan't need to be without the things you must use in your work. But . . . I can't help that I think that it's not right . . . I don't understand what it is you're busy with, but . . .

ALBERTUS: No, you don't. I don't know how many times you've told me you don't understand it. And how many times I've let you know that it doesn't *mean* anything. Nothing at all.

MARIA: No, no . . .

But can't you get someone else to help you . . . Try to get someone else to lend you the money, so that . . .

ALBERTUS: Someone else!

MARIA: Yes, someone who cares about what you are doing, someone who believes in you.

ALBERTUS: And don't you know that no one does! Maybe you don't know that! And how could they! They can't even understand what it's about. How could they believe in it!

MARIA: No, no . . . And what about him up there, he doesn't understand it . . .

Nor does he care about it either . . .

ALBERTUS *is silent.*

MARIA: No one understands it . . .

Then how can you . . . ?

ALBERTUS: How can I what?

MARIA: Well, I mean, how are you going to manage.

ALBERTUS: Manage? Do you hope that I won't be able to continue any longer?

MARIA: No, no, that's not what I mean, not at all.

ALBERTUS: That I'll be forced to quit?

MARIA: Oh no, no.

ALBERTUS: Yes! That's what you mean! But I'm not going to quit. I'll never stop working, you can be sure of that!

MARIA: I've never wished that you would stop . . .

ALBERTUS: Never! Do you hear! Even though you've wanted it! That's what you wanted, isn't it! Wanted me to give up and not think it worth the trouble any longer! Let the fire in the oven die out the way you thought it would that time I left everything and went away for a few days . . . then you were really satisfied! then you really had what you—!

MARIA: That's not *true*! I was anxious about you, I looked for you everywhere, no one knew where you were—you didn't know yourself, if you'll remember, you . . .

ALBERTUS: Knew! I knew very well. I was just wandering around in the hills a while.

MARIA: You *didn't* know, you didn't know where you had been.

ALBERTUS: But it wouldn't have gone out; it still burned when I came home again. It *didn't* die out even though you thought it did, you thought it was cold!

MARIA *makes an evasive gesture.*

ALBERTUS: Just as you thought when I'd been up at the court to see that young pup and made to run the fool's errand, with all of them sniggering at me in the corridors—the fops and the lackeys—"him there who's making gold!" —those dolts! —and when I had to bow and creep—humble myself—try to beg for it—as a favor—and still be run off shamefully—like a beggar— — —*Me*, a beggar! Me! —But I didn't put it out because of that—I didn't let it die! I came home and sat down beside the fire again, with my old books. No! It wasn't the way you hoped—it *didn't* happen! —I *didn't* stop! —and I'll *never* stop! —even though they keep trying to hinder me! —everyone is against me, everyone in this damned town! —even though I have no one to turn to, or even to talk with—and no one to support my work—even though they grin at me and heap scorn on me— —But that means nothing to *you* of course! How could it! That's too much to ask! And have I asked that of you! Have I ever asked anything of you! — —Meaning! How could it mean anything for someone like you!

MARIA: It doesn't mean anything to me either that you can't make gold.

ALBERTUS *looks sideways at her.* —*Mumbles to himself*: No, that may be.

MARIA: I wouldn't want that at all. I want us to be poor as we've always been.

ALBERTUS: Aha? —Aha . . . — —That's what you want.

If it's any comfort to you, I don't intend to make any gold. And can't either. That's not what I seek. And if I should just possibly learn how, it's still not that which I seek. It's something quite different.

MARIA: What?

ALBERTUS: What! Do you really believe that I can explain it to you. You ought to know it's no use talking to you about such things.

MARIA: No, I know that.

But is it so necessary?

ALBERTUS: Necessary! —If it's necessary!

MARIA: Yes. Is it so necessary that you have to sacrifice our child for it?

ALBERTUS: Sacrifice our child! What nonsense! How can you make up such things! You're so simple-minded . . . !

MARIA: But that's what you're doing. Sacrificing her.

ALBERTUS *is silent.*

MARIA: You can't deny that you know where you are sending her. That you don't know how they live up there—that rakehell and his cronies—that lecher!

I suppose you don't know that?

ALBERTUS: I've never heard anything about it.

MARIA: You haven't! You most certainly have. Everyone knows about it, every honest soul in this town. And Magdalena, she can tell you what they do . . .

ALBERTUS: Magdalena! What does she know about it!

MARIA: She knows because she takes away the leavings from the kitchen every day and she says they live like swine; it's like the worst kind of bawdy house, she says . . .

ALBERTUS: That common magpie gossip! You have your knowledge of the court from that bitch!

MARIA: She knows what she's talking about she does. And everyone who comes near knows it, and all the women in the street, they all talk about it!

ALBERTUS: Women's talk!

MARIA: Not a bit! The burghers talk about it openly, and so does every honest soul.

ALBERTUS: The burghers! Do you keep company with them?

MARIA: No, you know I don't. But I've heard. Everyone's heard it. And you have too!

ALBERTUS: Have I! How could I have heard it! I sit here all day and never go outside the door.

MARIA: But you have. You know it as well as the rest of us.

ALBERTUS: I don't know anything about it, I tell you! I don't know what people are gossiping about. And don't care either!

MARIA: Don't care! Don't you care what they do with your daughter! What it is you expose her to! That nest of fornicators you send her to! You're using her! Delivering her to sin and depravity! You're unscrupulous! So that you can have your way! You don't think of anyone but yourself! Yourself and your godless craft which the Lord God and his church turn away from in disgust, and which leads to nothing but damnation! — —Don't know! Don't you know! You send her because you know what they put a price on up there, what he's interested in and lusts after, and what will open up his purse that you couldn't get into! So that you can continue your work of darkness! You send her to sin and perdition because you yourself are lost, in Satan's—!

ALBERTUS: Check your tongue, woman!

MARIA: No! I won't, I . . . !

ALBERTUS: Silence, I say!

MARIA: You send her to a whorehouse, to a whorehouse I say, to a nest of vice and seduction . . . ! — — —Oh, why doesn't she

come! Why *doesn't* she come! ———Who knows what that
scum is doing with her!

ALBERTUS: Madness!

MARIA: With my child, my own child, whom I tried to protect but
who's born to perdition and is in the devil's hands.

ALBERTUS: You are raving mad, woman! You're out of your senses!
*There are several knocks from the clapper on the door in the background.
They both turn toward it.* MARIA *hurries to open it.* SIMONIDES *comes
in. He is a tall, thin man, about the same age as* ALBERTUS, *dressed
in a full-length caftan. He bows in the Eastern manner, with his hand
over his heart:*
Peace in thy house, master Albertus.

MARIA *closes the door, disappointed that it was not her daughter.*

ALBERTUS *mumbles something which can be taken for a greeting.*

SIMONIDES: I come to visit at a late hour. But I do not wish to disturb you in your work. Perhaps you have not finished yet?

ALBERTUS: No, I haven't.
Turns toward his oven, occupies himself there.
After a moment, without exaggerated friendliness:
Won't you sit down.

SIMONIDES: I have been sitting all day, studying the holy texts, and
would rather remain standing, if it pleases you as much.

ALBERTUS *mumbling*: Pleases? —As you please, of course.

SIMONIDES *bows*: I thank you.
After a pause:
Are you in good health?

ALBERTUS: Yes, certainly.

SIMONIDES: And your wife as well?

ALBERTUS: My wife? Yes, she is in excellent health. She most certainly is!
—We are both in excellent health.

SIMONIDES: Nothing pleases me more to hear, my friend.

ALBERTUS *after a moment*: And you?

SIMONIDES: I am also well, by the grace of the Almighty.
Pause.
Do I disturb you in your work?

ALBERTUS: Disturb?

Mutters something.

No, you don't.

SIMONIDES: I do not wish to bother you in any way. I know that your work is very important to you. — — —

If I had known that you were not finished at the oven, I would have put off my visit. But I thought that this hour was the best.

ALBERTUS *mumbles something.*

SIMONIDES: I thought that you might be tired this late in the evening and that you would be resting after your long day's work.

ALBERTUS *mumbling*: I haven't time to notice if I'm tired.

SIMONIDES: No, no. I understand.

I am not learned enough to understand anything of your science, but I know at least that it must be very difficult.

ALBERTUS: You are quite right. Quite right. It's not easy.

SIMONIDES *nods his head in affirmation*: No, no. I am completely convinced of it.

After watching him at work for a moment:

What have you sought today? And have you found what you were seeking?

ALBERTUS: Found?

SIMONIDES: Yes, I mean have you come to an understanding of the questions which occupy you? Has your day brought good fortune?

ALBERTUS: Good fortune?

SIMONIDES: Yes. Have you been successful, and are you satisfied with what you have achieved?

ALBERTUS: I hadn't thought I'd find what I'm seeking today. And not tomorrow either.

SIMONIDES: No, no. Perhaps not, perhaps not.

But one day you'll surely find it, won't you?

ALBERTUS: I don't know. I hope so.

SIMONIDES: Oh, yes. One day you will certainly find it, sometime in the future . . .

Granted that it takes time. The mysteries which you seek to reveal cannot be easy to penetrate. There must be many difficulties to overcome in your art, much which is not given to men to divine, which is hidden from them. The essence of things is far off, saith the Preacher, far down in the depths. Who can uncover them? But finally you will bring their secrets to light. If you only work at it long enough.

ALBERTUS: I'm glad that you have such confidence in my art. Maybe I won't be able to solve all of the riddles, but I shall do my best. I can't promise any more than that.

SIMONIDES: No, no, that's as it should be.

ALBERTUS: Yes, it is, no one can promise more than that. Except gamblers and charlatans.

SIMONIDES *nods in agreement*: It is true, it is true.

No one can do more. There are too many riddles.

ALBERTUS: Yes, there are. And there won't be fewer if we sit and brood about them.

SIMONIDES: No, no, surely not.

And the riddle of riddles, the deepest mystery which can explain *all*, all of the others! The very philosopher's stone!

ALBERTUS *turns away in irritation*.

SIMONIDES: It cannot be easy to find.

ALBERTUS: No, it can't! It would be strange if it could! It can hardly be easy to find the truth.

SIMONIDES: No, no.

ALBERTUS *turns away again. Busies himself at the oven, examining the contents of mortars and retorts, lifts up a retort and looks at the liquid in it*. And you? What have you found in your texts?

SIMONIDES: The same as always. God's will.

ALBERTUS: Hmm, you're lucky, Simonides. You know the truth. You don't have to seek it.

SIMONIDES *with a gesture of denial*: Only God the Highest knows the truth. I would be a fool among men if I thought I knew anything about it.

ALBERTUS: Oh, but you can read the holy authors and the fathers

so that you'll know how it all fits together, and what you
should believe.

SIMONIDES: What I should believe?

ALBERTUS: Yes.

SIMONIDES: I certainly don't have to search for that, my friend.

ALBERTUS: Oh? You don't?

Returns to the oven.

After a moment, turns to him again:

Do you really mean that we cannot know anything about the
truth?

SIMONIDES: Yes. It is certain.

ALBERTUS: And that there is really no point in seeking it?

SIMONIDES: Certainly.

God himself is the truth. And no one can see him.

ALBERTUS *regards him for a moment. Lifts up a retort, holding it against
the light, examining its contents.*

I must say, I would very much like to see the truth.

SIMONIDES: Then do you wish to see God!

ALBERTUS: Yes, I would like to see him.

SIMONIDES *takes a step back.* MARIA, *who has been sitting apart from
the men, in the shadow, crosses herself.*

SIMONIDES: The Almighty must punish you for talking like that.

ALBERTUS *with a shrug of his shoulders, returns the retort to its place over
the fire:* I don't understand why he should. I use only the gifts
which he himself has given me, the intellect that he's en-
dowed me with. Why should that displease him? He ought to
disapprove more of those who don't bother to use it.

SIMONIDES: My friend—you do not know God's ways. And you
don't know if you use your intellect according to his will.

ALBERTUS: I use it in order to try to see into his creation, into his
glorious work. Do you mean that should displease him?

SIMONIDES: No one knows if he wants men to see into it, into his
mysteries. Perhaps in his eyes it is an abomination.

ALBERTUS: An abomination!

SIMONIDES: Yes.

ALBERTUS: An abomination! To try to find out about the remarkable structure of his creation, the divine truth in his work. He should want us to learn about it!

SIMONIDES: Then why has he not given us the truth—if he wanted us to know it?

He has not, and in his wisdom has not intended it for us. Instead we grope in the darkness, and he is the only one who can lead us through it. If we attempt anything with our own power, we end up in sin and error.

ALBERTUS: Sin!

SIMONIDES: Yes.

ALBERTUS: Sin! —What nonsense! What foolishness is this? And you are supposed to have studied the philosophers and the great teachers of wisdom. Sin! The ancients wouldn't have agreed with you there. And still they knew much more about everything than we do. Sin! There's nothing in the writings of the great authors about sin!

SIMONIDES: No, but in God's word. In the Lord's holy scriptures. Many things are written about it there.

ALBERTUS: Oh yes, *there*. Of course. Of course it's there.
Turns away from him in annoyance.

SIMONIDES: Well, I didn't come to talk about these things. No, it was not for that . . .

ALBERTUS: No? Why did you come then?

SIMONIDES: Well, my path took me past your door, and I did not want to go by without having seen you. —One should never pass by a wise man's door, it is said.

ALBERTUS *muttering*: I'm no wise man, and neither are you for that matter.

SIMONIDES: Yes, you are. You are a learned man, and well versed in those things you study, and it has always been a great comfort and satisfaction for me to exchange thoughts with you—even if we do not have the same opinion about certain things.

ALBERTUS: Not any that I know of! Not a one!

SIMONIDES: No, perhaps not.

Oh, yes, when we talk about such things that I know a little about, the venerable texts and commentaries which we both—

ALBERTUS: Yes, yes, you are a good cabalist, I've never denied it. But the really great teachings—

SIMONIDES *with some fervor*: I have no other teacher than the Lord God, Israel's, my people's God. And I have carried on my humble studies in the cabala to interpret his word which he himself has given us, so that I can live by it.

ALBERTUS: Yes, yes, I know that. I know all that . . . Then why did you come?

SIMONIDES: Uh . . . I wanted to talk with you a moment, talk a bit after the day's labors that have tired me out so that I haven't the strength for any more of it. I felt I wanted to talk with another person with knowledge and intelligence so that our conversation could be something of a pleasure and refreshment. And you are the only one in this town . . .

ALBERTUS: There's no one! Absolutely no one in this town that a reasonable man can talk with or exchange a sensible thought with! Nothing but ignorance, the coarsest ignorance. No one who knows anything about what the ancients thought, or the philosophers. Only lunatics! Nothing but ignorant fools! And lunatics! Fools and lunatics! — — —Yes, you are . . .

SIMONIDES: Yes, yes. —That's what I thought too in my loneliness there at home. Exactly as you do. And then the idea came to me that I should visit you this evening after your work was over and you had finished with your philosophical oven and your learned tasks, you too. I wanted especially to talk with you, my friend . . . And I know that I am always just as welcome in your house.

ALBERTUS: Yes . . . you are. You are always just as . . . welcome . . .

SIMONIDES: Yes.

ALBERTUS: But I thought you said you had something on your mind. Didn't you?

SIMONIDES: Yes, I wanted to consult with you about something that's close to my heart, very close to my heart . . .

ALBERTUS: Aha, aha. What is it?

SIMONIDES: Well . . . it is about my son.

ALBERTUS: Your son? I see.

SIMONIDES: Yes, it is about him. My son . . . —And also your daughter, Catherine.

ALBERTUS: My daughter . . . ?

> MARIA, *who sits mending some old clothes at a table to one side, listens closely, too.*

SIMONIDES: It is something that troubles me, that troubles me very much, I must say . . . And I hope it is something that will also trouble you.

ALBERTUS: Trouble *me*? What is it that should trouble *me*?

SIMONIDES: Your daughter. Just as I am very troubled about my son.

> ALBERTUS *looks at him, wondering.*

SIMONIDES: I am sure we shall understand each other. A father always understands another father's worry, his anxiety for his child, the gift of God that he is responsible for. Youngsters have no sense of responsibility; they are thoughtless, and it is quite natural, but we, their fathers, we know life, we know this world, we know how all of these things are—and we know what is best for them. It is that which we think most of. Their true welfare—which they do not understand at all. We want to help them, don't we? Isn't that right, my friend?

ALBERTUS *mumbles*: Yes, of course.

SIMONIDES: Well, well, my friend, I know you think so too. I am sure that we shall be of the same mind, no matter how much we disagree about other things.

ALBERTUS: The same mind? What are we to be of the same mind about?

SIMONIDES: About the happiness of our children—your child and mine, who are so close to our hearts.

ALBERTUS: Mmm, yes . . . certainly . . .

> What are you getting at? I don't understand at all what you're talking about.

SIMONIDES: What I'm talking about? I shall explain, I'm coming to it . . . I'll speak openly to you, quite openly . . .

© *Studio Järlås*

Anna Lindahl (Maria), Uno Henning (Simonides), and Lars Hanson
(Albertus) in *The Philosopher's Stone*
Royal Dramatic Theatre, 1948
Director: Alf Sjöberg
Design: Sven Erixon

ALBERTUS: Yes, it would be well if you did. Then I might be able to make some sense out of all this.

SIMONIDES: Hmm . . . yes, yes, I know. —You know that Jacob and Catherine have always been very close, from the beginning when they were children, when I fled to this place with my brothers in the faith, and was allowed to move into this alley. When I fled to this town with my little son in my arms . . . They have been together often. They have indeed. It turned out that way, and it's not so strange. You and I sought each other out, and the youngsters did the same. Perhaps because the other children here would have nothing to do with them— of course, Jacob could have been with his people, with those who believe as he does. He could have, and I have often talked with him about it and seriously warned him. But he was a singular child, not at all like the others; it's always been hard for him to be with children his own age. But he liked to be with Catherine . . .

ALBERTUS: Yes, yes, we know all that.

SIMONIDES: Yes . . . And they have stayed together since even though it is against every custom, usage, and good practice of *our* people. I have never approved of it, not at all. But my son would have been so lonely, have felt so alone, I think . . . And it was so innocent really, his sitting beside her and telling his stories to her, as he does with his almost too lively imagination— but that is God's will. Catherine liked to listen to him, even though she was so different. She had quite a different temperament . . . it's surprising how two children so unlike each other could get along so well . . .

ALBERTUS: Well, then what? What is it you have to say?

SIMONIDES: Uh, well . . . Can you imagine, can you conceive of it . . . My son . . . my son Jacob has come to me and confessed that he loves your daughter.

ALBERTUS: Aha. Has he now.

SIMONIDES: Yes . . .

He has.

When ALBERTUS *gives no answer:*

I don't know how you look at it. A connection of that kind
with our people who are despised by many. No not by you;
you don't despise us, I know that, and I have always respected
you for it—you don't look upon us, the Lord's people, with
any ill will. No, you are a learned man, an enlightened man,
and you have thought much and therefore you are above the
error of the mob; you are a man of wisdom, a philosopher and
not like others—And your science, as remarkable as it is,
doesn't give you any standing to speak of, you know yourself
what it means to be despised . . .

ALBERTUS: Despised? Me!

SIMONIDES: Yes, I mean . . .

ALBERTUS: Am I despised! . . . —I am certainly not despised!
What do you mean?

SIMONIDES: Well, I mean . . . You do not regard our people with ill
will—and I credit you for that and place the highest value on it.
I do, you may be sure. But even so, you are a Christian and I
am a Jew.

ALBERTUS: What does that have to do with this!

SIMONIDES: You have no prejudices; you stand above such things,
above the notions of ordinary people, but . . .
Do you want to give your daughter in marriage to my son
Jacob?

ALBERTUS: My daughter . . . in marriage . . . ?

SIMONIDES: Yes, you agree, don't you, it is against every custom
and usage of both Jews and Christians, yes, and even against
nature, which you revere and know so much about. I am sure
that you won't give your daughter to a Jew, for you are, after
all, a Christian—perhaps not a faithful Christian, I don't know
about that, I have no idea. But I am certain that you won't.
And I, I don't want it either . . . But my son, my son Jacob . . .

ALBERTUS: He wants Catherine to be his wife!

SIMONIDES: Yes . . . He comprehends nothing, and I cannot explain it to him. He thinks they can be joined together like any
other young couple. He wanted me to come here to talk with
you about it, this thing that he has wanted so long. And lately

he has become more and more insistent that I come and ask you about it; I don't know why he has become so insistent . . . This is why I have come. I must hear your thoughts of what he asks.

ALBERTUS *doesn't answer.*

SIMONIDES: What do you say, my friend? —What answer do you have for him?

ALBERTUS: Why don't you answer him yourself? You can, just as well as I.

SIMONIDES: Yes . . .

ALBERTUS: You don't want to do it yourself!

SIMONIDES: No, it's true . . . But I have come to present it to you as he asked me to do.

ALBERTUS *shrugs his shoulders.*

SIMONIDES: And what is your opinion?

ALBERTUS: My opinion. As you say, I have no contempt for the children of Israel, why should I have; they are no worse than other people—that's not saying very much—and I have no prejudice, as you've mentioned; why shouldn't Jews and Christians marry if they wish. Not that I'd thought Catherine would marry a Jew—but that's probably because I've never given a thought to whom she'd marry.

What I wonder is how a marriage like that would work out. How could it be managed, do you suppose?

SIMONIDES: I don't know.

ALBERTUS: What does he think about it? Hasn't he said anything to you about it?

SIMONIDES: No. I don't think any of it is clear to him.

ALBERTUS: Surely he must have thought about it.

SIMONIDES *shakes his head*: No, no.

ALBERTUS: Surely he has, although he hasn't told you about it. Does he plan to be converted to the Christian faith?

SIMONIDES: To the Christian faith! *My son!* Rabbi Simonides' son should . . . should become a Christian, forsake the faith of his fathers! . . . My only son! The only one I have! He should

give up his Lord and God for the errors of the Christians . . .
and leave his father . . . leave me . . . My, *my* son should go to
the Christians . . . the godforsaken . . . the beasts . . . the
sevenfold damned . . . ! They have taken two of my sons!
Struck them down bloody and maimed so that I could hardly
recognize their bodies when I'd found them again! Two sturdy
sons whom the Lord gave me . . . They have taken every blessing from me! He is all I have left! It must never happen! The
Lord will not suffer it to happen! —And he has no thought of
it, I *know*! His faith is so ardent that nothing in the world
would make him betray it! He studies his Torah and his
Talmud—with my guidance—all of the holy scriptures, he is
always poring over them—at my side—I have brought him up
in his fathers' faith and opened his mind to the Lord and his
commands—and he has been my most inspired pupil—and de-
voted son—I shall never lose him! —my joy, my hope—my
only, most precious son—all that I have left! — — —The Lord
allowed them to take my two sons from me; he let it happen
without raising his hand—perhaps to try me. And he also
allowed my beloved wife to die when we fled because she
could not bear all the suffering. But he let me keep him—my
infant son—all I own— —I have carried him in my arms
through rivers and across many lands . . . You understand me,
don't you, you understand me . . . You are a father yourself,
you must understand me . . . !

ALBERTUS: But why do you come asking that I give my daughter to
him!

SIMONIDES *hesitates before he answers*: He has asked me to, kept on
asking me day after day . . . He says he can't live without her
—you know, such things they always say . . .
Looks down at the floor.
I am a bad father . . . I cannot deny him anything . . .
When ALBERTUS *does not answer*:
Finally I had to promise him to come and tell you about it.
And now I have done it. And I leave it to you.

ALBERTUS: To me?

SIMONIDES: Yes.

ALBERTUS: Aha. To me.

There's no other way, it seems to me; one of them must give up his faith. If *he* does—but then you said he wouldn't . . .

SIMONIDES: No, no, I know that he won't!

ALBERTUS: And if *she* gives up her faith she'll be a heretic, and of course she'll be treated like one—that's not very pleasant, they tell me.

SIMONIDES: No, no. —You oppose it, don't you! You won't allow it, will you!

ALBERTUS: Allow it? It's impossible, you can see for yourself; it just won't work!

SIMONIDES: Ahh . . . God be praised, God be praised . . . That's how things are.

ALBERTUS: Yes, that's how they are. That's how things are sorted out in this world. Very sensibly and considerately. You don't need to worry.

SIMONIDES: No . . .

But would you . . . would you tell him that you are completely opposed to it, and that you will never allow them to be married? Would you do that?

ALBERTUS *looks at him a little scornfully*: I understand . . . Yes, I'll gladly do it, more than gladly.

SIMONIDES *lays a hand on his arm*: *Will* you! *Will* you! Oh, my friend . . . I am so grateful to you . . .
Seems quite relieved.
And your daughter, too. So that she will understand that nothing can ever come of it.

ALBERTUS: I certainly shall.

SIMONIDES, *quite satisfied. —Stands, thinking a moment. Then*: I should very much like to have a few words with your daughter . . . to ask her about something . . .

ALBERTUS: About what?

SIMONIDES: Well . . . I want to ask her not to pay so much attention to Jacob . . . that she keep away from him, you see . . . so that he will think she doesn't care about him.

ALBERTUS: Do you mean that she does?

SIMONIDES: Yes, of course. Certainly she does. She must.

ALBERTUS: Must! Does she care so terribly much for your remarkable son?

SIMONIDES: Don't you think she does?

ALBERTUS: No, can you imagine it, I don't at all.

SIMONIDES: Don't you . . . ! Is it possible!

ALBERTUS: It seems unbelievable, but I wonder if it isn't so.

SIMONIDES: Do I understand you . . . Is it . . . possible!

Almost embraces him.

Oh, what a weight you have taken from my heart! . . . —My friend, my friend, with God's help all will go well, things will arrange themselves . . . for the young couple . . . Perhaps he is merciful to us, he is helping us perhaps . . .

But I can't believe it! It cannot be true!

ALBERTUS: To the best of my knowledge it is.

SIMONIDES: I must hear it from Catherine herself, from her own lips! Oh, how happily I should leave this house, if . . .!

Goes excitedly to the kitchen door and opens it:

Catherine! — —Catherine!

Surprised, when no one appears:

Isn't she here? —Where is she?

Looks questioningly at ALBERTUS.

MARIA: Catherine isn't home.

SIMONIDES: Isn't she? Not at home? Where is she?

MARIA: She is with the good mistress Cecilia, keeping her company because she is sick.

SIMONIDES: So-o . . . is she?

MARIA: Yes.

SIMONIDES: Aha, mistress Cecilia is sick. I am sorry to hear it. May God grant her a speedy recovery. She is a good woman.

MARIA: Yes, she is. And she is very good to our daughter, she always has been; she likes to have Catherine sit with her.

ALBERTUS *looks at her, surprised and annoyed:* How can you lie like that!

MARIA: I'm not lying! She is.

ALBERTUS: Nonsense! Such talk! What tales you tell!
  She's not at all with any mistress Cecilia; she's gone to the
  Prince to fetch my money. She usually does that now, so that
  I won't have to leave my work.

MARIA *looks wrathfully at her husband.*

SIMONIDES *regards them. —Then*: Is she there? — — —
  So late in the evening . . .

ALBERTUS: Late? It's not so terribly late.

SIMONIDES: Oh yes . . . in a place like that . . .
  After a moment:
  I thought his Grace didn't give you any more?

ALBERTUS: Oh yes, he does. Why shouldn't he? He is very much
  interested in my work, more than ever. There's nothing odd
  about that, at least I don't think so. I'm not scorned as much
  as you think, my friend. If you think my standing is like a
  Jew's, you're quite mistaken, I assure you.

SIMONIDES: No, I suppose you're not . . . Not as we are. We are
  always the most despised.
  Aha, the Prince has started to pay out your money again.
  Fortunate for you. You can go on working at your singular art.

ALBERTUS: I most certainly can. I have no worry about that any
  more.

SIMONIDES: Yes, I see. What a pleasant turn of fortune!

ALBERTUS: Yes.

SIMONIDES *stands, silently. Sometimes looking out of the corner of his eye at*
  ALBERTUS, *who is striding about with his hands behind him.*
  There is a pounding on the door.
  MARIA *goes to the door and pulls back the bolt.*
  CATHERINE *comes in, followed by a* VALET DE CHAMBRE.

VALET: Aha, so this is where the little miss lives.
  What a peculiar place . . .
  Looks around the room:
  His Grace wishes me convey to you his particular pleasure,
  master Albertus. But what a filthy back street you live in. Next
  time I think he can take his little whore-fluff home himself.

CATHERINE *looks angrily at the* VALET, *who disappears with a sneer into the darkness again, carrying his lantern.*
Defiantly she pulls a purse out of the inside pocket of her skirt and flings it onto her father's table so that several beakers and retorts are smashed:
Here is your money!

MARIA: Your evil money! Are you satisfied now!
Both of them go into the kitchen, closing the door behind them.

SIMONIDES *when he has recovered from his astonishment:* I can understand that your art must be very difficult indeed, my friend. I don't think I could ever learn it.
Goes toward the door:
Peace in thy house, master Albertus . . .
Goes out.

ALBERTUS *stands looking at the purse in the midst of the broken glass. Goes out through the door to the left.*
The stage is empty for a moment.

JACOB, *a tall, lanky, and slightly round-shouldered young man, carefully opens the door a bit, which no one had locked after* SIMONIDES' *departure. Puts his head in—discovers no one. Steps in. Looks around the room, surprised to find no one there. —Knocks carefully on the kitchen door. Knocks again.* MARIA *opens the door slightly to see who is there. After a moment:*
CATHERINE *comes in.*

JACOB: Isn't my father here?

CATHERINE: No, he isn't.

JACOB: Has . . . hasn't he been here?

CATHERINE: Yes, he has.

JACOB: Has he mentioned it . . . ?

CATHERINE: What?

JACOB: Uh . . .
Don't you know . . . haven't they . . . said anything to you...?
I mean haven't they told you what they were talking about?

CATHERINE: I don't know what they were talking about. I just came back.

JACOB: You just came back now?

CATHERINE: Yes.

JACOB: But . . . where have you been?

CATHERINE: Where I've been! That's nobody's business!

JACOB: No . . . No, it isn't, I suppose . . .

But don't you know why my father came here?

CATHERINE: How would I know that!

Was it something in particular?

JACOB: Yes . . . yes, it was . . .

Goes toward her:

But you *must* have heard what it was . . . Yes, I can see that you know about it . . . I can see it in your face . . . in your eyes . . . Do you think I wouldn't notice it . . . in everything . . . do you think I'm so blind!

Takes her hands:

Oh, I've been wandering about the streets, everywhere here in the alleys; I couldn't sit at home for fear of . . .

CATHERINE: For what?

JACOB: Of what your father would say about it . . . No, what *you* would . . . what *you* would say about it . . . !

CATHERINE: About *what*! Can't you talk so that I'll understand you!

JACOB: You must know . . . my father was here to ask . . . to ask you to be . . . my bride . . .

CATHERINE: Bride!

JACOB: Yes . . .

CATHERINE: That I should be your *bride*!

JACOB: Yes . . .

Father has no objection. Not any more. And your father . . . well, I don't know. But I'm sure he's convinced him.

CATHERINE *looks at him in astonishment*: Is it really possible that he has been here to ask about that?

JACOB: Yes, certainly.

CATHERINE: And what did he say?

JACOB: I don't know. But when father told him how much I love you, I know he wouldn't have said no. Do you think?

CATHERINE *with a scornful little laugh*: No, he wouldn't have had the heart.

JACOB: No . . .

But what about you, Catherine? What about you?

CATHERINE *is silent. Goes and sits down on a bench.*

JACOB: Why don't you say something?

After a moment:

That's what we always said we'd do, you and I . . . that we were meant for each other, and that we'd be married . . . You remember.

CATHERINE: Did we?

JACOB: Yes, you remember that we used to talk about it when we were little. We'd always promised each other. We've talked about it so many, many times.

CATHERINE: Yes, when we were children.

JACOB: Yes.

CATHERINE: But maybe we're not children any more.

JACOB: No, that's true.

No, now it's real, Catherine! Now it's going to be just as we dreamed it would be.

CATHERINE: Dreamed. What have we dreamed about?

JACOB: You know.

CATHERINE: Do I?

JACOB: Yes, surely you remember—what we talked about all the time. About how we would live together far, far away from this dreadful country, far away in another land. Don't you remember that?

CATHERINE: Yes, I suppose I do.

JACOB: That's the way it's really going to be now.

CATHERINE: Is it.

JACOB: Yes.

I've thought it through very carefully; I know exactly how we're going to do it. I've been sitting there at home, you see, alone because you wouldn't see me . . . and I've thought it all out. How we'll get there, I mean. And how wonderful it will

be for us out there, how happy we will be . . . you know as well
as I how it is there.

CATHERINE: Do I?

JACOB: Of course. You can't have forgotten.

Surely you remember.

CATHERINE: Yes. I do remember, Jacob. But that was only play.

JACOB: Play?

CATHERINE: Yes. Just play.

JACOB: That may be, but now our play can be reality, it can really be
like that.

CATHERINE: Can it? Do you think so.

JACOB: Certainly.

Goes and sits down beside her:

Do you remember when we played caliph and princess—do you
remember that? How I made off with you?

You sat imprisoned in a tower owned by a great troll who
sucked your blood at night when you slept because he needed
it to make an homunculus—remember? He wanted to make a
homunculus, a real miracle, and that's why he needed your
blood—I'm sure you remember it.

CATHERINE: Yes . . . yes, I do.

JACOB: Yes. You always wanted to play that so much. You lay on
the floor so pale, almost as if you were dead because he had
drained off all of your blood. It didn't seem you were even
breathing—and I was so afraid that you really were dead, but
you thought it was fun that I did. We always played that
game—you thought it up yourself. You slipped away to our
house so that we could play it, ran as fast as you could so that
no one would catch you and beat up on you. The other children
were so bad to you because your father was a sorcerer, you see.
And they were bad to me, too. Only the two of us were good to
each other. We had each other.

CATHERINE *lets him take her hand.*

JACOB: But I kissed you on the forehead, and you woke up, came to
life again. And then we climbed down from a window in the

tower on a long rope that I had with me—and I carried you away! Far, far away . . . All the way to Granada. That's where my palace was. Remember?

CATHERINE: Yes . . . all the way to Granada . . .

JACOB: And there we lived happily to the very end of our lives. For Granada is the most wonderful place there is. There's no other land like it. There *everyone* is happy.

CATHERINE: Are they?

JACOB: Yes.

Don't you remember how we longed to go there?

CATHERINE: Yes . . . I remember . . .

You used to talk about it.

Withdraws her hand.

JACOB: Yes. We used to talk about it all the time. And I described it just for you, how it looked there, how beautiful it was, more beautiful than any place else. There are myrtle forests where you can take long, pleasant walks, and magnificent gardens with roses and jasmine . . . and palms and cypresses, and trees of silver and others with fruits of gold . . . and round about, snow-covered mountains, whole mountains of snow . . .

And our palace was called Alhambra. It was up on a height, and it had gilded domes, and pillars of marble . . . and the walls of every room are of precious stones . . . and everywhere fountains play night and day like the sweetest music . . .

CATHERINE *moves away from him a little*: Say, how do you know all of that really? Have you been there?

JACOB: Well . . . no, I haven't.

CATHERINE: But you said it was your palace—and you haven't even been there!

JACOB: Well, of course I haven't *been* there; that's where we were going to run away to!

CATHERINE: Yes, sure. Run away.

It's amazing all the things you could make up.

JACOB: *Make up!* It's true. My father has told me about it. He hasn't been there either, but he knows exactly how it is there. It *is* a wonderful land. Nowhere else is it so beautiful. —And there a

Jew is just like an ordinary person. He can go about the streets like anyone else, into the houses, anywhere at all. Anyone can be happy there. Because in Granada all of the people love each other.

CATHERINE: No! Do they? Imagine all that love!

JACOB: Why are you making fun of me?

CATHERINE: I'm not Jacob, not at all. But you must understand that we're too big for fairy tales any more.

JACOB, *depressed*: But it's only the part about my palace that's a story . . . that's the only part I made up. All the rest is true.

CATHERINE: Yes, all the rest is true . . .

Smiles at him.

JACOB: Won't you come with me to Granada?

CATHERINE: Go with you to Granada? What do you mean? Dear Jacob, you don't really mean that you are *serious* about this?

JACOB: Serious? Of course I am. How could I be anything but . . . You know . . . I mean I want to take you away from this place where nothing is as it should be, where it's so hard for us, for both you and me, to a land where we can love each other, where everyone can love—I mean we'll flee from all of this, together.

CATHERINE: Flee! You and I!

JACOB: Yes. Certainly. Do you think there is anything so remarkable about that?

CATHERINE: I don't suppose you can believe it, but I really do!

JACOB: It's not at all as strange as you think. It's very easy, if one has the will. It's very difficult for us Jews to flee across the country, but we won't go that way; we'll escape by sea, where there aren't any people. That won't be hard at all, no one can do us any harm. And just think—across the sea! Have you ever seen the sea?

CATHERINE: No. Have you?

JACOB: No, I haven't either. —Oh, the sea is wonderful . . . on a ship with great sails filled with the surging winds, gliding over the waves . . . with nothing but sea and sky around us . . . just floating along . . . farther and farther away . . . until finally we catch sight of Granada's shore, the snow-covered mountains,

the gardens and the myrtle forests . . . the place where you'll
be my bride . . .

CATHERINE *stands up, takes a few steps. Then, without looking at him:*
Jacob . . . do you really know what a bride is? Do you?
*He seems to be embarrassed and doesn't answer. She laughs and goes up
to him:*
Tell me what you think a bride is. Tell me.
Ruffles his hair:
What a child you are.

JACOB: I'm no child compared to you! I'm almost as old as you are!

CATHERINE: Yes, imagine that, you are . . .
Only you haven't a clue about anything.

JACOB: Haven't I? That's funny; I know much more than you do,
I'll tell you, and you know it.

CATHERINE: Oh yes. You know so much, so terribly much . . .
Only you've never done anything, experienced anything.
That's why you're such a little child.

JACOB: Experienced?

CATHERINE: Yes.

JACOB: Well, that may be. —Experienced . . . you certainly haven't
either.

CATHERINE *smiles an equivocal smile. —Goes to him and puts her hand on
his cheek. Chucks him under the chin:*
And you think you could carry off a woman!
Bursts out laughing, twirls around the floor:
Then carry me off! Carry me off! Oh, how I want to be carried
off to a palace full of gold and jewels—by someone who loves
me, *loves* me!

JACOB *touches her:* I love you!

CATHERINE: Take me then! —No, take me as a *man* takes a woman!
Kiss me!
He kisses her.
Oh, you don't know how to kiss! You've never done it before!
Pushes him away.

JACOB: I suppose you have!

CATHERINE: I?

JACOB: Yes!

CATHERINE: Oh so many, many times . . . if you knew, if you only knew . . . You have no idea what love is! What it really is that you're talking about all the time! Do you know how two people love each other, do you! Is there anything about that in your fairly tales! You want me to tell you? And what a palace is! A real palace! With courtiers and lackeys . . . who offer their arms and escort you home through the myrtle forests! . . . or through the back streets . . . the filthy back streets! . . . You and your Alhambra! And your stories! Do you think I want to listen to your childish babbling! I want to live, *really* live! In a real palace! Full of love! —I know what it's like! Can't you see that I have my best skirt on! And gold and jewels!

Fingers her necklace:

Can't you see that I have my bride's dress on!

JACOB: Catherine! What have you . . . ?

Whose necklace is that?

CATHERINE *unclasps it and holds it up while she dances*:

This!

JACOB: Where did you get it!

CATHERINE: I got it from the Prince of Persia, no, I mean of India . . . ! He has a whole chest full of them! Everyone he loves gets one! Everyone! Everyone! Everyone who's a bride in his palace! Who's a bride, who's a bride . . . !

JACOB *rushes despairingly to her*: Catherine! Catherine!

CATHERINE *becomes limp; it seems as if she's going to fall*: You're so foolish . . . —So foolish . . . —Foolish . . .

JACOB *holds her up, helps her to a chair.*

CATHERINE *sits there with an empty, expressionless look, her arms hanging limply.*

In a moment she raises the hand that holds the necklace, looks at it. —*Tonelessly*:

It's really gold. And the stones are quite genuine. —It's rather pretty, isn't it? Don't you think so?

Then, her face contorted:

It's nothing to me!
Flings it away from her onto the floor:
I'll ask my father what it's worth. He'll know. He knows about such things.
Remains sitting apathetically, staring in front of her.

JACOB *stands looking at her in despair, unable to say anything.*

CATHERINE: Aren't you ever going to leave . . . I'd be so grateful if you would go away . . .
JACOB *goes slowly toward the door.*
Turns and looks toward her again.
He goes.
CATHERINE *remains sitting as before.*
Gets up slowly. Listlessly takes a few steps. To the necklace. Gives it a push with her foot. Pushes it again.
Bends down and picks it up. Looks at it. Puts it on again.
She picks up a mirror, looks at herself to see how it suits her, if it becomes her. Adjusts it a little.

MARIA *comes in:* You slut! How can you stand there and hold up the mirror to your shame!
Hurries toward her with the intention of snatching the necklace:
Give it to me!
CATHERINE: I won't either. It's mine. It was given to me.
MARIA: Give it to me, I say! So that I can throw it on the dung heap, where it belongs!
CATHERINE: No, I tell you!
Avoids her.
MARIA: Are you going to wear that . . . that . . .!
CATHERINE: Why shouldn't I. What's the matter with it? It's made of real gold and the stones are pure, can't you see?
MARIA: Pure . . . ! And what did you get it for!
CATHERINE: Because I'm pretty.
MARIA *in a rage, shakes her fists at her:* Oh you, you . . . you think you're pretty!
CATHERINE: Yes!
Looks at herself in the mirror.

MARIA: Look at yourself—that's what you love to do. Sin and vanity, that's what you're thinking of! The only thing . . .

CATHERINE: Oh, stop nagging at me. I'm tired to death of listening to it.

Why can't I have something I like, something that suits me. Why can't I ever have something dressy like other girls. Always having to go around in your dirty, ugly, old hand-me-downs, patched and spattered like the lowest guttersnipe.

MARIA: Because we *are* poor.

CATHERINE *shrugs her shoulders*: I don't like to be poor.

MARIA: No! You want ornaments, gold and jewelry and fine skirts, you have always wanted them—because you imagine you're pretty.

CATHERINE: Imagine? And I suppose I'm not!

MARIA: No, no, you aren't, you aren't . . . —Do you think God has made you pretty, do you think it's he who . . . Oh, why are you pretty!

CATHERINE: Why shouldn't I be pretty! What harm does that do! Why can't I be what I am! You're always after me! I always have to sit here and listen to your bickering, in this awful house, in this dirty alley where everyone's so ugly and filthy, and everything's foul and sickening! I don't like it here, I don't like *anything* about it! I don't like being poor! I *want* to be pretty! Yes! I want to be! And I want gold and fine clothes too! I want to be exactly as I am!

MARIA: As you are, as you are . . . My poor child, how you talk . . . you don't know who speaks from your mouth . . . You have no idea . . .

Sinks down on a chair:

Oh what's the use . . . I've known there'd be no help for it . . . I've known it all the time . . .

It has to be that way.

CATHERINE: Has to be . . . ? What do you mean by that?

MARIA, *her head swaying*: What's the good of struggling against it . . . What good has it done that I've tried to save you and preserve you in every way . . . It has to happen to you, I knew it all

along; you must fall into ruin, you were driven to it. You
can't help it.

CATHERINE: No, I can't. It's not *my* fault.

MARIA *nods her head in agreement.*

CATHERINE: Yes, I know.

MARIA: Nothing has helped. Nothing. And how could I have had
the strength to save you, I was completely helpless . . . How
could I have saved you when I'm so sinful myself, so full of
evil.

CATHERINE *approaches her mother, her hardened face now has an anxious
look:*
Mother, don't talk like that . . . You know that's not so. How
could it be.

MARIA: Yes, yes.

CATHERINE: No mother . . . not at all . . . You are so good . . .

MARIA, *with a deprecating gesture.*

CATHERINE: You've never hurt anyone . . .

MARIA: Never hurt anyone? You don't understand anything . . .

CATHERINE: Of course I do, mother. Of course I understand what
you mean. But you haven't sinned because you've helped him
—he forced you to it.

MARIA: I suppose.

CATHERINE: He alone has to answer for it. You are innocent.
You've helped because you give in so easily to what he wants—
yes, that's it, you're too weak and submissive, that's what you
are.

MARIA: Innocent! Do you think anyone can be innocent if he sins
for the sake of someone else. Oh no, not a bit. How could that
be. Sin is sin and when it is put before the Lord God he'll say
it must be punished, and punished it will be. I've been punished, punished already in this life, and then in all eternity . . .

CATHERINE: No, no! Don't say that!
Mother . . . surely that can't be true?

MARIA: How could it be otherwise, my child? God must take vengeance on whoever's given way to sin. He's forced to. He must

reject him, leave him alone and never look at him again. So it is. That's been borne in on me. He can show no mercy, not to a sinner like me, it's impossible for him.

CATHERINE *hesitantly and anxiously*: No . . . Are you quite sure of it, mother?

MARIA: Yes, yes, quite sure.

There is no hope for me. And there's nothing more to say about it. It must be so. But the worst of it is that I have no one to talk with, to pray to, no one who cares about me.

Already I'm beyond all mercy.

CATHERINE: No, mother . . .

MARIA: You know it's true, you know I am . . .

CATHERINE *looks shyly at her.*

MARIA: That's why I couldn't help you. I'm completely alone, completely forsaken . . .

Looks up at the picture of the Madonna on the wall, with its votive light nearby.

Oh, if only I could have talked with the Madonna about it, with the holy Mother of God, then maybe it wouldn't have happened. She's not as stern as he. And she understands it all so well. But she wouldn't talk with me. She never gives me an answer, either good or bad. It seems she doesn't know me. And of course she doesn't. I know she can't.

I have the light burning before her night and day, but she says nothing. And when I have the money I light a candle in her chapel at St. Thomas, but she says nothing. Nothing. She's never said a word through all the long years.

CATHERINE *puts her hand on her mother's shoulder*: Oh mother . . .

MARIA: I'm all alone, quite forsaken . . .

CATHERINE: Mother, he's the one who's robbed you of your soul's peace.

MARIA *sways her head.*

CATHERINE: But then why do you help him, why do you let him force you to it? That's what I've never been able to understand.

MARIA: What can I do. I have to help him.

CATHERINE: Why?

MARIA: I'm his helping hand, there's no one else.
Who do you think would help with work like that.

CATHERINE: But you, you should . . . !

MARIA: He's accustomed to it. And he could never manage without me, not any of the things he has to do. How could he manage.

CATHERINE: Yes, accustomed to using you! Making use of you! And to not caring what you feel or what you suffer for it!

MARIA: Yes . . .

CATHERINE: What harm he does! But he never cares!

MARIA: No, no . . . I suppose not.

CATHERINE: He only uses you! Bleeds your body and soul! Sucks the blood out of you, that's what he does!

MARIA: Oh . . . how you go on . . .

CATHERINE: He does! And you submit to it! Give in to everything! Why do you do it, mother!

MARIA: There would be so much trouble, dear child.

CATHERINE: There is anyway!

MARIA: Yes, yes, but there would be even more. And he would never be able to manage, I tell you.

CATHERINE: Without you! No, he certainly wouldn't. But why should you sacrifice yourself! That's what I don't understand. And does he thank you for it! For staying here and wearing yourself out in this dreadful house. For his sake!

MARIA: And for yours, too, for all of us. I have to try to hold things together, you see.

CATHERINE: But it's as if you were no more than a bondslave—you let him treat you as he pleases.

MARIA: Oh, no, I don't! Far from it.

CATHERINE: Yes, he treats you exactly as if you were his servant.

MARIA: Yes, but I am. I am a servant.

CATHERINE: But you're his wife too, aren't you?

MARIA: Oh yes, yes, of course. But I came here first as a servant,

and even though he's a godless man and full of sin—as I am—
he's always been a good master to me.

CATHERINE *scornfully*: A good master!

MARIA: Yes, it's true, he has.

Ever since I came here as a poor orphan girl, I've never been
treated other than well in this house. And after we were united
by the Church's bond, through the holy sacrament of marriage,
he has always respected me as his wife and has been a good
husband.

CATHERINE: Good! —The way he is to you!

MARIA: Yes.

CATHERINE: Oh mother . . . you are so . . . you are completely
blinded!

MARIA: Am I?

CATHERINE: Yes, you certainly are. It's impossible to talk with
you.

MARIA: Oh, I think you can.

CATHERINE: Do you think he *deserves* your sacrifice! Do you think
he's worth it!

MARIA: Worth it? —How can I know that. Anyway, you don't
think about such things when you've lived together so long. You
stay with the one you've tied yourself to, and if you suffer for
it, you have to bear it. When you're tied to someone, you have
to stick with him.

CATHERINE *shrugs her shoulders*: What talk! You'd almost think you
love him the way you sound.

MARIA: Love him?

CATHERINE: Yes, the way you talk.

MARIA: Of course I love him. I thought you knew that.

CATHERINE: Do you love *him*!

MARIA: Why, certainly. But dear child, you know that I do.

CATHERINE: *Do* you!

MARIA: Yes, I couldn't do anything else. Of course I do.
And he loves me too.

CATHERINE: He does!

MARIA: Yes, certainly.

CATHERINE: You don't mean it, mother! It's impossible that you
   do!

MARIA: If I mean it? How could I mean anything else, my child.
   I know that he loves me.
   I am the only one he has cared about, he's told me himself.
   And it's true, I don't doubt him. That's how it is.

CATHERINE *giggles*: That's a funny way to show you care!

MARIA: Well, yes, maybe it is. I suppose you're right. But he loves
   me, I'm sure of it. He still does even now. I don't doubt it.
   —Even though it's been a long time since he said it.

CATHERINE: I guess it has!

MARIA: Yes. It has been . . . but that's not odd, not at all so
   strange.
   You see, when you're old you don't ever say any more that you
   love each other.
   Smooths out her apron and looks up at her daughter:
   Dear child, surely you understand that your parents love each
   other.

CATHERINE: No! I don't understand it! I never have understood it!
   Because I've never seen any sign of it!

MARIA: No, no. You don't notice it I suppose. —I guess you don't.

CATHERINE *her face set*: Then maybe he loves me too! Even though
   you can't see it! Even though I've never noticed it. Maybe he
   loves the servant's child too! What a pity he hides it so well!
   Don't you think he hides it well? Don't you!

MARIA: Well . . .

CATHERINE: You'd think he didn't have any feeling at all for me,
   wouldn't you? That he's really a heartless man who doesn't
   think of anyone but himself. Couldn't you get that idea about
   him—the way he acts! That he's a beast!

MARIA: How can you say such things. I hardly know you're talking
   about your father.

CATHERINE: My father! Has he ever shown that he's my father!
   Has he ever done anything at all for me, ever! Cared the least
   bit about me! . . .

She throws herself down beside her mother, sobbing, with her head on her mother's knees.

MARIA *strokes her hair*: There, there, he has, my child . . . he has . . .

CATHERINE: Sending me up there . . . to that disgusting . . .

MARIA: There, there, my poor, poor child . . .

CATHERINE: And you . . . all you do is defend him!

MARIA: Defend him! I do not. Absolutely not . . .

CATHERINE: But you do! —You do! Even though he threw me away like this, gave me to them . . . so that I feel so dirty, so . . . Isn't that his fault! His! Who else's!

MARIA: Yes, yes, it is. It is his fault. But you don't know . . . you have no idea . . .

CATHERINE: What is it I don't know?

MARIA: You have no idea *why* he did it . . .

CATHERINE: Why? You know very well!

MARIA: No, I don't. You don't know . . . There's something about your father that you don't know . . . No one else knows about it, you see. I have kept it a secret, carried it inside myself all these years. You can't imagine what a burden it has been . . . And never anyone to talk to . . . I was all alone with it . . .

CATHERINE: With what . . . what was it, mother?

MARIA: I have never wanted you to know about it . . . But now when you're lost anyway . . .

CATHERINE: Lost?

MARIA: Yes, now you are. The thing that I had expected all along has happened, and I haven't been able to stop it. It makes no difference any more, no difference. And if you're going to talk that way about your father, you had better know it, everything about him, so that you'll understand why he acted as he did.

CATHERINE: You're going to defend him again of course! All you do is try to defend him.

MARIA: I *don't* defend him. You'll soon see. Just the opposite. His guilt is even greater than you ever imagined. My poor child . . . There is nothing more dreadful you can hear about your father . . . And about yourself . . .

CATHERINE: About . . . myself?

MARIA: Yes, yes. You'll wish you'd never heard it.

CATHERINE *looks uneasily at her. Then*: It can't be anything more horrible than I know about him already. What has he done to me!

MARIA: No, no. But you don't know what it really *is* he's done with you.

CATHERINE: Don't I? Then what . . . what is it?

MARIA: You don't know *why* he did it. You surely understand that a father couldn't do anything like that of his own free will. It's impossible that he could. He did it because he was forced to it —through the will of someone else. Someone who has power over him.

CATHERINE: Power over him?

MARIA: He's not responsible for his deeds. Someone else is telling him what to do, and he must do it.

CATHERINE: Silly talk . . . Someone else?

MARIA: Yes.

CATHERINE: Who?

MARIA *looks anxiously about.*

CATHERINE: Tell me what you mean . . . Why are you behaving so queerly . . . Why do you look at me like that . . . ? What *is* it?

MARIA *goes to see that the door to* ALBERTUS' *room is tightly closed. Listens a moment. Then back to* CATHERINE. *—Whispers*: He has sold himself to the devil!
Hastily crosses herself several times.

CATHERINE *also crosses herself and looks frightenedly at her.*

MARIA: He is in league with Satan so that he'll succeed in the god-less work he's doing here.

CATHERINE: No . . . is it . . . is it true! . . .

MARIA: Yes! He is in Satan's power! That's why, you see, that's why . . . It's because of that he sent you up, because the devil said he must—he was *forced* to it! He is forced to do everything he does. Because Satan has him in his power, and so that he can continue with this, with his sinful craft. It was Satan that made him do it, made him send you—because he wanted to en-snare you. You, too, you see!

CATHERINE: No . . . !

MARIA: Yes! And he had a right to you. He's always had. Every-thing here belongs to Satan. And now he has you in his power too, he's lured you to him . . . and put his snare around your neck . . . Now he has his snare around your neck!

CATHERINE *fingers her necklace in fright.*

MARIA: It wasn't hard for him to trap you; you were willing. You were drawn to where he'd laid out his snare for you—and now he has you fast, you'll never get out of it now! You wear it gladly because you belong to him.

CATHERINE *dazed with fright*: No . . . !

It's not my fault! Not mine!

MARIA: You wanted it yourself! Don't you see! You wished for nothing more! Didn't I beg and plead with you! Didn't you go even though I forbade you! And you had to be painted and dressed up to please your Lord Satan!

You wanted what he wanted! You wanted to be his! Now and forever! As everything must be in this unhappy house!

CATHERINE *hides her face in her hands and cries*: Oh mother, mother... !

MARIA: In this house . . . in this wretched house . . . !

Walks about in the room excitedly, while CATHERINE *remains crying*: Where everything is doomed to damnation . . . to eternal damnation . . .

Goes to the oven. Shakes her fists at it:

Will it never go out, this accursed oven burning with a fire fetched up from hell!

Act Two

Some years later. The same setting, but poorer than before, not as much apparatus and as many instruments, less furniture, everything suggests poverty.

ALBERTUS *sits as before beside the oven in his old, worn-out clothes, but he is older and has become gray.*

He gets up and goes across the room several times. Stops, bends over a folio lying open on the table. —Goes back to the oven and sits down again.

MARIA *comes in through the door in the background. She too has become older, seems smaller and withered; her face is thin and wrinkled, her hair stringy and gray. She carries a basket containing bread and turnips which she puts down on a bench to the right. She is tired and sits down on the bench.*

ALBERTUS *doesn't look at her. After a moment*: Well?

MARIA: It was no use. I knew it wouldn't work. And he said that he didn't want me to come again. There wouldn't be any point to it anyway, he said, because he'll never give another farthing. He didn't say so himself, but that's the word he sent down.

ALBERTUS *mumbles something to himself.*

MARIA: And Martin Merchant wasn't home. At least that's what they said. I don't know if it was true.

ALBERTUS *mutters.*

MARIA: They all say they have no money left after this war. They have nothing left over for the poor, they say.

ALBERTUS: For the poor! The poor!

MARIA: Yes.

ALBERTUS: It's not because I'm poor! You might know that!

MARIA: No, no. —If it were only that we were poor they might give a little.
But no one will have anything to do with us. No one who fears God.

ALBERTUS: They never have.

248

MARIA: No, I suppose not. But after all these misfortunes and then
this terrible plague, they are all afraid of, they say that . . .
that . . .

ALBERTUS: I don't care what they say. It doesn't matter to me.

MARIA: No . . .

ALBERTUS *mutters to himself in annoyance.*

MARIA: But then I went in a while to the good mistress Cecilia, and
she took pity on me. She's God-fearing, too, a very God-fearing
woman, but still she is so kind and good to me. She gave me
five stivers.

ALBERTUS: Did you buy that silver salt and the mercury? And the
cinnabar?

MARIA: It was for the household, not for those things.

ALBERTUS: Didn't you *buy* them!

MARIA *unwillingly*: Mmm . . . yes I did . . . That is, they didn't
have any cinnabar.

ALBERTUS: Didn't *have* any! Well, are they going to get some!
—Didn't they say so?

MARIA: He didn't say anything about it.

ALBERTUS *shrugs his shoulders despairingly*: They don't have anything
in this damned backwash. Nothing . . .
Do you have the rest. Let's have it.

MARIA *gives it to him*: It cost three stivers, now I have only . . .

ALBERTUS: Yes, yes, I know.
Takes the things she bought.

MARIA *goes back and sits down by her basket*: She talked with me for a
long time and wondered how we were. And when I left she
gave me this nice bit of bread—she's a good soul. God bless
her.

ALBERTUS *doesn't hear her. He examines the silver salt, weighs it.*

MARIA: I was so afraid she'd ask about . . .
Stops when she notices that he isn't listening:
But she didn't. She's so kind. Yes, she's such a good soul.

ALBERTUS *after a moment*: Maybe she doesn't know about it?

MARIA: About Catherine?

ALBERTUS: Mmm?

MARIA: Oh yes, she does, everyone does.

ALBERTUS *turns away.*

MARIA: I can see that they all do. And some of them mention it to me too.

ALBERTUS *looks at her a moment.*

MARIA: I can see that mistress Cecilia knows too, although it's not quite the same with her. She's always so friendly to me.
Sighs.
But no one thinks whose fault it is.

ALBERTUS: Fault?

MARIA: Yes. No one thinks of that. They all blame *her.*

ALBERTUS: And isn't she to blame!

MARIA: No, she isn't.

ALBERTUS *is silent. Looks at her for a long time.*

MARIA: You know.

ALBERTUS *begins to work intently at the oven. Stirs a mortar. Adjusts a retort. Opens the firebox and looks into it. Takes the bellows and blows more life into the coals inside.*

MARIA *remains sitting, staring ahead of her; there is an expression of tired-ness and loneliness in her old, worn face:*
It's so hard now that no one pays any attention to me, none of the women in the alley do any more. They hardly speak to me. Unless it's to say something rude.
I have no one to talk with anymore.

ALBERTUS: Why should you need that! What good is it! Those gossips!

MARIA: Yes, I know. But it's good to have someone to talk with. It's a comfort. An equal, not someone as fine and good as mistress Cecilia, who never can understand how wretched one is.
They turn their backs when I walk by . . .

ALBERTUS: Because of Catherine?

MARIA: No . . . Not because of that. Because . . .

ALBERTUS: Turn their backs indeed! Why should you care about that! Let them do it! And they stick out two fingers to "protect" themselves, I suppose—that's what they do to me!

MARIA: Yes, yes.

But before, they would talk with me. I could talk with just about anybody, just like any other person.

I feel so empty not having anyone to talk with.

ALBERTUS: Can't you gabble with the old Jewish women? There are plenty of them here in the alley, and they wouldn't mind.

MARIA: No, but I don't want to talk with them.

ALBERTUS: Why not? You did before.

MARIA: Yes, sometimes. But I don't want to any more.

ALBERTUS *shrugs his shoulders and goes back to his work.*

MARIA *after a pause*: It's strange . . .

ALBERTUS: Yes, yes, there's so much that's strange. Everything is strange. I can't sit here all day and listen to your foolish talk. I have to think of my work.

Leans over his work table:

Now that I've finally gotten this . . . this silver salt . . . Cinnabar! Why don't they have cinnabar! . . . They never have anything . . .

MARIA *rises*: I guess I'd better go . . . and prepare a little food for us . . .

Goes toward the kitchen door. Hesitates. Remains standing with the basket on her arm:

But it is strange how everyone keeps on talking about these evil times, and all the misfortunes and everything. It seems to me we've never had anything but evil times. How could it be otherwise with all the wickedness in the world?

ALBERTUS *doesn't listen to her.*

MARIA: Just now when I was up in the square to buy these turnips and a bit of pork, some of them stood there talking about it. Nils Hawker and Maria Lacknose and many others. — Magdalena, she was there. But she didn't see me. She doesn't any more. And she said . . . She said if they only hang the wizards and those that crucified Our Lord Jesus Christ this terrible plague would soon be over by itself.

ALBERTUS *runs his fingers through his hair*: These . . . these idiots! They are mad . . . completely mad!

And you want to talk with the likes of them! They're the ones you'd like to gossip and keep company with! Fools like these!

MARIA: I know, I know. But after all, she is my neighbor; and before, we'd always stop and talk a bit when we met, and she was even in here sometimes, and I'd go see her. She was almost a friend, she was.

ALBERTUS: You miss her, I suppose?

MARIA: No, but . . .

ALBERTUS: That gabbling old woman! Can't you avoid her!

MARIA: Yes, yes, I suppose I can. But it's so lonely that way. I feel so alone.

ALBERTUS: Lonely! Because you can't gossip with that rabble! That won't do you any harm! —Now how about me! I haven't talked with anyone for years. Hardly go out even! —Lonely! —Talk with someone! —Why should I do that!

MARIA: No, that's right. But you don't need to.

ALBERTUS: No! What need would I have for it! Nor do you either! You just imagine it.

MARIA: Yes, yes . . . maybe so. Maybe I do.

But it's hard not to be like others.

ALBERTUS *shrugs his shoulders scornfully. Returns to his work.*

MARIA: I didn't answer her. I hurried to buy what I came for. Well, all I bought were turnips—I didn't bother about the pork. I couldn't really afford it either. And I thought maybe that would show her that we are poor, and that it wasn't true what she was thinking of us.

ALBERTUS: What she's thinking of us? What do you mean by that?

MARIA: Well, if it were true, we wouldn't be so poor.

ALBERTUS *understands what she refers to*: Of course it's not true! Even you can understand that! You're not that stupid.

MARIA *sighs*: No, no, I suppose not . . .

Well, I'd better get started with my work.

Goes into the kitchen.

In again, after a moment.

Simonides . . . that Simonides is coming! And his son . . . Surely they are not coming in here!

ALBERTUS: Simonides?

It's been . . . many a day.

MARIA: Yes! We've been rid of them all of these years. Surely they'd never think of coming here!

ALBERTUS: Oh, no . . . I don't believe so.

MARIA: What shall we do if they . . . ! Shall we lock the door!

ALBERTUS: Lock the door? What do you mean? Why?

MARIA: Because . . . because . . . What have they to do here?

ALBERTUS: Oh . . . well, perhaps he wants to see me and have a word together. It's been several years now. Perhaps he has something he wants to talk with me about.

MARIA: *Talk* with you about! About what! What's the use of that!

ALBERTUS: No, no, you're right. He's not much to talk with. He's really a very ignorant man. Oh, of course he has read some of the great authorities, I must admit that—but he hasn't understood them. He's full of errors and confusion. Full of them!

MARIA: Shall I lock the door!

Goes to the door.

ALBERTUS: Lock it! What do you mean? He's my friend.

MARIA: Friend! Is *he* your friend!

ALBERTUS: Yes, he is. He certainly is. Do you want me to close my door to a friend. What makes you think of such things?

MARIA *anxiously*: Why do we have to have anything to do with those people? . . .

ALBERTUS: Those people? What's the matter with them?

MARIA: They . . . they crucified Our Lord Jesus Christ . . .

ALBERTUS: What kind of talk is that? That's sheer madness!

MARIA: But they have . . .

The door clapper is heard. —Whispering:

Don't open it! If we don't open it they'll think we're not
home!

ALBERTUS: Nonsense!

Rises and goes to the door:

Come in.

SIMONIDES *comes in, followed by his son. Goes toward him and seizes his
hands:* Master Albertus . . . my friend . . . my old friend . . . !

ALBERTUS: So . . . Simonides the rabbi. Is it really you.

SIMONIDES: Yes, my path took me this way—and I wanted so much
to see you again . . . It has been such a long time . . .

ALBERTUS: Yes, it has. That's true.

SIMONIDES: Yes. Everyone is busy with his own tasks. I seldom go
out anywhere. I sit at home reading the old texts, the holy
texts. I have no time for much else. But today I said to my son
Jacob, My son, I want to go and visit my friend Albertus, the
philosopher. I want to talk with a man who is searching for
wisdom—which so few thirst after in this world—in these
days—in the vain, thoughtless world that surrounds us. This is
what I thought in my loneliness, and I told my son, Jacob. And
he asked if he might accompany me here to your house so that
he, too, might listen to your words and hear what such a man
could have to say to us and teach us.

ALBERTUS: Yes, yes. You are most welcome in my house.

Both bow deeply with hands over their hearts. With a gesture ALBERTUS
asks them to sit down, but they remain standing. JACOB, *shy and
troubled, stays behind his father a couple of paces. He has become even
more round-shouldered, and seems run-down from too much study, and
appears absent-minded, although the childishness has disappeared from
his pale, thin face. He looks around carefully and timidly in the room he
knew so well once, as if afraid that he would attract attention.*

SIMONIDES: Are you in good health?

ALBERTUS: Yes. Yes, I think so.

SIMONIDES: And your wife is well?

ALBERTUS: Yes. She too.

SIMONIDES: It pleases me to hear that you are . . . pleases me very
much . . .

Catches sight of MARIA *for the first time, bows to her.*
While he is bowing he looks about in this poor home.

Peace in thy house . . . Peace in thy house . . .

MARIA *withdraws to the kitchen.*

ALBERTUS: And you, rabbi?

SIMONIDES: I? —I am well, by the grace of the Almighty.

The Lord allows me to grow old like a tree, without pain. But
not without sorrow. No, not without sorrow . . . And how
could I ask that of him. Sorrow is his gift, like all else. And of
that which makes the face sorrowful, the heart fares well, saith
the Preacher. I need not complain of him.

And you, my friend? How is it with you? Well? Or do sorrows burden you, too?

ALBERTUS *looks at him a moment. Then:* No. I can't say that they
do.

SIMONIDES: No . . .

Nothing gladdens me more, my friend.

And your work? It goes forward?

ALBERTUS: Forward? Yes, I suppose it does. I try as well as I can to
bring it to a finish, and it seems as if I've made some progress.
But it is not easy to be sure about such things.

SIMONIDES: No, no. Surely not . . .

But you still sit here at your philosophical oven, and I am sure
that you have discovered many things in these years, solved
many riddles . . . Yes, yes, surely you have. —My friend, it is
such a pleasure to see you again . . . and to see this room,
dedicated to the venerable science, your work table, your old
oven, still burning day and night, to be sure . . . everything
quite like it was before . . . or almost so . . . Oh what a joy it
is to step into this house from a world of discord and unrest,
into a room where a man seeks wisdom . . .

ALBERTUS: Oh . . . wisdom . . .

I look only for the truth, for some little knowledge about it.

SIMONIDES: Yes, yes . . . human wisdom . . . human truth . . . But just the same, it is not a little thing either, nothing to scorn.

ALBERTUS: No. Absolutely not. If one can only find it, then it is a great thing, a great thing indeed.

SIMONIDES: Yes, yes, perhaps . . . Verily, verily, it is so.

I am so untaught in these things. I do not live in the world of things, and I know too little about it. But I have thought of you so often, as I sit in my lonely study, in my thoughts . . . Well, not really in *my* thoughts, in *God's* thoughts . . . I have thought of you and *your* studies . . . We are both seekers, we are both students, although our paths are different . . . and all of our paths are imperfect and full of difficulties . . . Yes, and what are my studies really but a kind of search for human wisdom, a man's search for understanding of the Lord God's purpose and will with us, his meaning in all of the unrest and sorrow he lays up on us. What do I know of his mysteries. He does not reveal them to me, not even to his own servant and to his people. Yes, this is what I have thought in my loneliness, especially in these latter days when thoughts lay heavy on my mind . . . as perhaps you too have felt in your loneliness . . . Of course I am not really alone . . . not in that sense . . . I always have my Lord and God.

But what was it you said about *your* sorrows?

ALBERTUS: My sorrows?

SIMONIDES: Yes.

ALBERTUS: My . . . ?

SIMONIDES: Yes. Your difficulties—and that it is not easy to be sure what progress you are really making in your art?

ALBERTUS: Well, yes . . . Aha.

It's clear enough that it must be hard to decide what is real progress and what may be only imagined, results which lead nowhere at all. One may be right, or may only have gone astray; a new discovery may prove to be something imagined. One can't be sure. And sometimes it seems one knows so little, so very little.

SIMONIDES *nods in agreement.*

ALBERTUS: Nor do I have the chance any more to complete my experiments as I should like to do—the cost is so great. And perhaps instead I spend too much time on theories, fantasies perhaps—they cost nothing. That's no good, you know. One must try to find out how things really *are*, how they really fit together. And I don't have the instruments or the ingredients any more; I can't afford the things I need.

SIMONIDES: No, I see that is true.

ALBERTUS: But I continue as I always have . . . just as before.

SIMONIDES: Yes, yes. And you have no doubt that you will finally reach your goal?

ALBERTUS: Goal?

SIMONIDES: Yes, to find the philosopher's stone, I mean.

ALBERTUS: The philosopher's stone . . .
No . . . no, I'll find it sometime . . . —But it's far off. Very far . . .

SIMONIDES: Yes, yes, I understand you. I understand you so well. But you still have time. There is still much that you can do. You're really not so old yet.

ALBERTUS: Old? No, I suppose I'm not . . . —Old . . . ?
Well, I guess I don't have the strength I once had, that may be . . .

SIMONIDES: No, you can't expect to have.

ALBERTUS: But I stay here by my oven and do my experiments every day and learn a little bit more each time, I have no doubt of that.
But in many other ways I have my doubts.

SIMONIDES: So . . . Is that right? Aha . . .
But if you are in doubt, you can go to the noble fathers of your science, to the great authorities.

ALBERTUS *nods his head in agreement.*

SIMONIDES: There you will find what is true. —And I see that you do. They lie open here, just like my texts in my study at home.

Mm, I do not wish to compare them to these, that would be...
But anyway you know what you have to hold yourself to.

ALBERTUS: Hold myself to?

SIMONIDES: Yes?

ALBERTUS *thoughtfully*: When you read them, you can also begin to
have your doubts, it's not just when you seek the truth yourself.

I have my great teachers and my deep and learned books to re-
fer to, just as you have.

But my texts can be read in so many ways.

SIMONIDES: Yes. They are works of men; they must have many
meanings.

ALBERTUS: Yes, it must be so. Naturally they *must* be that way.
You have no such troubles, my dear rabbi.

SIMONIDES: No, I have not.

ALBERTUS: I know.

SIMONIDES: My troubles do not concern myself.

ALBERTUS: Myself! I have no troubles about myself either! Who
has said that I do?

SIMONIDES: Haven't you?

ALBERTUS *mumbles absently*: Myself . . . myself . . . What does that
mean! . . .

SIMONIDES *observes him carefully. Then*: I am troubled about my
people.

ALBERTUS: Oh. Oh, I see.

SIMONIDES: Yes, my unfortunate people. What will happen to us,
the people of my faith here in the alley? It is them that I am
thinking of.

ALBERTUS *shrugs his shoulders*: How should I know? —Are you in any
particular danger?

SIMONIDES: Haven't you heard what we are accused of? They
blame us for the misfortunes after the war, the bad harvests,
for all the poverty, that so many are dying of hunger, and now
for the plague. You must have heard.

ALBERTUS: They have to blame somebody.

SIMONIDES: Why is it always us? What law have we broken?

ALBERTUS: Law? Do you think they would ask about that?

They are mad and don't know either what they think or do.

SIMONIDES: No, that is true. And that is why my people are so uneasy. Just as I am, just as I am. We have lived through so much, you see. My heart is heavy with the thought of it. This is why I have come to you, my friend. I could not bear it any longer there at home in my loneliness.

I felt such a strong wish to seek you out . . . perhaps you too . . .

ALBERTUS: Yes, they blame me for it too—me and my tricks of magic!

SIMONIDES: Hmm . . . yes. Aha, you have heard that story? I wondered if you knew about it.

ALBERTUS: I certainly do. When things go bad for them they always begin to think of me. Then they begin to brood about what it really can be that I'm doing here at my oven.

SIMONIDES: Yes, they understand nothing at all of what you call the divine science, and the mysteries of these things you work with.

ALBERTUS: No, they don't! And nothing of the mysteries that occupy you in your synagogues, and how you pray to God. Why shouldn't they blame you! Or me! Or the hunchbacks—it's happened to them too—because they are not quite like other people!

SIMONIDES *troubled, shakes his head.*

ALBERTUS: It's hardly worth any notice. You can't expect fools to have any sense. Sense! Sense is a very rare gift! Very rare. If the world had sense, everything would be completely different.

SIMONIDES: Yes.

And none of them realizes that it is the Lord who punishes them for their sins.

ALBERTUS *mutters*: No, no, I suppose they don't.

SIMONIDES: And that men are full of sin and arrogance that he must punish, no one thinks of that.

They don't understand their misfortunes because they don't understand their sin. Or that the Lord must take his hand from

them. They want to bear their sin, but not the punishment—
they want somebody else to do that. They want to avoid it, and
to be spared vengeance. And they ask this of the Righteous
Lord! They would like to upset his order of things, if they
could. Change his laws, as if they were men's work.

But they cannot be changed. He has established them and keeps
them in force. And whoever rebels against them shall be chastised. Who else should be chastised! He reads in men's hearts
as in a book and nothing escapes him. He sees who is guilty.

He is a fool who thinks he can burden another with his guilt.

ALBERTUS *looks at him a moment.* —*Then*: Yes, yes. You needn't despair. God punishes the wicked and not the righteous.

The righteous have nothing to fear.

SIMONIDES: No. We who wander in his paths, who know his law
and live according to it, we can have nothing to fear. He holds
his protecting hand over us; he does not forsake us. Not his
own people. And this is what I tell my brothers in faith, fear
not! And I also tell my son, you shall not be fearful! Among
us God is our Lord; no harm can befall us.

ALBERTUS: Oh no. Surely not. You needn't be uneasy about it. Not
any more than I am. I sit here quietly by my oven and am not
worried about anything. At least not for that sort of thing.
Even though I am an alien here too and have nothing at all
to depend on. We are surrounded by irrational creatures, as we
always have been. But I have lived here the greater part of my
life without being molested. And you have too since you came
here. In that sense it's a good country, a good place to be to
seek the truth, —although inhabited by fools, like all coun-
tries.

SIMONIDES: Yes, yes. You hear, my son! Master Albertus thinks
just as I do!

You see that I was right. He doesn't think there is any reason
to be uneasy. He has no fear himself. And he receives us in his
house just as before. You see, our people still have friends—he
is still my friend. Oh master Albertus . . . my faithful old
friend . . . You see, I wanted so much to have my son come to

hear you speak just such words as you have spoken now. It does us good to hear them, we who always sit at home in our loneliness, in our many lonely thoughts. And I wanted him to meet a learned and wise man, a philosopher, because he himself studies so earnestly and thirsts so much for learning.

ALBERTUS: So-o . . . Does he.

SIMONIDES: Yes, he earnestly pursues studies in many subjects and makes very good progress. I hardly need to guide him any longer, he is so much at home in the scriptures and the old sources.

JACOB *very embarrassed.*

SIMONIDES: His knowledge of the Talmud, in both the Mishnah and the Gemara is really so . . .

JACOB: My father, I beg you, please do not talk about me in that way.

SIMONIDES: Why shouldn't I tell about it, my son? You know yourself that it is true. I am only telling the truth. His wide reading in the Talmudic literature is really astonishing for a man of his age. He already knows a great part of it. He has a receptive mind, and he has absorbed the knowledge and wisdom of the fathers and, of course, all of the beautiful legends which appeal so vividly to his imagination, but also the commentaries and elucidations and the most difficult and obscure texts. Yes, and I assure you, he is even beginning to be well acquainted with cabala.

JACOB: My venerable father has too high an opinion of me, master Albertus.

I am a completely ignorant young man without knowledge of anything.

SIMONIDES: Ignorant! He knows both Hebrew and Aramaic as well as I do, and even in Greek he hardly needs help from me any longer. Soon enough he will be able to find any of the key passages and to read and enter into the thoughts of the great teachers.

ALBERTUS: You'll soon be as learned as your father.

JACOB *shakes his head*: No, no . . .

ALBERTUS: Oh yes. You surely will. And you will be a rabbi, just as he is.

SIMONIDES: Yes, certainly, he certainly will.

Yes, God has been merciful to me. The Lord has been merciful to us, master Albertus.

ALBERTUS: Yes, I see that he has.

SIMONIDES: He has given me a son after my own heart—and after his, after his—a blossoming branch of my old tree, the old tree of our fathers. I need not be anxious in my old age about my offspring, as so often is a father's lot. His thoughts are turned toward the Lord and things immortal, not toward this world with its sin and error and all of its wantonness. He lives for nothing else but his studies, never thinks of anything but them. He never has—no, he never really has . . .

And he has written a poem in the best Hebrew, a poem, can you imagine—yes, I happened to find it among some things he'd hidden away, and I think it is so beautiful, so full of the finest feeling, something in the style in which the great Jehuda ben Halevi in Granada wrote his wonderful poems— with an imagery, a glowing imagery, as in the Canticles . . . Yes, yes, it *is* true . . .

JACOB *extremely troubled and agitated, doesn't know what to do with himself.*

SIMONIDES: Well, perhaps I am talking too much about myself and my son, about my life. It is because my heart is full of gratitude to the Lord. The credit is all his. It is his blessing that has given me this undeserved happiness in my old age.

Pauses a moment.

I should like to ask you about your daughter, my dear friend.

ALBERTUS *gives him a hard look.*

SIMONIDES: I hope she is in good health?

ALBERTUS *coldly*: Yes. She is.

SIMONIDES: I am glad to hear it. I don't suppose she is at home?

ALBERTUS: No. She isn't.

SIMONIDES: No . . . No, I see . . .

Yes, yes, I leave my house so seldom and it's been a long time since I saw her . . . But I hope that all is well with her.

MARIA *comes pattering in from the kitchen*: Yes indeed it is! She lacks nothing; I think she'll manage. She earns her own keep and isn't a burden to her old parents. No, she wouldn't think of troubling us, and so it's no wonder she's not at home. Is there anything else you'd like to know?

SIMONIDES: No, no . . . not at all . . . not at all . . .

ALBERTUS *begins to work with his mortars and materials on his work table, doesn't look up.*

A long silence.

SIMONIDES *finally*: I hope I am not disturbing you in your work?

ALBERTUS *mumbles*: Disturbing me? —No, you're not.

Silence again.

"THE NIGHTCOCK" *jerks open the outside door and comes bursting in with* CATHERINE, TILDA TROOPTUB, MALENA SACKSTRAW, *and the student,* CLEMENS. *All of them are excited and more or less drunk.*

NIGHTCOCK: Damned Whorerake, guess we sent him on a fool's errand! No catch for him! Let him just try to smell us out—he won't find us! When he ever gets back on his hind legs again, that swine! You gave him a good one, boy!

CLEMENS: I'm well taught in that fine art! He went down like a bellows!

NIGHTCOCK *with a loud guffaw*: I saw it! I saw it! He caved in as if his guts plugged up! And his eyes bulged out like an ox's! Just the way it should be done, boy! Perfect, bless me, perfect! Just what he needed! —That polecat! Fat ass! Insult a lady! And a nobleman! *A nobleman!*

Damn him, he insulted me, too! Whoever insults my lady insults me, too! I should have run him through!

TILDA *laughing loudly*: You, you!

NIGHTCOCK: Yes! I certainly should have!

TILDA:—Why didn't you then!

NIGHTCOCK: Why? Why not? Are you mad? I can't fight with a simple town constable! With Lucas Whorerake!

TILDA: No, that's one thing you're careful not to do!

NIGHTCOCK *taps the hilt of his sword*: This sword wasn't made for the blood of swine, my dear. It has drawn blood for His Grace in many a battle, it has fought—!

TILDA: And you—you've campaigned in the whorehouse!

They all laugh uproariously except CATHERINE, *who has stiffened and remains standing motionless when she notices* JACOB'S *presence.*

NIGHTCOCK *with an ostentatious gesture*: Yes! Yes, I have! Tilda Trooptub, you are magnificent!

Throws his arms around her:

I . . . !

No, I don't.

Puts his arms around CATHERINE *instead:*

But if I didn't love little Catherine, you know . . . !

CATHERINE *frees herself.*

TILDA: And many thanks to you! You have loved me more than enough, you old nightcock!

NIGHTCOCK: You don't say! You don't say!

Puts his arm around CATHERINE *again:*

I'm saved, my little chick! Saved! —Aha, is this where you live . . .

CATHERINE *frees herself again.*

NIGHTCOCK: This is an odd place . . . A damned peculiar place... And it smells like the devil in here! —But it makes no difference! No difference! Do you have any ale! Strong ale! I'm thirsty as the devil himself!

Jauntily sits down on a chair:

Well, you see, we sat carousing in peace and quiet at Malena Sackstraw's house—that's her over there, that's Malena Sackstraw, known and respected by the whole town, when who should come in but that blowzy meddler and begins to mouth off and kick up a fuss about this being a whorehouse, and goes poking and hunting through the whole shack, but there was no one else but the two of us there, for it was early, you see, they don't come 'till later, and him talking shit about immoral liv-

ing and laws and decrees, kiss my ass! Because you know those
idiots are about to close the whorehouses, the fools, the bloody
fools. Before long there'll be no place left for a decent man to
go! Close the houses! So that custom and usage will match the
people's worry and want! Then life'll be poor! Damn me if it
won't be really poor! Huh, what do you say, eh? Well, he
puffs himself up, that scoundrel, and makes to jaw with me—
with a nobleman! Answers me as if I were an equal! Gabbles
and goes on! That made me mad—this is no whorehouse, I
said, yes it is, he said, no, I said, the hell it is, this is a very
decent house kept by our highly respected Malena Sackstraw,
and there are no more women in here than in a Trappist
monastery—except for these noble and virtuous ladies whom
you may consider guests at my table, or me at their's, which is
none of your business, you filthy bootlick! He makes to *answer*,
the bumpkin, not knowing better! Even though I *told* him how
things stood. And you know what he said? He said: "Wherever
the Nightcock hangs his hat it's always a whorehouse."
Breaks out in wild laughter.
That's what he said, the clown! Devil take me if he didn't!
"Where the Nightcock hangs his hat . . . where Nightcock
. . . !" I laughed so hard I nearly split my breeches! But then I
told him: Go along now, Lucas Whorerake—you know they
call you Whorerake, don't you, a name you bear with every
right and honor, as I do mine. Let us part as friends before
we've insulted each other. But do you think he went! Hell no!
He stood there gabbling that it was a whorehouse, a bawdy
house, a proper nest, and that Malena Sackstraw and Tilda
Trooptub he knew well enough and could lay his hands on any
time, but he'd take Catherine with him, for by now who didn't
know she was a slut, and it was into the stocks with her, and
then she'd have to wear the hat of shame like the others, and
tonight they'd come and shut down the place. And so he pulled
her off my lap and took her by the arm and hauled her off! I
sprang up, of course—mad as a hornet—but they'd gone! As
soon as we'd come to our senses and found out what happened,

off we went to rescue the little girl. And down in the alley we
caught up with them and there they stood barking and howling
at each other like dog and cat, that is, Catherine growled like a
mongrel and hissed like a wildcat—she was furious: "Never in
my life, you pig! Never! I don't mind the stocks, that's all
right! But never with you, lard-belly, you rotten, hulking
bastard!" And then we heard it all, if you'd like to know! And
what a pure and edifying story it was! That swine had said to
her that if she'd lie with him, he'd not put her in the stocks,
and look the other way this time. What do you say to that,
eh! Nice boy! That's why she got so foaming mad and hell's
provoked! She's a fine little girl, now, isn't she! Splendid,
bless me, splendid! She's a pure heart and she has scruples, indeed she has!

MALENA:—Well, I say as I did before, Catherine might as well have
given him his way. She could, you know. One more or less
doesn't make all that difference.

TILDA: The hell she should have! That catspaw, that whoregoat,
sniffing around all over the place! And what an old sow of a
man he is!

MALENA: Eh, what talk. They're all the same anyway. And you and
I have done him many a time, as you well know, how'd we
manage otherwise.

TILDA: That may be. But has it ever helped?

MALENA: Oh, sometimes.

NIGHTCOCK: No, you've been sitting there in the stocks many
times over, and been lashed besides for the sake of your lovely
sins!

MALENA: Shut your snout, Nightcock, it's none of your affair!

CLEMENS: I smacked him on the jaw anyway, that half-wit, and a
good job it was!

NIGHTCOCK: Yes, that's what I said to Clemens, give him one on the
jaw, I said, don't stand here and gabble, just give it to him,
and he did! And then he fetched him a jab the likes of which
he best deserved, and down he sank, and so we cut and ran!

CLEMENS: He'll not be popping up again in one jump!

NIGHTCOCK: Believe me, he won't! Not the way he hit the cobbles!

MALENA: Oh yes, he will, there's nothing but dung in the whole alley down there. He'll come to, soon enough. And he'll have his way just the same. It never was any use to kick up a row with them turnkeys that has authority; there's no fun in that.

TILDA: Authority!

MALENA: Yes, I suppose he's appointed by His Grace somehow, just like every other turnkey.

Believe me, she'll not get away from Lucas Whorerake. No one has. I know him. She could have gone home with him a while, that would have been the brightest thing to do. But now she's fixed it for herself. Now she'll have to lie in the bed she's made.

TILDA: Not with that cur anyway!

MALENA: Who knows. They always get their way.

CATHERINE *gives a scream*: No, I tell you! No!

MALENA: Well, we'll see, we'll see.

CATHERINE: No! no! no!

MALENA: Would you rather sit in the stocks?

CATHERINE: Yes! I would!

MALENA: I guess you wouldn't know anything about it until you've been there. It's not the kind of pleasure you seem to think. You haven't tried it, little girl; you don't know what you're talking about. Oh no, sitting out there in front of St. Thomas, that's not easy, I'll tell you, in front of God's own house, when everyone you know walks by and all the decent women with the candles going in to the merciful madonna—but there's no mercy for you, you can be sure.

CATHERINE: I don't care! Don't care at all! It's not my fault I'm going to the stocks!

MALENA: Not your fault?

CATHERINE: No!

TILDA: No, of course it's Lucas Whorerake's!

MALENA: Maybe, but don't deny you've lived in sin like us and made your keep by it. So I guess it wouldn't be so far from wrong to say that it's not your fault that things have gone the way they have.

CATHERINE: No! It isn't! It isn't!

NIGHTCOCK: Catherine is right! The little baby girl's innocent, quite innocent; I certainly ought to know!

TILDA *gives a laugh.*

NIGHTCOCK: She's a fine girl! Comely, bless me, comely . . . !

MALENA: Oh no. If you give yourself to this, you've yourself to blame. You have to answer for what you do, and if the truth shall out, there's some pleasure in it, but all too little at that. And you suffer for it, you do; there's no doubt of that. But if you're this world's child, well there it is and no help for it. Better see it for what it is. Whose fault is it that you're the way you are if not your own?

CATHERINE *points to* ALBERTUS: His! His!

MALENA: What are you saying? His fault? That's your father, isn't it?

CATHERINE: Yes, he's supposed to be. But he's the one who's made me the way I am, a whore that anyone can lie with! That idiot there, and Lucas Whorerake! Anyone! And now I'm going to the stocks!

Goes toward him. ALBERTUS *reels back:*

Are you satisfied now!

Are you satisfied with your goddamned oven, tell me how your devil's tricks are turning out, have you made any gold yet, or has your luck run bad!

Takes out some gold pieces from the pocket inside her skirt and flings them onto his work table so that some of the glass breaks:

I can make gold! I know the trick! Satan's taught me how— how far has he gotten with you? It's so simple! I've learned it all! But then, you see, I got started early! I was only a child when you gave me my first lesson!

MALENA: Lord preserve us . . . what do you mean? . . . what . . . ?

CATHERINE: What do I mean!

MALENA: It's your own father you're talking about . . . What has he done to you?

CATHERINE: He's sold me to the devil!

MALENA: What . . . sold you to . . . !

THE OTHERS: Sold you to . . . ? — —Sold her to . . . ?

CATHERINE: Yes! He has! Him there! To get money for his black arts and hellish deeds, he's sold me to his Lord Satan, whom he serves!

ALBERTUS: Quiet child. You are out of your wits.

CATHERINE *goes toward him*: Am I! Am I! —Can't you see his noose around my neck, do you recognize it, do you! Do you remember when you put it around your child's neck! Remember! So that I'd belong to him as you two agreed! Do you remember that! Is it strange that I've become what I am! Don't you know that I'm lost, and it doesn't make any difference how I live, because anyway I belong to him for all time and eternity! That I go about with his noose around my neck, with his noose, his noose, so that I'll never get away . . . !

Draws the chain tightly around her throat:

It's of purest gold, because I was to wear it with joy.

With joy . . . with joy . . .

Begins to sob:

I am lost . . . I belong to Satan, I belong to Satan, as everything does in this house . . .

MALENA: Catherine!

ALBERTUS: She's dazed . . . She doesn't know what she's saying . . .

MALENA AND TILDA *cross themselves in fright*.

NIGHTCOCK *also makes the sign of the cross*: Damn . . . ! What in hell is . . . !

Wipes his brow:

And the oven there . . . and that oven burning there . . .

CLEMENS *bursts out laughing*.

NIGHTCOCK: And it smells like . . . —What is that smell in here! . . .

CLEMENS: It's only a little sulpher and ammonia, that's all.

NIGHTCOCK: Sulpher! . . .

CLEMENS *guffaws*: Yes. You ass! Do you think there's any danger in that, hmm?

Goes and looks at the work table:
Sulphuric acid, quicksilver, ether—antimony. It's the divine
science that smells like that. Actually rather bad. Lead, tin, of
course—blue vitriol. The divine and exalted science . . .
Goes and looks at the oven:
And the philosophical oven—aha. The oven for boiling up a
mess of philosophy, aha! The great elixir and the lesser elixir—
the philosopher's stone.

CATHERINE: It burns with a fire fetched from hell!

CLEMENS: The devil you say! It burns ordinary charcoal, and not
very well at that. It's old, soon burnt out, not much left. You
ought to get yourself a new one, old man; let them wall up a
new one for you if you've got the change.
Turns to the others:
The old boy's just trying to find the philosopher's stone, you
know. Primordial matter, the truth itself, the great harmony
in God's glorious work—figure out the universe and a few
things like that. Innocence itself. All sorts of fools are doing it.
Nothing can be more harmless—well, yes, of course, if they
should find it. But they'll never find it.

MALENA: It's sinful! It must be sinful! . . . And if he sold her to
the devil . . . !

CLEMENS: Don't talk such crap! Sold to the devil! . . . what
horseshit!

LUCAS WHORERAKE *jerks open the door. His face is scraped and bloody; he
looks around wildly. Catches sight of* CATHERINE: Oh there you
are, you damnable whore! I caught up with you after
all!
Now you're coming along with me, you understand! Tomorrow you're going in the stocks, devil see to that! And
screw me too, both one and the other, then maybe you'll see
who's master here!

CATHERINE *in dread, tries to get away from him.*

ALBERTUS *goes toward* LUCAS *as if to strike him.*

JACOB *at the same moment hurls himself at the constable, rushes at him
like an enraged boy, skinny but with the incredible power of his blind*

*fury, clutches his throat with his thin, spare fingers so that the constable
wavers and falls backward on the floor.*

SIMONIDES *calls—hurries forward and tries in vain to stop him:* Jacob!
—Jacob!

NIGHTCOCK: That's right! That's right! Give it to him!

JACOB *hears nothing, lies on top of him, his fingers around his neck.
Rises finally, panting.*

NIGHTCOCK: Well done, boy! Well done! You gave it to 'im—
damned if you didn't!

CLEMENS *goes and bends over* LUCAS: But . . . he is . . . he's dead . . .

TILDA: Dead?

CLEMENS: Yes.

MALENA: Dead!

NIGHTCOCK: Is he *dead*?

CLEMENS: Yes. He is.

Whispers among them: Dead . . . —Dead . . . —Dead . . .

SIMONIDES *covers his face:* My son! My son!

MARIA *throws herself at the foot of the image of the madonna over by the
wall to the right:* Holy Mother of God! . . . Holy Mother of
God! . . . — — —
Why don't you hear me . . . !
She collapses.

CATHERINE AND JACOB *stand motionless, looking at each other.*

THE NIGHTCOCK *and his following, frightened, sneak toward the
door, but remain in the doorway looking in astonishment at them both.*

Act Three

A room in the palace.

ALBERTUS *stands in his shabby clothes before the* PRINCE, *who sits leaning back in a chair.*

ALBERTUS: But your Grace, it is impossible; he can't have done it. Although he's over twenty, his body's small and weak and he has hands like a child's. It's obvious that he can't have strangled him.

PRINCE *looks at him doubtfully.*

ALBERTUS: He wouldn't have had the strength to do it. —It *was* I who did it.

When the PRINCE *does not answer:*

How could he have overpowered him. It was all I could do to manage it, but suddenly I was given strength I didn't think possible.

I am the murderer, I bear the guilt. That's why I've come, to ease my conscience.

PRINCE: This is strange. Very strange.

ALBERTUS: I beg your Grace to take me at my word. I am an old man and ought to be taken at my word.

PRINCE: If what you say were true, it would seem that during your long life you haven't acquired very much wisdom. And still the purpose of your work is to acquire it, is it not?

ALBERTUS: Wisdom? No, your Grace, I haven't acquired any wisdom.

PRINCE: Well, frankly speaking, I've never thought that what you're doing carries with it any great measure of good sense, or that it's particularly rewarding. Perhaps you know that.

ALBERTUS: Yes, your Grace. And I don't think so either. Not any longer. In my old age I've come to exactly the same conclusion as your Grace.

PRINCE: Well. Then we are obviously in much better agreement

than we were before. Than when we met last and you wanted
me to give you gold, so that you could make—gold.

ALBERTUS: I've never said I could do that! Never!

PRINCE: Didn't you? No, of course you didn't exactly . . .

ALBERTUS: I said that I needed gold to continue my studies in
science, to seek the truth! That's all I said, nothing more!

PRINCE: Well, then. Have you found it?

ALBERTUS: No. I haven't. Has your Grace himself found it?

PRINCE: I? What prattling! As far as I know I never set out to find
it. I'm not such a fool to waste my life on such things. That I
leave to you and your kind, if it gives you any pleasure.

ALBERTUS: We don't get any pleasure from it. But we seek it anyway, as well as we're able.

PRINCE: An absurd idea when it can't be found anyway. Completely
absurd!

ALBERTUS: I suppose I'm the only one who is a fool. Most of my
respected colleagues think they can find it or already have.
But I know I never will.

PRINCE: I have never noticed such modesty in you before, master
Albertus.

ALBERTUS: I'm not as modest as you think, your Grace.

PRINCE: Aha. No, perhaps not.

ALBERTUS: It is the others who are modest, your Grace.

PRINCE: Oh. —Well, this is nothing to me. But tell me now, my
good master Albertus, why do you come to me to take the
blame for something which you are probably not guilty of and,
as far as I know, no one has accused you of?

ALBERTUS: Because I am guilty.

PRINCE: So?

ALBERTUS: I am guilty and no one else.

PRINCE: It's possible. I don't know the details of this matter. I
have only heard that a Jewish boy is said to have killed a constable, that he's been seized and is imprisoned for it.

ALBERTUS: He has nothing to do with this crime. I committed it, I
alone. The murder was committed in my house, and *I* am the
murderer.

PRINCE: This is strange, but I really find it very hard to believe that you could do anything like this. I don't believe it of you.

ALBERTUS: Why not! Why can't you believe it of me!

PRINCE: It is not easy to say, good master Albertus. One simply doesn't believe it.

ALBERTUS: Why not? Why not me?

PRINCE: Yes, why? How shall I explain it really.

You see, perhaps you amount to something, perhaps you are of some use when you are sitting by your magical oven or whatever it's called—that is possible, of course. I know nothing about it. But I don't think you have it in you to kill a constable who has come to take away your daughter. Which he, by the way, had every right to do. One simply can't believe it of you.

And you say that this Jewish youngster didn't have the strength. But where then did you get *your* strength?

ALBERTUS *is silent.*

PRINCE: Can you tell me?

No, I don't believe your story. And now I have no more time for you. I have heard you as you asked—now you can go.

ALBERTUS *standing helplessly. Then*: I did it for revenge!

PRINCE: Revenge! For what?

ALBERTUS: My daughter's dishonor!

PRINCE: Dishonor? But surely she is responsible for that. Who else?

ALBERTUS: No! She isn't! You are; your Grace is responsible for it. You debauched her!

PRINCE: Consider to whom you are talking, old man.

ALBERTUS: Sacrificed her to your infamous way of life. One of your victims! You make human sacrifices! Lay waste everything! You are the cause of it! Of her misfortune! And mine, too! Mine, too, do you hear! It was my *vengeance*! My *vengeance*! On you, and your ne'er-do-wells who understand nothing! You with your idle, empty lives which are completely useless!

Completely! You with your power and brilliance and incompetence to which everything must be sacrificed and which costs men their happiness! You who believe you are the masters of the world because you spread poverty and wretchedness everywhere! Rulers! What rulers! You have no idea what you rule over and nothing more about your work than the worst bungler! You are bunglers! Bunglers! But you must have everything, subdue everything, you believe that everything belongs to you! And you make a mockery of him who cannot make gold for you . . . Gold! gold! that's all you care about! The only thing you understand! Or *think* you understand! Even though you haven't the slightest idea what it is! But you know how to *use* it! For your crimes and atrocities, your wars and your fancies and adventurous enterprises—for all of your vain, meaningless world! You are fools! Fools and criminals! Do you hear! Does your Grace hear what I'm saying! What I'm throwing in your face! I'm not afraid to tell it to you! To speak the truth! Which you do not waste your life to seek! I say it out loud! And throw it straight in your face!

The PRINCE *has risen, but he says quite calmly and coldly:*
You seem to be a little muddled, old man. You are a little excited and confused, aren't you? You are not thinking very much about what you're saying, or perhaps of what these words can cost you.

ALBERTUS: I know, and that is exactly what I wish, your Grace. And therefore your Grace's power over me amounts to very little.

PRINCE: I'm not so sure of that.
Observes him a moment:
Tell me, really, why are you so disturbed that I don't believe you'd committed that murder?

ALBERTUS *is silent.*

PRINCE: Because I haven't let you be thrown in irons when you pretended you were guilty of it. Well?
I don't intend to do that. I intend to punish the one who was

really bold enough to do it. *He* shall be punished, and not any-one who comes to me and tries to make me believe that he has done it. And to make himself believe that he has avenged his daughter by killing a constable. What you are pleased to im-agine is no concern of mine. You may have thought of doing it, but at least for *you* it came to nothing.

ALBERTUS *stands looking down at the floor.*

PRINCE: With respect to my supposedly having debauched your daughter, as you put it, you offered her yourself. Didn't you? For the sake of your divine science. So that you could seek the truth. Isn't that so?

ALBERTUS: Yes . . .

I didn't mean it that way. But I must judge myself as if I had.

PRINCE: Yes. Why do you come here and accuse me? What right have you? You sacrifice people too.

ALBERTUS *bows his head.*

PRINCE: For a higher purpose than mine, of course. But anyway. Obviously we are both guilty of a crime. But as far as I am con-cerned, I have no pangs of conscience about it; what cause have I? I don't think people are so terribly valuable. As I see it, they are rather trivial and unimportant.

Don't you really think so too?

ALBERTUS *gives him a despairing look.*

PRINCE: One can make use of them if one wishes. They don't de-serve anything better. Nor will it make their lives in any way more meaningless.

Isn't that also your view? At least it's mine. And I act accord-ingly. And you as well, I should think.

ALBERTUS: Sentence me for my crime! Sentence me! I *am* guilty! I have confessed my crime! . . . Why can't I be sentenced! . . .

PRINCE: What crime?

ALBERTUS: What crime . . . —It *was* I who strangled him . . . it was . . . I *am* guilty! Why won't you believe me . . . why won't you take my word for it . . . I am an old man . . . I have nothing to live for . . . nothing at all to live for . . . that's why I did it . . .

PRINCE: Oh . . . is that *why*. That's another matter.

Well, now I understand you better.

For your own sake . . .

ALBERTUS: Yes . . . I thought my life was worthless . . . And I wanted to avenge my daughter and all the injustice I've suffered . . . And when I saw that filthy constable force himself into my house and outrage my daughter I was filled with disgust and rage . . . rage . . . It's quite natural, easily explainable, isn't it . . . and if your Grace will think about it . . . of what I must feel . . . how enraged I was . . . enraged . . . when I saw . . .

CATHERINE *in, throws herself down on her knees before the* PRINCE: Mercy! Mercy! Pardon him for the sake of God's mercy . . . !

PRINCE: What is the meaning of this? How did you slip by the guard!

CATHERINE: I begged and pleaded with them until they let me through . . . Mercy! Mercy!

PRINCE: What are you talking about? Who shall I pardon?

CATHERINE: Jacob, the rabbi's son, who they have imprisoned and intend to condemn to death.

PRINCE: Do they intend to. I haven't heard anything about it.

There now, arise.

He helps her up. Regards her:

Aha, such lovely decoys they have in the bawdy houses. It was obviously wise of me to have them closed—during this difficult time.

CATHERINE: Your Grace, I implore you, have mercy on him! Have mercy . . . !

PRINCE: I really don't understand what you mean.

CATHERINE: Yes, yes! . . .

PRINCE: No, I really don't.

The one for whom you ask my pardon is innocent, you know. He hasn't at all committed the crime he is accused of.

CATHERINE *astonished.*

PRINCE: He was not the one bold enough to do it, and who for your sake is guilty of this mad action. The guilty one stands *there.*

CATHERINE *confused. Looks at her father without understanding anything.*

PRINCE: Your father has just confessed. He has come to ease his guilt-laden conscience. Isn't that true, master Albertus?
ALBERTUS *looking at the floor:* Yes, your Grace.

CATHERINE *looks speechlessly at her father.*

PRINCE: He insists definitely that he and no one else is the murderer. And he becomes very upset if one doesn't believe him. You may ask him yourself.
ALBERTUS *looks pleadingly at* CATHERINE: You know that I am guilty. You know it—better than anyone else.
That's why I'm here, to receive my punishment.
You can bear witness so that they'll believe me.

CATHERINE *does not answer.*

ALBERTUS: You saw yourself how I strangled him. You were standing right there.
CATHERINE: Yes . . . yes . . . well, yes, I did . . .
ALBERTUS: There, your Grace can hear for himself!
CATHERINE: No . . . !
PRINCE: Aha, you say it really was your father who strangled the constable?
CATHERINE: I didn't say that! . . .
ALBERTUS: Yes you did, Catherine! And you know it's true!
CATHERINE: No, no, I said that . . . only that I was standing nearby, quite near . . .
PRINCE: So? Is that what you said?
But who strangled him then?
CATHERINE: I don't know, your Grace, I don't *know* . . .
ALBERTUS: Don't you know who is *guilty*, Catherine. You surely do. You have told me yourself many times.

CATHERINE: No . . . no, I haven't . . . I don't know . . . I don't
know anything . . . — —Only that I . . . that I am full of
sin . . .

PRINCE: Yes, most certainly. But we are not talking about that
now.

CATHERINE: We are full of sin . . . and all of us shall be damned . . .

PRINCE: Yes, yes. But who has committed this murder?

CATHERINE: I don't *know*, your Grace, I don't know anything . . .

PRINCE: I can't make anything of this.

Rings a bell.

A SERVANT *in.*

PRINCE: Henricus, the court recorder—call him in.

SERVANT: Yes, your Grace.

Out.

PRINCE: You stood quite near—and know nothing.
You are not a very good witness.
Can't you tell us the truth, Catherine. Master Albertus is very
careful with the truth. He searches constantly for it.
Well, tell us now!

CATHERINE *helpless, does not answer.*

ALBERTUS: Catherine, you know that I am guilty. Before you and
before God, I am the guilty one. You know what I've said is
true. But his Grace will not take me at my word. Won't you
convince him of my guilt. I am an old man . . . a worthless old
man . . . why won't they take me at my word . . .

CATHERINE *looks at him without being able to answer anything.*

RECORDER *in.*

PRINCE: Well, here comes the court recorder who has been in
charge of the investigation. Perhaps now we can finally discover how all this fits together.
It's about that Jewish boy accused of murdering a constable.
How does the matter stand? It is said that actually he's innocent.

RECORDER: Innocent? The accused has made a full confession,
your Grace.

PRINCE: Well, then.

RECORDER: And several witnesses have been heard, among them a nobleman.

PRINCE: A nobleman, indeed. What sort of nobleman is it who moves in such lofty circles?

RECORDER: A man named Valentine, your Grace . . . also called the Nightcock.

PRINCE: The Nightcock . . . a peculiar name. Is it that Valentine who was with us in the field for a time?

RECORDER: Yes, your Grace.

PRINCE: Then I know him. Or have known him, to be more exact. So he was present at the event in question.

RECORDER: Yes, your Grace. And furthermore, it was he who informed against the murderer, presumably to avoid being suspected himself.

PRINCE: Aha. That was very thoughtful of him. He also left the battlefield to avoid any suspicion that he might have killed some of the enemy. Evidently he is always thoughtful.

There is hardly any reason to suspect him of the murder.

RECORDER: No, your Grace, there isn't.

PRINCE: No. I understand. He does not draw his sword for such displays of courage as this. Not at all.

The Nightcock . . . a most peculiar name . . .

RECORDER: All of the witnesses testified that the Jew, Jacob, son of rabbi Simonides, was the murderer.

PRINCE: Aha. Very good. *Very* good. You may go.

RECORDER *goes out.*

PRINCE: Well, master Albertus? What do you say about that?

ALBERTUS *stands with his head bowed.*

PRINCE: I believe I shall be forced to acquit you of this murder. It was nice of you to assume the guilt for it, but you should also have *carried* it out. Anything less will not do.

I'm sorry that I can't help you, but it's impossible; you have committed no crime. I cannot be guilty of any unjust decisions.

But that's right, I can sentence you for choosing your words rather carelessly and improperly when you spoke to your lord and prince. I can always do that, of course. The offence is trivial. No one can attach any great importance to it. Least of all I. The punishment cannot amount to much. But I will sentence you as you deserve.

Gestures toward the door opening, A GUARD, *in.*

Put him in one of the dungeon holes for several days, so that he can think a little bit more about what he has said. Perhaps he may find a few more great words to speak against those who have power in the world, though they have no idea how to use it. But remember that he shall be treated well—he is not to be disturbed in his bold thoughts. No fetters—and give him good food. He shall have nothing to complain about here.

THE GUARD *seizes him.*

ALBERTUS: I am an old man . . . I have nothing to live for . . . Why should I live any longer? . . .

PRINCE: I don't know, old duffer. That's your business, hardly mine.

ALBERTUS *is taken out.*

CATHERINE *throws herself down at the feet of the* PRINCE *again*: Pardon him, your Grace . . . ! Be merciful and pardon him, for God's sake!

PRINCE: Calm yourself, my dear.

CATHERINE: For God's and Jesus Christ's sake . . . !

PRINCE: Now, calm yourself a bit . . .

CATHERINE: For Jesus Christ's sake . . . !

PRINCE: Such talk. Should I pardon a Jew for Christ's sake—what do you think he'd say about that? Don't you know they were the ones who crucified him?

CATHERINE: Be merciful, as our Lord Jesus Christ was full of mercy!

PRINCE: Now, now. It's impossible, my child. You must realize that.

CATHERINE: No, no, nothing is impossible for a prince . . .

PRINCE *lifts her up*: Such a child! —Yes indeed, it is. Do you believe
  that I may do exactly as I please. That I have such power. But
  what would the people say then?

CATHERINE: That their Prince is full of mercy!

PRINCE *laughs*: They would pull down the towers in their rage!

CATHERINE *mumbles something to herself as she continually fingers and
  twists the chain around her neck*: For Jesus Christ's sake . . . for
  Jesus Christ's sake . . . and your Holy Mother's . . . Holy
  Madonna . . . hear me . . . hear me . . . have mercy . . .

PRINCE *stands looking at her*: Imagine being so loved.
  Do you really love that Jewish boy so much? Yes, he has given
  his life for you, he has done that. But would he be so remarkable if he didn't have to give his life, if I should pardon him?
  Then he would be nothing. It seems to me you ought to think
  about that. Hmm? Why should we rob him of his singularity
  —that would truly be a sin, I think, if *he* were allowed to live.
  Don't you think?

CATHERINE: I beg it of you on my knees!

PRINCE: Yes, and I'm greatly moved. But it is not I who deter-
  mines his fate, but the law. I must condemn him as a common
  criminal—which he is, by the way.

CATHERINE: No, he isn't! . . .

PRINCE: In the sight of the law he is nothing else. He has committed a brutal murder—he really *is* guilty. Why do you want
  him to be treated as if he had done nothing? I really don't understand it. What kind of justice would *that* be?
  If I were you, I wouldn't ask that he be pardoned.

CATHERINE *by herself, with her eyes closed and one hand clutching the
  chain*: I know that all my prayers are in vain . . . always in
  vain . . .

PRINCE: It is no pleasure for me to condemn him to death, not at
  all; surely you know that. How could it be? I should like to be
  able to avoid it. That would be pleasantest for me. But a prince
  may not think in that way. He has many burdensome duties.
  It is my duty to condemn him as the law requires. I am powerless to do anything else.

CATHERINE *dully*: May I see him once more while he's alive?

PRINCE: Yes, of course. Of course, you can. As a matter of fact, I would like to see him myself, I must admit.

Rings.

A SERVANT *comes in.*

PRINCE: Let Jacob, the rabbi's son, imprisoned for murder, be brought in.

SERVANT: Yes, your Grace.

Out.

PRINCE: I shan't bother you—only for a moment, then you can be alone with each other. Lovers usually want to be alone. Will that be all right?

Holds her chin in his hand:

Can one see in your eyes how you love him? . . .

Is that how they look when they love . . . it must be something curious indeed . . .

Is he very handsome? As handsome as you are, perhaps?

How can it be that you love him so much? . . .

CATHERINE *turns her face away.*

PRINCE: Why do you turn away? May I not see your face . . . surely you won't begrudge me that . . . The look of eyes full of love . . .

CATHERINE *fiercely turns away*: No, no . . .

PRINCE: So . . . let me see . . . It's not easy for a prince to see anything like that, you know . . .

Plays with her necklace:

To put a chain around someone's neck, that's not so hard . . .

Nor is there much pleasure in it . . .

It pleases me that you wear it, I can't deny it . . . You always shall.

CATHERINE *whispering to herself*: Yes, yes . . .

PRINCE: One who has been given such a chain should always wear it.

CATHERINE *whispering*: Yes, yes . . . I shall always wear it . . .

JACOB *is brought by the* EXECUTIONER'S GUARD. *His hands are securely linked with irons.*

PRINCE *to himself*: They all wear their chains . . .
Shrugs his shoulders. Observes JACOB *for a moment*:
Is it he you love?

CATHERINE *does not answer.*

PRINCE *shakes his head*: I have never understood anything of love.
Goes toward a room to the right. Turns around in the doorway. To the EXECUTIONER'S GUARD:
You may leave too. Stand by outside.
These two doves are to be alone a while.
Out.

EXECUTIONER'S GUARD *goes out to the rear.*

CATHERINE *goes to* JACOB *and takes his hands. They stand for a long time just looking at each other. Then*: Why did you do it . . .?
JACOB: Because I love you.
CATHERINE *with her head on his chest*: Oh, Jacob . . . ! Jacob . . . !
How cruelly I've rewarded you . . . always, always . . .
JACOB: Still you have made me happy. I have always been happier than you.
CATHERINE *looks at him*: Yes . . . yes . . . —Can you call it happiness?
JACOB: Maybe it ought to be called something else.
CATHERINE: No one would call it that.
What curse has chosen me to make you happy in this way.
JACOB: You couldn't do it in any other way, Catherine. But I don't blame you for it.
CATHERINE: Oh, Jacob, if you would blame me, if you would . . .
All this is my fault. I am to blame for all of it.
JACOB: Yes, for everything. To blame that my life's been filled with love.
It was as I dreamed it would be. You became my bride. But not here. How could we love each other here? We lived to-

gether far away where we could be happy. Where you could love me.

CATHERINE *sobs, her head on his chest.*

JACOB: I was always so happy in my dreams. And in them, you were happy too, Catherine.

CATHERINE: Was I?

JACOB: Yes. You were. Otherwise maybe you weren't.

CATHERINE: No, no . . .

JACOB: I often asked you if you were. And you'd always answer, I'm happy when I'm with you, only with you.

I knew that you were just as lonely and forsaken as I was. Even more than I. I had you. But you had no one. If you don't love, you have no one. Nothing to live for and nothing to die for.

CATHERINE: Oh Jacob . . . — — —You must not die for me!

JACOB: I won't, Catherine. I'll die because I don't belong here. Because I have nothing to do here. Don't you think so, too? Everything is so alien to me, I don't understand it. I never have.

I have always wanted to live in dreams. And now I'm going to a place where that's all I'll need to do. It will surely be much much better. Everything's much better there, far, far away. There everything is so different . . .

CATHERINE: I want to come with you, Jacob . . . I want to go too . . .

JACOB: No, you can't. Not *now.*

CATHERINE: Can't I?

JACOB: You can't come with me *now.*

CATHERINE *clings to him.*

JACOB: You must not think that it's so hard to move on from here; it isn't. It's no great sacrifice. I go freely. I want to with all my heart.

It is here that it's difficult.

CATHERINE: Yes, yes, it is here that it's difficult . . .

JACOB: Everything is much better there, far, far away . . .

CATHERINE: Yes . . .

JACOB: I've thought about it down in the dungeon, how wonderful
it is. I long for nothing else.

CATHERINE: To your Granada, Jacob . . . ?

JACOB: Yes . . . but not the one I used to talk about.
It doesn't exist, Catherine. There is no country where everyone loves each other. I realized that long ago.

CATHERINE *hides her face on his chest*: Pardon me . . . !

JACOB: It can't exist. It is only love that exists. Its realm is some-
where, where lovers long to go. There nothing is like it is here.
There they know they can be happy.
I can see it when I close my eyes. But I can't describe it. It
can't even be described for one you love. It's something that
you must see for yourself.
I want so much to go there. You understand me, don't you.
But I'll carry your image with me in my heart.
Takes her head in his chained hands.

CATHERINE *bends down under them so that his arms and the chain are
around her. Embraces him fiercely*: Take me with you, take me
with you, Jacob! I don't want to be here either, not here . . .
Take me with you . . . take me with you to your Granada! . . .

THE PRINCE *and* TWO COURTIERS *in from the right.*

FIRST COURTIER: Ohhh, what amour! What amour, your Grace!

SECOND COURTIER: True love, your Grace!

PRINCE *does not answer. Merely stands and looks at them.*
JACOB *shyly frees* CATHERINE *from the chained embrace.*

FIRST COURTIER: By the madonna, I call that love!
When the PRINCE *still does not answer:*
Not so, your Grace?

PRINCE *is silent. Just looks at the two young people. —Shrugs his shoulders:*
Now you have taken a sufficiently tender farewell of each
other. Enough of this!
*Goes to the door at the rear and gestures to the guard out in the corridor.
To the* COURTIERS:
We meet at table, gentlemen.
Out.

COURTIERS *bow deeply as he leaves.*
The EXECUTIONER'S GUARD *comes in. At the same time a disturbance outside the open window to the left captures their attention. Voices and laughter are heard.*

FIRST COURTIER: What is it?
Goes to the window. Leans out.

SECOND COURTIER *follows him. Also leans out the window:* That old Jew—who is he?

FIRST COURTIER: Isn't it that rabbi, Simonides or whatever he's called?

SECOND COURTIER: Yes, I think it is. What does he want?

FIRST COURTIER *to some of them down there:* What does he want?

Their answer is not heard clearly.

SECOND COURTIER: Unleavened bread? Unleavened bread for the prisoner? Why?
They answer something.
They say it's because of the feast of the Passover!

FIRST COURTIER: Must he eat unleavened bread because of that? Curious. Extremely curious.

SECOND COURTIER: Yes. And it isn't Easter now in any case.

FIRST COURTIER: What a fanciful notion! Strange people indeed.
The loud laughter of the guards is heard below.
They are just laughing at him.

SECOND COURTIER: Look! Now he's tearing his hair! He's out of his mind.

SIMONIDES *is heard calling below:* My son! My son!

JACOB tries to free himself in order to get to the window.
The EXECUTIONER'S GUARD *stops him.*
More loud laughter from below.

FIRST COURTIER: They are mocking the poor old man.

SECOND COURTIER *calls down:* Let him alone now, don't pay any attention to him. He'll go away.
They leave the window and go toward the door to the right.

FIRST COURTIER *with a jerk of his head toward the young couple:* Touching, isn't it? I think the Prince felt quite sentimental. But I'd guess he has no objection to that boy being the murderer.

SECOND COURTIER: Certainly not.

FIRST COURTIER: The timing couldn't be better.

SECOND COURTIER: No.

FIRST COURTIER: Shall we have a round of backgammon before dinner?

SECOND COURTIER: Yes, perhaps so. We have just enough time.
Out.

The EXECUTIONER'S GUARD *takes* JACOB *by the arm to lead him away.*

CATHERINE *clings to him*: Jacob! Jacob! . . . You must not . . . you must not die . . . !

JACOB *strokes her hair*: It's not hard, Catherine, not hard at all . . . I do it gladly.
I can't feel sad, as you do, I can't cry . . . if you knew how happy I am not to have to live here . . . how happy . . .
This is the place of tears.

The EXECUTIONER'S GUARD *separates them.*

CATHERINE: Jacob! Jacob! . . .

EXECUTIONER'S GUARD *takes him away.*
CATHERINE *remains standing, her hands covering her face.*
Goes out falteringly.
The stage is empty.

SIMONIDES' VOICE *is heard outside*: My son! My son!

Act Four

In the laboratory some days later. No one on stage. And the oven has gone out.

ALBERTUS *comes in from the alley, a broken man. Absently he leaves the door open behind him.*

Looks about in the room as if he were a stranger there. Goes to his work table and looks at his instruments and materials as if he didn't recognize them. Goes to the oven, feels that it is quite cold. Then he sits down tiredly, not beside the oven as he usually does, but away at the other end of the room. Rests his head on his hands.

After a while,

A BLIND MAN, *cane in hand, comes groping along out in the alley. Comes into the doorway*: Isn't there anyone here . . . not a soul . . .

> *Feels his way into the laboratory*:
> I've lost my way . . . I don't know where I am . . .
> *With his cane outstretched he goes straight toward the work table with its glass retorts and instruments.*

ALBERTUS *becomes alert when he sees this*: Watch out!

> *Goes to him and turns his cane away.*

BLIND MAN: *Is* someone here! — — —Is there some person here!

ALBERTUS *as if to himself*: Yes . . . — — —Yes, there is.

BLIND MAN: Oh, God be praised.

> *Tries to find him, touches his shoulder*:
> I'm all alone, you see, quite helpless. —That scamp of a boy has run away from me, left me all alone; of course, he couldn't miss seeing that Jewish boy beheaded . . . well I'll not say anything about that, I suppose it might be good for him; but to run away from me like that and leave me all alone . . . there isn't anyone left here except me, they are all up there, every one . . . it's all right I suppose, let them do it . . . but it's no pleasure for me; I can't see anything anyway.
> But where am I now?

ALBERTUS: You're in Narrow Alley.

BLIND MAN: Oh, am I? . . . How have I gotten in here? . . . Narrow Alley—then I think I can manage to find my way back.

And you? Who are you?—Why aren't you up there? It's supposed to be a real entertainment, they say, and edifying too, for men of Christian mind. I've never seen it. I've never seen anything.

Who are you?

ALBERTUS: I? I am an old philosopher by the name of Albertus.

BLIND MAN: Oh . . . Philosopher? What's that?

ALBERTUS: Yes, there's a question one may ask.

BLIND MAN: I've never heard any talk about that. But I'm glad I found you so that you can help me find my way.

Narrow Alley . . . that's where the Jews live . . . You're not a Jew, are you?

ALBERTUS: No, I am not.

BLIND MAN: Mmm, I see. No, you're a good man. Well, now they have to leave, you'll be rid of them.

ALBERTUS: Leave? Are they going to leave?

BLIND MAN: Yes, certainly. You must know about it.

ALBERTUS: No, I didn't know it.

BLIND MAN: Strange, and you living in the same alley. Don't you really know!

ALBERTUS: I haven't been at home for a while.

BLIND MAN: Oh . . . oh that's it. Yes they shall. And this very day too. As soon as the execution is over and he's had his just punishment, they're to be off. They're to leave the country, you see. Not surprising . . . all the evil they've done, even cutting down the Prince's own guards. I've no idea all the trouble they've caused; I can't keep track of it. But times will get better now, they say, happier times are coming, that's what they all say. We'll all be well off. —Is this the way I go to get to South Gate?

ALBERTUS: Yes.

BLIND MAN: I know then. I know I can find my way. —Yes sir, can you imagine that rascal! And I pay him well, too! He gets a fourth of all we beg; I'm sure he cheats me out of much more than that, he tricks me, I know he does . . . It's not easy being blind, I can tell you, philosopher . . . did you say philosopher? No sir, not so easy. Thank the Lord thy Creator that he's let you keep the light of your eyes, that you don't wander in the darkness as I do . . .

ALBERTUS *helps him out.*

BLIND MAN: Thank the Lord, thank the Lord . . . —Now I know where to go . . . it's not easy . . . now I'll find my way . . . not easy to be blind . . .

ALBERTUS *closes the door after him, stands for a moment thinking. Goes and sits down again far to the right in the room.*
MARIA *and* CATHERINE *come in, formally dressed, in black. Depressed and silent.*
CATHERINE *sinks down on a chair by the table; lays her head down on it.*

MARIA *goes about, her head swaying, mumbling something to herself:*

God be merciful to him . . . God be merciful to him . . .
Catches sight of ALBERTUS:
No . . . are you here? When did you come? Now?

ALBERTUS: Yes.

MARIA: Did they let you go?

ALBERTUS *nods in affirmation:* My punishment wasn't very severe.

MARIA: No, no, how could it be, you hadn't done anything, nothing at all.

ALBERTUS: No . . .

MARIA: They couldn't condemn an innocent man, could they?

CATHERINE *lifts her head, looks toward her father.*

MARIA: I was so worried when I came home and saw that you were gone; I thought you'd lost your senses again like that time you were wandering around the streets not knowing . . .

ALBERTUS: Lost my senses! . . .

MARIA: Well . . . I mean . . . If Catherine hadn't come and told me about it, I'd have never known where you were. —How did they treat you in prison?

Have you had a bad time of it?

ALBERTUS: No. I haven't.

MARIA: You must have. Did they give you anything to eat? Are you hungry? Shall I fix something for you? —You look terrible.

ALBERTUS *shakes his head*: That's because I haven't had any sleep.

MARIA: Hadn't you better go in and go to bed then?

ALBERTUS: Later. Not now. I can't sleep anyway.

MARIA: No, no, it's not easy to sleep on a day like this . . .

She sways her head:

You haven't been up there, I suppose?

ALBERTUS: No. They let me out so that I'd go see it. But I didn't.

MARIA: No, no . . . It was a grievous sight to behold, to see him die like that . . . I didn't think I'd be able to bear it. But just the same, he didn't show how much he suffered, he didn't want to, I guess; what do you think, Catherine, he didn't want to show them. He went to his death so peacefully and quietly, one would have thought he was happier than we are. I can't understand where he got the strength to do it. Because no one read for him; he wasn't allowed to hear a word about our Lord Jesus Christ, no, just sneers. The Jews prayed, of course, but who knows what they prayed. And Catherine, she kneeled and prayed right beside him. And I prayed with her as well as I could so that she wouldn't be alone, even though I had no idea how to pray for a Jew's soul. But what good could it be. Alas, poor child, it was no help to him. But I think it was a comfort that Catherine was kneeling there close by, so that he could see her to the last. That made it easier for him. But how could that help his *soul* . . . what will happen to his soul? . . . Without a priest or anything, no one reading for him about Our Saviour . . . Who can save him who comes before the face of God with such sin . . .

CATHERINE *sobbing*: Simonides read for him all the time, mother!

MARIA: Yes, yes, he did . . . he did, but what use could that be. And anyway he read in a language not a soul could understand. How could that help him.

ALBERTUS: It must have. His father is a servant of God, too. It must have helped him to hear his father.

MARIA: Do you think so? It would be a blessing if it were so.

Goes to CATHERINE, *lays her hand on her head.*

My poor child . . . my poor . . . —I won't try to comfort you, one shouldn't and one can't . . . but may God's Mother give you peace, may your mind have peace and consolation when you come under her watch and care.

Turns to ALBERTUS:

Can you imagine the gift of grace that has fallen to our lot. Catherine is to be received as kitchen help in the house of the good sisters in the Order of Our Lady; she shall be under their supervision and strict rule. Perhaps then Satan will not reach her any more. I can hardly believe that it is true that such good fortune should be granted us who are so undeserving.

It is the good mistress Cecilia who has arranged this to our great joy; she's talked with her good friend the prioress, she's spoken well for the child and they've agreed to take her. The prioress was very hesitant, you see, but that's to be expected in the case of a creature lost to God, and from a house like this besides. But finally she was convinced and said she'd do it, and it pleased her, she said, to have a chance to snatch this prey of Satan from his claws. What mercy, what great mercy she has shown us . . . I can't believe it's true.

ALBERTUS: Do you yourself want this, Catherine?

CATHERINE: I want nothing else on this earth. I want it with all my heart.

Mother, do you think she's sure to come today, is it certain?

MARIA: Quite certain, she'll surely come when she promised. She has many things to do in town first, but then she'll come and fetch you here. —It's Sister Teresia she's talking about, she's coming to take her to the convent today, they'll go together.

You'll have a lot of work, and hard work too, you must remember to be ready for it, as I've said before. Washing and scouring and all such things you're not used to, you'll have to do all the time, except the cooking—may the Madonna forgive me for not having you do those things at home; I've always done them myself, and now that you'll begin to serve her you know so little. Being a lay sister in Our Lady's household is no idler's job, you know, most surely not. But I'm sure you'll do your very best to please her so that she'll be well satisfied with you.

CATHERINE: Yes, yes, mother I will. I *will*. I will do everything to please her; I won't live for anything but her.

MARIA *strokes her hair*: My child, my dearest child . . . that you may live in Our Lady's house, our dear Lady's house . . . to leave you to her and perhaps never be worried about you any more, not to wake at night and not know where you are . . . and not be able to pray for you . . . she lifts the anxiety from my heart, from a poor mother's heart, and I need not trouble any more... Blessed be her name for all eternity . . .

Do you have everything ready, my child?

CATHERINE: Yes, yes, I have, long ago.

MARIA: That is well. We don't know when Sister Teresia intends to come; she may be here at any time. And then she will certainly want to leave right away; we must not let her wait for you.

CATHERINE *leaning against her mother's breast*: Oh mother . . . you don't know how I long, how much I long to go there . . .

MARIA, *moved, strokes her hair.*
Movement out in the alley; THE JEWS *stream into it, returning from the execution. A hum and commotion are heard and the subdued agitation of voices speaking in an unintelligible, foreign tongue.*

SIMONIDES *in, dressed in a full-length robe with many folds, his head covered*: Lord, Lord, how can you let this happen! Why is your hand still, why don't you raise it against your enemies and crush them! Against the godless who taint your earth with their crimes, who fill the world with their misdeeds! Why don't you strike them to the ground and show that you are the Lord, the Lord! No, you strike down your servant and stretch out your arm to destroy him! You take vengeance on him in your wrath, on your own people, who fear you! You let us be punished by your retribution, and the feet of the unrighteous are on our necks, and they triumph over us! Lord, Lord! What do you mean by this? What do you want of your people whom you yourself have chosen, and of your servant who has lived all his life for you! How long shall you persecute me! How deep into my breast will you drive your insatiable sword, filling me with anguish and suffering! Will you not be satisfied soon with your bloody work! Behold me, Lord, behold me! Like a tree without branches I stand before you—who has hewn them off! Like a ravaged old tree that once spread its crown and bore green leaves and excellent fruit. Who is the Almighty without whose will nothing comes to pass, nothing in heaven or on earth? Who in his omnipotence has allowed this to befall me? Is it not you! Behold me, Lord! Behold your work! What is a man without sons, a tree without branches to bear the fruit of life! Why do you allow me to remain standing? Strike me down with your heavenly lightning so that I shall be freed from living on this accursed earth which you have chosen for the unrighteous and his seed!

Stops suddenly. Draws his hand over his forehead.

No, no . . . I don't know what I am saying . . . I must be completely out of my senses . . .

AN OLD MAN *in from the doorway where the Jews have gathered to listen to what* SIMONIDES *is saying. Falls on his knees, takes hold of his clothes*: Rabbi, rabbi, has the Lord forsaken us! Is it true that he has forsaken us?

SIMONIDES: What are you babbling about, old man . . .

OLD MAN: But that's what you said, rabbi! Is it true?

SIMONIDES: How can you believe anything like that . . . The Lord forsake us? His people, his own people? . . . You know that He won't.

He is trying us; he sends us afflictions in his mysterious way . . . But forsake us? No, he will never do that.

We do not understand his ways, we cannot grasp their meaning. We think that he is unjust, that he is too hard on us. But that is because we do not understand his purpose with us, with his people. He cannot tell us; it must remain his secret. We stand before his face to seek out his meaning, but he must hide it from us, for no one may see God. If he could show it to us, we would not complain. Who am I that I should justify myself in his eyes?

Helps the OLD MAN *up.*

Arise and do not despair. —Is he not our Father, in whom we place our trust? Are we not his children that he loves and troubles over? If he did not love us, would he send us such trials? Do you think he would?

He turns also to the others:

No. The Lord has only sent us yet another trial which we do not understand. But we know that he wishes us well. He lays his heavy hand upon us . . . his heavy hand . . . but we know that it is our own Father's hand, and that it is for our well-being. He will never take it from us, he will never let us go. For we are his people and he is our God. Our stern, unfathomable God. Blessed be his name.

THE JEWS: Blessed, blessed be his name . . .

SIMONIDES *remains a moment with his head bowed. Then:* Have you brought the Torah rolls and the other sacred things from the synagogue?

ONE OF THE JEWS: Yes, rabbi. They will soon be here.

SIMONIDES: Then we can set forth at once.

Turns away from them.

I ask your pardon, Lord! Pardon my weakness and my arrogance! I am a poor servant, full of human frailties. Only you are strong, and only you know what must be. Rule over me and allow me not to rule. Wear away my selfishness and fill me with humility in face of thy will. For my eyes have been opened and I see what still lies before me. You take the branches from the tree—but the trunk you allow to remain because it is still a part of your design. Lord let me serve thee.

There now, my children, be of good courage. We shall soon begin our wandering again, but the Lord shall be with us. He is with us every day. And on this day which we feel is such a burden. All of our days are gifts of the Lord.

Wait here, then, until the men have come back from the synagogue.

Goes to ALBERTUS:

I wish to take farewell of you and your house because the time has come for us to set forth from this place. I thank you for the time that I have been a guest here. You have been a good friend. We have exchanged many thoughts, although we could not agree as perhaps we ought to have. And now we shall be parted forever.

They embrace each other.

ALBERTUS: I thank you too. I shall miss you in my loneliness.

SIMONIDES: May the Lord guide you on your way, a difficult way, it seems to me.

Peace in thy house, master Albertus.

Turns toward the women:

Peace . . . peace . . .

ALBERTUS: May you also go in peace, you and your people. To think that our meeting should lead to such sorrow . . .

SIMONIDES: I shall never forget that you wanted to sacrifice yourself for my son . . . that you wanted to die for his sake.

ALBERTUS: No, no, that was not why I did it. Not for his sake, not for anyone's. For my own sake. I do everything only for my own sake.

SIMONIDES: So . . . Did you?

Maybe that was why your offering was not accepted.

ALBERTUS: Yes, but his was accepted.

SIMONIDES: Yes, yes. His was accepted.

Goes to CATHERINE, *takes her hand:*

Love, my child . . . love . . . I had forgotten what it is. It was so long ago . . . —She lies buried far away in a foreign country, by a river, under a tree . . . It is all so long ago . . .

ALBERTUS *when* SIMONIDES *goes toward the doorway:* Where are you going?

SIMONIDES: I do not know. We have nowhere to go. We are

strangers in every place, and everywhere doors are closed
against us.

Our only home is with the Lord our God.

*Several young men come in carrying the rolls of the Torah, the shofar,
the kiddush cup, and prayer shawls.* THE JEWS *gather outside in the
alley with their packs and bundles.*

SIMONIDES *bows before the Torah. Touches it reverently and bows again.
The people reach out their hands and try to touch it.* SIMONIDES *calms
the old people who cry as they kiss it.* —*Then:* So . . . we are ready
then.

A JEW *stretches out his hands with a few small stones in them:* Rabbi, see
the stones from my father's grave. I'll never see them again!

ANOTHER *likewise:* From the graves of my children, rabbi!

SIMONIDES: We shall see our children again someday with God.
And our fathers.

ONE OF THEM: Where shall we go, rabbi?

OTHERS *out in the alley repeat the question:* Where shall we go?

SIMONIDES: Where shall we go? You know where. Where did our
fathers go at the time of the Passover? Didn't they go up to the
Lord their God, to be with Him. Didn't they go up to Zion?

THE JEWS *lamenting:* Alas, Zion lies waste . . . the temple is leveled
to the ground . . .

SIMONIDES: But our God is there just the same! Don't we have our
Lord even though he, like ourselves, has no dwelling here on
earth. Don't we have Zion even though we will never see it
here!

THE JEWS: Yes, yes, rabbi . . .

SIMONIDES: Shall we not march up to Zion as he has bidden!

THE JEWS: Yes! Yes!

SIMONIDES: Shall we not celebrate our Passover, our feast of joy, up
there!
With our God!

THE JEWS *stirred by his inspiration:* Yes! Yes! Up to Zion!

SIMONIDES *takes the Torah rolls and raises them over his head:* Up to
Zion!

Up to Zion!
Goes out while the people watch him with their eyes shining. They follow him.
Their cries are heard farther and farther away in the alley:
Up to Zion! Up to Zion!
Finally, very far off, the sound dies away.

SISTER TERESIA *comes in. Stops a moment in the doorway, a little hesitant.*

MARIA: Oh, Sister Teresia! . . . be welcome in our house. God bless you . . .

SISTER TERESIA *looks about in the strange room, especially at the peculiar oven. Crosses herself*: God bless you too, woman. I come a little late; I had so many errands first, and they have taken all day. But anyway, I hope we'll be home before dusk.
There are too many earthly troubles in our lives. Don't you think so?

MARIA: Yes, yes, good sister. There are. I think so too.

SISTER TERESIA: I am the one at Our Lady's who must take care of our wordly concerns, you see. We give it too much thought, but these things too are done for her sake.

MARIA: Yes, yes. It must be a great comfort to serve her.

SISTER TERESIA: Yes, it is, it is. Blessed be her name.

MARIA *whispering*: Yes, yes, blessed . . .
Stands reverently with her hands folded. CATHERINE *likewise.*

SISTER TERESIA: And so this is our new little lay sister? May I have a look at you. You seem gentle. You are not as I had thought. You must know that I am aware of everything about you, my child.
Touches her face, strokes her cheek:
May God give your heart peace.

CATHERINE *bows and kisses her hands impulsively.*

SISTER TERESIA: And you wish to live with us and serve only God's holy mother?

CATHERINE: Yes, yes! I do! I do! I will forget everything for her...

SISTER TERESIA: That's right, my child. For her we must forget everything, all our own sorrows and thoughts and all that binds us to the world.

May She give you her peace.

Feels her necklace:

We'll take this off. It can stay here.

Puts it on ALBERTUS'S *work table.*

MARIA: Oh, God's mother has worked a miracle, God's merciful mother has worked a miracle . . .

SISTER TERESIA: A miracle? What do you mean by that?

MARIA *and* CATHERINE *look uneasily at each other.*

MARIA: I mean . . . I mean . . . that it is a great wonder that our child has been freed from this world and from the power of evil . . . that she may come to the very dwelling of the Merciful One, and be under her protection . . . alas, Sister Teresia, my heart is so full of gratitude to her, to our gracious God, to the good abbess and the good sisters who are willing to receive this soul that otherwise would be lost . . . my dearly beloved child . . . I thank her, thank her for it . . .

Stands in front of the picture of the Madonna on the wall, with her hands folded tightly, mumbling.

SISTER TERESIA *without disturbing her:* Yes, yes, you shall. It is proper that you thank her for it.

When MARIA *again turns toward them with a timid look, her eyes lowered:* I am greatly astonished to find such a godfearing woman in a house like this.

MARIA: Alas, no. No, I am not godfearing; my soul is lost and I am full of sin.

SISTER TERESIA: Yes, all of us are full of sin. But why should your soul be lost?

Her merciful heart is open to us all, and if you pray to her, her son will also have died for you. Then you will be redeemed, you as all others who turn to her.

MARIA: No, Sister, I shall not be. It is not so. It can't be helped; there is nothing to be done about it. But if only my child is saved from evil and someday can have eternal life, I'll be happy. I'll ask nothing more.

SISTER TERESIA: Yes, yes . . . she surely can if she devotes her life to God and the Holy Virgin, she who prays for us.

MARIA: Yes, Sister, and to the Holy Virgin, to God's mother . . .

SISTER TERESIA *to* CATHERINE: Are you ready, my dear, so that we may go? Do you have your things in readiness?

CATHERINE: Yes, yes, Sister I have.

Gets a little bundle with her belongings in it.

SISTER TERESIA: Then you must say good-by.

CATHERINE *goes to her mother, embraces her long and tenderly.*

MARIA: My child, my child . . . I need not wish you happiness, for you are going to the greatest happiness there is on this earth, to live in the dwelling of Our Lady, to be ever near her presence. I have been a bad mother to you, but now you'll have one who can take care of you and protect you from all evil. Pray that she may forgive me that I send you to her with so many faults— that I haven't brought you up properly and that you know so little of the things that must be done at home. Tell her that you will learn quickly. And always do your very best. God be with you. My thoughts shall always be with you where you are . . . Farewell . . . And forget everything, my child . . . the two of us here . . . everything here . . . But I shall never forget you my child . . .

CATHERINE *holds her tightly. Goes to her father*: Good-by, father, I shall pray for your soul when the good sisters have taught me to pray so that God will hear my prayer.

ALBERTUS *smiles a little*: Yes, yes, do that. And go in peace.

SISTER TERESIA *and* CATHERINE *go, followed to the doorway by* MARIA. *She stands there for a long time watching them. Comes back into the room.*

ALBERTUS *after a moment*: We can only hope that she'll be happy there.

MARIA: Oh . . . there is no greater happiness.

ALBERTUS: No, perhaps not.

> *After a moment:*

We know so little about what happiness is.

MARIA *sits down on a bench:* The good mistress Cecilia has told me so much about how it is in God's mother's house . . .

Sometimes it's almost as if I'd been there . . .

> *Gets up and goes about the room. Then:*

Well, now there are just the two of us left in the house . . .

ALBERTUS: Yes.

> *Stands by the oven. Lays his hand on it.*

MARIA: Yes . . . it has gone out. I didn't know how to take care of it, or when you'd come home.

ALBERTUS: No, no.

> *Goes and sits down in his usual chair.*

MARIA *hesitantly:* Will you light it again?

ALBERTUS: Yes. I shall. Not today . . . I'm so tired. But tomorrow. Tomorrow I'll light it again.

MARIA: Yes, yes . . .

> *Stands still a moment, looks emptily in front of her.*
> *Then begins to go about putting a few things in order in the room.*
> *After a moment she comes to where* ALBERTUS *is sitting.*
> *Notices that he seems to have gone to sleep.*
> *Carefully goes closer to him.*

Are you sleeping?

> *Goes closer.*

Are you asleep?

> *Tenderly caresses his forehead, his cheeks—*
> *Smooths away a lock of his gray hair that's fallen down.*
> ALBERTUS *stirs—she quickly steps back.*
> *Patters silently out to the kitchen, at the right.*

ALBERTUS *wakens. Looks about him. Draws his hand over his forehead where she has just touched him:* Was someone here . . . — — — No . . .

> *Gets up from his chair:*

Well, I guess I'd better go in and rest now . . .

> *Slowly goes out through the door on the opposite side.*

Bibliographical Note

Little is known of Lagerkvist's personal life apart from what he reveals in his writing. *Gäst hos verkligheten* (tr. *Guest of Reality*; Stockholm: Bonnier, 1925) is frankly autobiographical and of primary importance to an understanding of his development. A brief, factual sketch of his career may be found in *Current Biography*, 1952, (New York: H. W. Wilson Co., 1953), pp. 321–324. There are two indispensable bibliographies: Uno Willers, *Pär Lagerkvists bibliografi* (Stockholm: Bonnier, 1951), and Anders Ryberg, *Pär Lagerkvist in Translation* (Stockholm: Bonnier, 1964). Willers lists all of Lagerkvist's published writing and translations up to 1951. Ryberg's work, a continuation of the earlier bibliography, is of great usefulness in identifying translations of specific works. Alrik Gustafson's *A History of Swedish Literature* (Minneapolis: University of Minnesota Press, 1961) provides the best general orientation in its subject in English; it contains an excellent bibliographical section with numerous references to articles about Lagerkvist. Contributions on Lagerkvist, chiefly those in English, published in America, are recorded in the bibliography appearing each year in the May issue of the quarterly journal *Scandinavian Studies* (1911 to the present).

Three Lagerkvist plays not included in this volume, have appeared in English translation: *Mannen utan själ* (*The Man Without a Soul*, 1936) in *Scandinavian Plays of the Twentieth Century*, Series 1 (Princeton: Princeton University Press, 1944); *Midsommardröm i fattighuset* (*Midsummer Dream in the Workhouse*, 1941), published separately (London: Wm. Hodge and Co., Ltd., 1953); and *Låt människan leva* (*Let Man Live*, 1949) in *Scandinavian Plays of the Twentieth Century*, Series 3 (Princeton: Princeton University Press, 1951), reprinted in *Religious Drama*, 3 (New York: Meridian Books, 1959).

Plays by Pär Lagerkvist

The Last Man (Sista mänskan, 1917)

The Difficult Hour I–III *(Den svåra stunden,* 1918)

The Secret of Heaven (Himlens hemlighet, 1919)

The Invisible One (Den osynlige, 1923)

He Who Lived His Life Over Again (Han som fick leva om sitt liv, 1928)

The King (Konungen, 1932)

The Hangman (Bödeln, 1933)

The Man Without a Soul (Mannen utan själ, 1936)

Victory in the Dark (Seger i mörker, 1939)

Midsummer Dream in the Workhouse (Midsommardröm i fattighuset, 1941)

The Philosopher's Stone (De vises sten, 1947)

Let Man Live (Låt människan leva, 1949)

Barabbas (Barabbas, 1953)